Pruning
Handbook

By the Editors of Sunset Books and Sunset Magazine

LANE BOOKS · MENLO PARK, CALIFORNIA

ACKNOWLEDGMENTS

In the many months of research which resulted in this new book, the editors utilized the accumulated knowledge and practical pruning experience of many interested individuals—from home gardeners to professionals. We are extremely grateful to them and to the many business firms and private and public agencies whose representatives also contributed so generously. We would like especially to thank the following:

Wilbur L. Bluhm, County Agricultural Agent, Salem, Oregon.

John E. Bryan, Director, Strybing Arboretum, San Francisco, Calif.

California State Department of Highways, Sacramento, Calif.

Francis Ching, Director, Los Angeles State and County Arboretum, Arcadia, Calif.

Ken Doty, Berkeley Horticultural Nursery, Berkeley, Calif.

John R. Dunmire, Assistant Editor, Sunset Magazine, Menlo Park, Calif.

Philip Edinger, Special Editor, Sunset Books, Menlo Park, Calif.

Dr. James R. Feucht, Extension Associate Professor, Colorado State University, Fort Collins, Colorado.

Brian Gage, Ornamental Horticulture Instructor, San Jose Regional Vocational Center, San Jose, Calif.

Bert Googins, Berkeley Horticultural Nursery, Berkeley, Calif.

W. Richard Hildreth, Director, Saratoga Horticultural Foundation, Saratoga, Calif.

Dr. Z. Horvath, President, Bay Area Lily Society, San Francisco, Calif.

Frederick M. Lang, Landscape Architect, South Laguna, Calif.

Walter Lawrence, Superintendent, S. P. McClenahan Co., Portola Valley, Calif.

Henry McClenahan, S. P. McClenahan Co., Portola Valley, Calif.

Arthur Menzies, Assistant Director, Strybing Arboretum, San Francisco, Calif.

Art Modin, Head Gardener, Sunset Magazine, Menlo Park, Calif.

Mrs. Karl Mueller, San Francisco Fuchsia Society, San Francisco, Calif.

Sciaini Hardware, Cloverdale, Calif.

Lee Sharfman, Armstrong & Sharfman, Land Design Associates, Los Angeles, Calif.

L. K. Smith, Landscape Architect, Thousand Oaks, Calif.

U. S. Dept. of Agriculture; University of California, Berkeley, Calif.

Walter Vodden, Superintendent, Blake Garden, Berkeley, Calif.

Wayne C. Whitney, Extension Horticulturist, University of Nebraska, Lincoln, Nebraska.

Supervising Editor: Joseph F. Williamson, Garden Editor, Sunset Magazine

Research and Text: Lee Klein

Coordinating Editor: Sherry Gellner

Illustrations: E. D. Bills
Design: Joe Seney
Cover Photograph: Ells Marugg
Cover Design: John Flack

Executive Editor, Sunset Books: David E. Clark

CONTENTS

Why Prune?

Sunset's definition of pruning is "removing plant parts for a purpose." It is one of six basic things that a gardener or a farmer does to plants to make them grow the way he wants. The other basic acts of plant husbandry are: choosing and preparing special growing places; watering; fertilizing; weeding and cultivating; protecting plants as necessary from elements and living organisms that might spoil or destroy them.

Pruning does not necessarily rank as number one (or at any other definite position) among those basic six. One reason is that different kinds of plants need different kinds of pruning. Some need lots of it every year, some need just a little in a lifetime, and some never have to be pruned at all unless they get injured.

That's what most of this book is about—the specific pruning needs of different kinds of plants and the reasons for them. You'll find this information under the various plant names, listed alphabetically in the Pruning Encyclopedia that covers the 75 pages from page 13 to page 87.

By contrast, all the general information about pruning that needs to be said is contained in a total of 18 pages, from here to page 12 and in the Glossary from page 88 to 96.

You do most of the removal of plant parts by pinching between your thumb and finger or by cutting with shears or a saw. These tools of pruning, and a few others, are presented in their great variety on pages 8 to 12 .

Ordinarily, you shouldn't go out in your garden to *prune*, as you go to *water* or to *weed*. Two or three or maybe half a dozen of the kinds of plants in your garden may need some kind of pruning at the same time (each for its own reason and in its own way, probably), but even that big a demand is unlikely. Except in a completely overgrown garden where you must cut everything back just to walk around, the needs for pruning never come to all kinds of plants at once.

That brings up the question—when and why will the plants in your garden need pruning? The "when" part of the question is answered—plant-by-plant—in the Pruning Encyclopedia. The "why" part is answered by the following objectives or reasons for pruning.

Pruning for physical reasons. Leaves on the inside and lower portions of plants need air and light to function. Therefore, a common reason for pruning is to thin out dense growth to let in air and light. Pruning to thin out crowded conditions sometimes pays dividends also in providing more room, light, moisture, and air to adjacent plants. It can also lessen damage by subsequent winds and storms. If you live in a harsh winter area, you'll want to thin to reduce the danger of breakage due to heavy snow loads. Where brush and forest fires are a danger, good garden housekeeping can reduce fire risk. Dead wood and withered leaves should be trimmed off shrubs, vines, and trees as part of such garden housekeeping.

Pruning to correct or repair damage. If a storm breaks a limb, you should cut the stub back to another branch or to the trunk. Branches that died from unknown causes should be removed as soon as you

PRUNING FOR PHYSICAL REASONS

CUT HERE

PRUNING TO REPAIR DAMAGE

see them. Such a branch may be diseased, and the removal can prevent the infection from spreading to healthy wood. (Make such cuts back into live wood, and dip the shears in a disinfectant between each cut.)

Pruning to encourage flower and fruit production. In nature, a plant forms flowers and the flowers become fruits so that seeds in the fruits can go forth and produce new plants. The quantity and quality of the flowers and fruits are not an integral part of this natural cycle. But when man steps in and takes these plants (or hybrids and improved varieties that he has developed) into his garden, quality and quantity of flowers and fruits become all important.

One of civilized man's first gardening discoveries was that by pruning in certain ways he could make flower and fruit producers grow better flowers or fruits. If a plant's flowers or fruits can benefit from some form of pruning, you'll read about it in the Pruning Encyclopedia.

Pruning to direct or control growth. Any time you pinch the end bud off a branch or make a cut through a stem or branch, you stop or inhibit growth in one direction, encourage it in another. When you remove side branches, you speed up growth of the central leader (main trunk); when you remove the tips of the leader and the main branches, you speed up growth of lesser side (lateral) branches. The cuts you make cause food to be diverted from one part of the plant to another, thereby allowing you to shape and train it as you wish.

Just with your thumb and forefinger (or pair of pruning shears), you can deliberately nip out buds to stop growth in that region and force it in another place.

Effective use of this knowledge will not only shape the plant in the form you want, it will also keep it the size you want: low, flat against a wall, compact, whatever your objective. Using this knowledge of growth diversion to control or modify growth of plants is one of the most satisfying aspects of pruning.

Pruning for a pleasing artificial form. This includes pruning to reveal the attractive branches of normally leafy plants, hedge shearing, topiary pruning, espaliering, and even lawn mowing.

Pruning to compensate for transplanting. A living healthy plant has its root mass and its leaf mass in a state of equilibrium at most times. There are just enough leaves to manufacture food, and just enough roots to take in water and minerals. The two parts supply each other and depend on each other.

When you dig a plant up to transplant it, you sever many roots. Transplanted, that plant has trouble getting enough water to supply the leaves. As a result, the plant wilts. And it can die unless something happens within the plant or its environment to reduce the moisture loss. You can prune the top of the transplanted plant enough so that the leaf area gets reduced more or less in ratio to the loss the roots suffered when the spade or trowel sliced through them.

Pruning because of someone's bad judgment. Some pruning takes place because at some time previous the planter selected and placed a plant without adequately allowing for its ultimate size, its rate of growth, or what it would look like when mature.

You may want to experiment with pinching and pruning to get interesting forms from a misplaced plant. To minimize your pruning problems, however, select and place plants with your objectives—3, 5, 15 years from now—in mind. Many plants placed appropriately and properly trained while young never need any pruning at all, beyond the removal of damaged or dead wood.

PRUNING TO ENCOURAGE FRUIT PRODUCTION

PINCHING TO DIRECT GROWTH

PRUNING FOR A PLEASING ARTIFICIAL FORM

PRUNING BECAUSE OF SOMEONE'S BAD JUDGMENT

Plant Growth

Elsewhere in this book you'll read repeatedly of the various plant parts and how they relate to each other when you prune or fail to prune.

Here, very briefly, is how the system of plant growth works. The various acts of pruning, their causes and their consequences, all have something to do with this system.

The seed. Each seed contains inside its protective coating an embryo plant and a supply of stored food (starch, protein, oils) to start the embryo in growth and sustain it until it can manufacture its own food.

When a seed sprouts, the coating splits, a rootlet starts downward, and a stem carrying the seed leaves grows upwards.

The roots. The single rootlet begins to branch out into tiny white roots which take in chemical substances needed for plant life and also the water to carry these substances to the rest of the plant. As the root system grows and branches more, different parts take on different functions and appearances. Older parts grow a skinlike covering similar to bark. Always at the ends of the tiniest roots are tender root tips. These contain a growing point which continually produces elongating cells, pushing the roots farther into soil that is favorable to them.

Right behind the root tip is a short length of root that produces the root hairs. These hairs are the organs that absorb water and nutrients for the entire plant. As the root tip extends the root farther into the soil, the region of root hairs moves on with it. The old root hairs cease to function when the part of the root to which they are attached thickens and becomes mature.

The stems (trunks and branches). Between the seed leaves (or enfolded within a single seed leaf) is the growth tip which eventually elongates to form the stem. Buds develop along the stem, and they open to produce the first true leaves. The stem continues to elongate, producing additional buds. The end bud, also called the terminal bud, carries the growth upward. Side buds (lateral buds) develop into leaves or, as the plant becomes larger, into branches. Buds at the end of each branch are also terminal buds, and side buds on branches are also lateral buds.

As a pruner, you can manipulate and direct plant growth by nipping or cutting off selected buds. If you remove side buds, you channel energy into terminal growth. Conversely, if you remove terminal buds, you cause growth in side buds to increase, making for denser, bushier plants. In some plants, the buds may lie dormant in stem or bark for many years (latent buds); these start growth only after pruning or injury removes upper growth. Latent buds account for the sprouting of shrubs and trees from stumps.

The stem transmits water and nutrients from the root hairs to the growing points (buds, leaves, flowers) and returns to the roots the food (sugars) manufactured in the leaves. In the stems of most trees, shrubs, and herbaceous (soft-wooded) plants, the tissues that conduct the growth substances are concentrated on either side of (or very near) the cambium (a layer of cells located just inside of the bark or "skin"). This layer of cells also adds tissue that increases the girth of the plant.

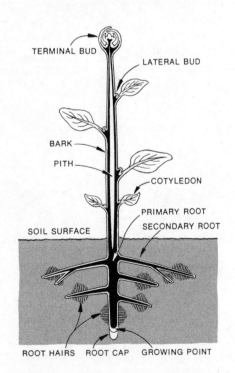

The stem also supports the plant. Stems of many plants are rigid because the walls of their cells are stiffened by cellulose, lignin, and similar substances. In trees and shrubs, the dense interior heartwood serves only as support, having outlived the function of supplying conductive or storage tissue. Some stems are too long and thin to be held erect, even by woody tissue. So it is that vines have developed twining stems, tendrils, coiled leaf stalks, or adhesive disks to carry leaves and flowers up into the sunlight.

IF YOU CUT HERE

THIS WILL DIE

When food moves through the plant from the leaves, it is in the form of sugars. When stored, it is converted into starch. When it is ready to move again in spring for the plant's use, it changes back to sugar.

As the wielder of a pruning tool, you will work more effectively if you think of each stem (you may call it a stem, trunk, branch, or twig) as a live conveying tube. If you cut a stem some distance above its uppermost growing point (leaf, bud, or branch), you leave nothing for that part of the conveying tube to convey toward—there is no longer any reason for growth substances to enter it, hence no longer anything in it to maintain growth. The stub withers and dies. Not only does the dead stub look ugly but also decay can enter into the live part of the plant through it.

The only situation where you don't need to concern yourself about cutting back to a growing point is in shearing. In this case, your shears cut through such small, twiggy growth that the dead stubs are of no consequence.

The leaves. As soon as the first true leaves expand from their buds on an infant plant, the plant begins to function on its own. This means that the leaves manufacture sugars and other carbohydrates. This manufacturing—photosynthesis—is carried out by green material known as chlorophyll, which converts carbon dioxide, water, and energy from sunlight into carbohydrates and oxygen.

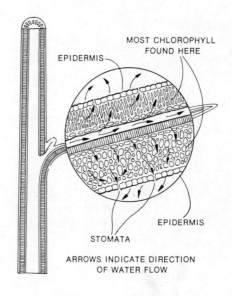

MOST CHLOROPHYLL FOUND HERE

EPIDERMIS

EPIDERMIS

STOMATA

ARROWS INDICATE DIRECTION OF WATER FLOW

Photosynthesis requires large quantities of water, drawn up through the stem from the roots and into the leaf tissue. Here it encounters carbon dioxide in the air which passes into the leaf through minute breathing pores (stomata). Since the interior of the leaf must be moist and since the outside air is frequently dry, the pores are able to close when necessary to prevent dehydration. The leaf is further protected against drying by an outer coat (epidermis) which may be waxy, resinous, hairy, or scaly.

In deciduous plants, the manufacture of carbohydrates stops during the dormant season. In evergreen plants, it slows down greatly during the modified dormancy which comes to these plants during cold weather. Simultaneously, of course, the requirement for water lessens, and roots no longer strain to keep up with the demands of the leaf system's manufacturing process.

Flowers and fruits. All garden plants form flowers if permitted to do so, but not all flowers are noticeable. (Some are too little or too green to be detected.) The flower contains within itself female parts that, when fertilized by male sexual cells (pollen), produce seeds. And the seeds reproduce the plant.

REMOVE SOME FRUIT TO MAKE OTHERS BIGGER

Much of pruning consists of removing some or all flowers or fruits before the plant's reproductive cycle comes to its end—that is, before ripe seeds can go forth to make new plants. Typically, this forces the plant to produce more flowers or fruits, or bigger flowers or fruits, than it would if it were left alone. Sometimes, premature removal of the flowers or fruits makes the plant stay green or attractive longer than it would otherwise.

Pruning Tools

A pair of pruning shears—any of the kinds you work with one hand—is such a basic gardening tool that even an apartment gardener should invest in one. These hand shears are constantly useful for many gardening chores—cutting off faded flowers, cutting vigorous vine tendrils, cutting and removing broken stems and small branches, routine shaping and trimming of plants.

Hand pruning shears are not an all-purpose pruning tool, however, and most gardeners will want in addition a saw and a pair of hand loppers for pruning limbs and branches on trees and big shrubs. The amount of pruning equipment to invest in beyond these three basic tools depends upon your garden and your budget. Most gardeners will probably need, in addition, hedge shears and grass shears; and if you want to prune your tall trees without a lot of climbing and ladder work you will need some of the long pole-type saws and loppers. A wide variety of other tools will come in handy for various pruning jobs, though they are not strictly pruning tools—surface forming tools for finishing and smoothing pruning cuts; knives for shaping wounds; power saws for fast, efficient removal of limbs and branches.

The options available in pruning tools are apt to be somewhat overwhelming to the beginning gardener. Many different kinds of pruning cuts can be made, and each implement is designed to do certain kinds of cutting. If you use only one kind of pruning implement for many kinds of plant cutting, you probably make bad cuts at times—occasionally damaging both the plants and the overextended or misused tools. Though the tools themselves have changed very little in basic design and function over the years, the various manufacturers in this very competitive market have introduced their own individual styles and refinements.

To help you select the right blade for the right job, let's examine these various groups of implements, beginning with the most basic of all.

One-hand pruning shears. You'll find two basic designs of one-hand shears: anvil, which cuts by the action of a straight blade against an anvil; and the hook and curved blade type. Many gardeners use both and find it hard to see any difference in the kinds of cuts made. Each type also has its followers who swear by one or the other exclusively. Whichever type you buy, get a good one. Skimpily made models prove to be bad investments because they will probably have to be replaced in a very short time.

Besides these two basic designs, you will find many other kinds of hand pruners, each of which is designed for a specific job such as cutting flowers (some are designed to cut and hold the flower stems and some incorporate stem crushers); fruit shears for lemons, grapes and other stems which don't break off readily; a Japanese-designed shear that makes a concave cut (which is said to heal much more rapidly than a straight cut). This one is favored by bonsai growers. The various manufacturers offer such refinements as teflon-coated blades as well as the usual stainless steel replaceable blades (on the anvil types), self-lubricating bearings which need no oil, sap grooves

ONE-HAND HOOK
AND BLADE SHEARS

ONE-HAND
ANVIL SHEARS

BONSAI SHEARS

(said to keep the blades cleaner); various types of handles and grips; one-hand operable catches. One model has a ratchet which adjusts the cutting power of the blade—when you meet resistance, a slight release of pressure on the grip shifts it into another notch, giving you more leverage for the cut.

Most of the one-hand shears measure somewhere between 5 to 9 inches in length. The 5-inch one is a mini-shear for very delicate work or for pruning miniatures. In a class by itself is the extension pruner, with a cutting blade at one end of a 4-foot lightweight pole and a squeeze handle to work it on the other end. Use it for cutting flowers and doing other light pruning beyond arm's reach.

Lopping shears (two-hand pruners). Use lopping shears wherever the added leverage of long handles will give you more cutting strength than you get from one-hand shears and wherever the long handles can help you reach farther. As with one hand pruners, you can choose from two basic styles. In the hook and blade style, the hook holds the branch while the blade slices through it. The blade and anvil type has a draw-in slicing action—a sharp blade cuts against a flat plate, or anvil. In loppers you'll also find a wide variety of styles to choose from: wood, tubular steel handles (vinyl or rubber covered), adjustable anvil (so you can resharpen the blade many times before it has to be replaced); adjustable cutting action. Lopping shears range in size all the way from about 15 to 35 inches long, with most falling between 20 to 30 inches.

Hedge shears. Here's a hand pruning tool that gets stiff competition from an electric counterpart (see power tools on page 11). Hand-operated hedge shears remain in use by those with not enough hedge to make an electric trimmer worthwhile, and with others who believe that they can do a better job manually. Actually, many hedge keepers use both—the electric for one-plane (sides or tops) work, and the manual to make sharp corners. In appearance, manual hedge shears seem to be more standardized than is the case with loppers and hand pruners. But here you have options. Most come with a limb notch which is handy for cutting the occasional big stem that the blade balks at and most models have one serrated blade to keep your work from sliding away from you. The better models have neoprene, rubber, or spring shock absorbers between the handles. You have several choices in blade materials: drop-forged, hollow ground, teflon covered (self-lubrication). Blade lengths average 8 inches and handles—also available in several different materials and coatings—are normally about 10 to 12 inches in length. Most manufacturers offer a model with extra-long handles (20 to 22 inches) for trimming tall hedges. If you are 5 feet, 5 inches tall you can clip almost as high as 9 feet with these.

Grass shears. Most grass shears cut grass by the action of one blade slicing across another. Some models operate with a vertical squeezing action; one handle is over the other. Others operate horizontally; handles are on the same plane as the blades, but offset so you don't bruise your knuckles. Try them both before you buy to see which suits your hand muscles best.

Unusual are a one-piece "sheep-shear" type spring action shear, and a cordless electric shear with batteries that recharge overnight.

For the gardener who prefers to clip grass from a stand-up position, one type puts the shears on wheels at the base of a 3-foot-long handle. You wheel it along, squeezing the grip on top of the handle to activate the shears. This type also comes as an electric, cordless model with rechargeable batteries.

HOOK AND BLADE LOPPING SHEARS

ANVIL-TYPE LOPPING SHEARS

WOODEN HANDLE HEDGE SHEARS

METAL HANDLE HEDGE SHEARS

HORIZONTAL HANDLE GRASS SHEARS

VERTICAL HANDLE GRASS SHEARS

LONG HANDLE
GRASS SHEARS

EDGING SHEARS

BOW SAW

STRAIGHT SAW,
6 POINTS
TO INCH

DOUBLE-EDGE SAW,
COARSE AND
FINE TEETH

Edging shears. With a pair of lawn edging shears, you can stand up to cut the edges of lawns (you can cut right into the sod) and the edges of thick, spreading ground covers such as ivy and vinca. The handles on these shears are 3-feet long.

Pruning saws. If you must cut a branch thicker than 1 inch, you should use a pruning saw. Pruning a branch of that size with any other tool—shears or loppers—taxes the tool, and you. And shears and loppers tend to crush as they cut, producing ragged, mashed edges that leave the way open for disease.

Just as bad is trying to cut branches with a carpenter's saw fetched from the garage. This brings on frustration, makes bad cuts, and doesn't do the carpenter's saw any good either. Pruning saws—unlike ordinary ones—are designed to cut quickly through fresh, green, wet wood. Also unlike ordinary saws, most pruning saws are designed to cut on the pull stroke. One (the tree surgery saw) cuts on the push stroke, and several cut both ways.

Some gardeners prefer to prune with a saw even when shears might do; a saw often cuts old hard wood easier and more cleanly. Or they use both tools to prune the same plant; shears for the small young wood of roses, a small saw for old canes. Which pruning saw would best suit your needs?

It is not an easy task to pick the proper saw for your needs. For a group of tools which all have a blade with serrated teeth in common, there is a wide choice of sizes, styles, and shapes. Here are some details on the various types to help you choose the proper one.

The first thing you want to do when evaluating a saw is to heft it for weight and balance. Look at the size of teeth. Big teeth (5 or 6 per inch) go along with a big blade and make a saw suitable for heavy work only. Smaller teeth (up to 10 per inch) are for smaller branches, deadwood, or hardwood such as citrus.

Look straight down the blade and see how the teeth are set. For the best cut you should see a V of teeth alternately bent to either side—the length of the blade.

Some saw makers now put a nonstick coating on the blades. This may at times make sawing easier by allowing the blades to slip through wood with less friction.

Here are the more familiar types of pruning saws:

Tree surgery saw. With teeth angled forward on a heavy 2-foot blade, the tree surgery saw looks and works much like a carpenter's handsaw and it cuts on the push stroke. Many professionals swear by it for use on big limbs. But using it for overhead sawing or undercutting can be difficult.

Bow saw. Better suited for cutting firewood, the box saw is inexpensive and some people prune with it. Hard to maneuver among crowded branches. Many sizes with 15-inch blades on up. Cuts both pushing and pulling.

Two-edged saw. One side has small teeth, cuts on push, and is intended for small limbs and dead wood. The other has coarse teeth, cuts on both strokes, is for larger branches and green wood. Idea of versatility sounds better than it really is; the saw is a compromise and doesn't do either job too well.

The following saws all cut when you pull, and most gardeners like this kind best. Pulling is the most natural motion for cutting overhead branches. You can hook a limb with a pull saw, bring it toward you, and control it while you saw; a push saw tends to shove the limb out of reach.

Curved saw with rigid handle. Knowing the saw can't fold in action (two of the curved saws illustrated have folding handles) is comforting, but it's more trouble to store and carry. Blade lengths are 12 to 16 inches.

Folding saw. The most popular folding saw is available with blades 7 to 16 inches long. Small ones with fine teeth (8 or 10 per inch) fit into your back pocket, are good for roses and shrubs. Large ones (6 teeth per inch) can handle fruit trees, most dormant pruning.

Speed saw with raker teeth. The fastest cutter of 3-inch and larger limbs, it is good for green wood because rakers (slots in place of every fifth tooth) pull sawdust out, keep blade from jamming. This saw cuts anything a small chain saw can, albeit with more effort, but is quiet, needs no fuel, makes no mechanical demands, and costs about the same as renting a chain saw for a few hours.

Speed saw with lance teeth. Cuts deadwood better than the speed saw with raker teeth.

Folding saw with grip handle. Same as the other folding saw but handle offers easier grip, doesn't shield all of blade when folded.

Pole saw. Detachable saw heads can be fastened to 6 to 24-foot pole of wood, aluminum, or fiberglass (some telescope for storing). Wood or the newer fiberglass ones are safer near electric lines. Pole saws are tiring, and it's tricky to pin down smaller branches; it is often better to work from a ladder if you can.

Pole pruners and pole saws. You get the extra reach you need to cut or saw branches high overhead with pole pruners and pole saws. The poles may be wood, aluminum, or fiberglass. Some telescope and lock into the required position, others come with extensions and quick-connecting devices. (Choose the wood or fiberglass poles if there is any chance at all of contacting electric wires in your pruning.) One pole saw and pruner comes with three 8-foot sections for a 24-foot reach, a length which would probably be unwieldy for most home gardeners.

A popular type is a combination pruning saw and cord or chain-operated cutting shears. The shears are inside a beak-like hook which you place over the branch you want to cut, then pull the cord to draw the blade through it. Most of the shears will handle limbs up to 1 inch. Heavy duty models have a capacity up to 1½ inches. (Good tip: wrap the cord a turn or two around the pole so it won't bow out when you pull the cord.) Saws on most pole tools are similar to the last one described under *Pruning saws* (see above), and most cut on the pull stroke. You can get one which cuts on both strokes, however. Besides the combination you can buy either type separately, and others come with interchangeable pruning and saw attachments for the same pole.

Power tools. Already mentioned are the cordless, rechargeable electric grass shears and electric (or gasoline operated) hedge trimmers. The electric hedge trimmers come both cordless and with a long cord.

Professional tree trimmers and forestry workers who do a high volume of pruning and clearing often use air and hydraulic power pruning tools. Some of these can cut limbs up to 2 inches in diameter, but the tools are not practical for the average homeowner.

More suited to the home gardener are the lightweight power saws. Professionals have been using these for heavy branch work for a long time. The lighter, smaller models are a practical pruning tool for home gardeners as well.

Surface-forming tools. An unusual pruning implement is the "surface forming" tool which is widely used by carpenters for smoothing rough edges of boards. It finishes pruning cuts to perfection. Large pruning cuts (about 2 inches in diameter or larger) are often smoothed

SPEED SAW, LANCE TEETH

SPEED SAW, RAKER TEETH

RIGID HANDLE CURVED SAW

GRIP HANDLE FOLDING SAW

FOLDING SAW

POLE SAW

POLE PRUNER

POLE SAW WITH
HANGING HOOK

POLE SAW
AND PRUNER

CHAIN SAW

ELECTRIC HEDGE TRIMMER

RASP

with a sharp chisel or knife. But you can do a faster, more efficient job with this kind of rasp, and without the risk of cutting yourself. It is also better for the tree—a well-smoothed pruning cut heals faster and resists invasion by damaging organisms. These lightweight rasps are available at most hardware stores and they come with replaceable blades.

Sharpening your pruning shears. Until the shears in the photographs shown below were cleaned and sharpened, they couldn't prune with smooth, even cuts. Nothing was drastically wrong with them—except what happens after typical (not highly conscientious) garden use: Over several seasons of pruning they had collected some rust; dust and plant juice had accumulated and dried; the cutting edge had been nicked. That was enough to dull the blades and make them stick together when they opened and closed.

If your shears are in a similar state, it's simple enough to restore them to good condition by cleaning, sharpening, and oiling, as shown in these photographs. But if your shears are in worse shape—large notches in the blade, a gap at the point where blades should touch—take them to a professional with the tools and experience to do a good job. Remember that bad sharpening can very easily ruin a good tool.

And don't take chances with especially fine shears, or those with special nuts and bolts or other complicated mechanisms that require precise adjustments with specific tools. Take them to an expert, or send them to the manufacturer (if it is one of the tool companies that offer to repair or sharpen their own products at a nominal charge).

Sharpening your pruning saws. Pruning saws are another matter. To sharpen the teeth on a saw you need some very special tools and skills. If a pruning saw cuts less efficiently than it used to, don't try to sharpen it yourself. Take it to a commercial saw sharpener.

RUB rust and grime from disassembled shears with medium grade emery cloth. Don't sand sharp part of cutting edge.

SHARPEN CUTTING edge by moving mill file at slight angle across blade; go from back toward cutting edge.

SQUARE edge and remove nicks from blade with round file. If blade has square edge, is not nicked, leave alone.

OIL joint after assembling shears. Wash and dry sharpened shears after each use, wipe with oiled rag before storing.

Encyclopedia

Instructions for pruning each of the most popular shrubs, trees, vines, and perennials are given on the next 74 pages. All plants except fruits are listed alphabetically by botanical name. If you want to look up a plant using its common name (Oak, for example), a cross-reference will lead you to its botanical name (Quercus, for example). Fruits—apple, cherry, blackberry, and so forth—are listed only under their common names. Unfamiliar terms used in the pruning instructions are defined in the glossary on pages 88 to 96. Where drawings are used as part of the pruning instructions, a thin black rectangle across a stem or branch represents a pruning cut.

AARON'S BEARD. See Hypericum.

ABELIA. Evergreen, partially evergreen, or deciduous shrubs. Will withstand heavy pruning but need only light and selective pruning to maintain size and graceful arching form. In spring prune lightly by thinning out unwanted branches to maintain desired shape. Cut about ⅓ of old, grayish-colored stems back to ground each fall or winter to maintain attractive, open, arching branch pattern. New shoots that develop in spring will produce best flowers. To control height, pinch out growing tips. You can clip abelia as hedge, but you'll lose some of graceful beauty by shearing it. In coldest climates, cut plants back to ground and protect with straw or mulch. New growth will sprout when warm weather returns. Make attractive informal flowering hedge if controlled by selectively thinning out some branches.

ABELIOPHYLLUM distichum. White forsythia. Deciduous shrub. Lower and slower growing than true forsythia. Requires less pruning. Renew by pruning immediately after flowering. To encourage new flowering wood, cut ⅓ of old shoots to ground.

ABIES. Fir. Evergreen trees. Slow growing. Unnecessary to prune except for removal of dead, weak and damaged wood. Conifers generally require more careful pruning (when necessary) than other trees. Before you prune, reread the section on conifers (see *Pruning Glossary*). Two important don'ts to remember: don't cut back into leafless wood, or the whole branch is likely to die; don't cut leader to keep the tree lower, for you'll ruin its natural shape and good looks. If leader becomes damaged, encourage one of the branches in topmost whorl to replace it by staking and tying branch into upright position. Never place a fir where it does not have room to grow because you will not be able to keep it small without ruining its natural shape.

ABUTILON. Flowering maple, Chinese bellflower, Chinese lantern. Evergreen, sprawling shrubs. Can be trained as standards and as formal or informal espaliers. Rapid growers, they require severe cutting back in early spring. If convenient or necessary, continual pinching of branch tips during growing season will keep shrubs compact. Pinching also encourages formation of new wood which bears flowers. Rejuvenate often each spring by cutting oldest stems to ground. If hit by frost, wait until new growth begins, then cut damaged wood back to fresh shoots.

ABYSSINIAN BANANA. See Ensete.

ACACIA. Evergreen shrubs and trees. Best to prune while in bloom or directly afterwards but can be pruned anytime. Most forms can be pruned quite heavily because they are such vigorous growers. Whether they are trees or shrubs depends on particular species and how they are pruned in youth. Cut off lead shoot and it grows as shrub. Shorten lowest branches below scaffold, then remove when trunk is sturdy and self-supporting or until lower branches begin to be shaded out and it will grow tree-like (if leader is undamaged). Stake tree types until deeply anchored. Thin out whole branches on large trees to open interiors, reduce dieback of shaded branches, and prevent wind damage. Thin by cutting branches back to trunk.

ACALYPHA. Evergreen tropical shrubs. Control size with regular pinching or they will grow to bulky 10 ft. With heavy pruning, they make good house plants.

ACANTHOPANAX sieboldianus (*Aralia pentaphylla*). Deciduous shrub. Can withstand heavy pruning. Renew by thinning out some of the oldest stems each winter or cutting to ground before new spring growth begins. New growth will quickly follow.

ACANTHUS mollis. Bear's breech. Perennial. Cut plant completely to ground at end of flowering period in mid to late summer for complete renewal of growth. If grown for foliage alone, cut off flower stalks before bloom.

ACER. Maple. Deciduous or evergreen trees or large shrubs. Take many forms; how you prune depends upon the form you want. When grown as trees, they require normal staking and training to single trunk. Very little pruning, aside from removal of dead, weak, and interfering growths, will be required after they have reached maturity. Most bleed profusely, so avoid pruning in spring just before and during period of most active growth. As shrubs, encourage multiple trunks. Do not stub branches back or you'll encourage unsightly, broom-like growth.

A. buergerianum. Trident maple. Deciduous tree. Low, spreading growth. Needs staking and training to make it branch high. Good bonsai subject.

A. campestre. Hedge maple. Deciduous tree. Slow growing, forming dense, compact, and rounded head. Can be trained and sheared into high hedge.

A. circinatum. Vine maple. Deciduous shrub or small tree. Responds well to shaping in a variety of forms. Let it go untrimmed to make natural bowers or espalier against shady side of a wall. Stake and train as a single-trunked small shade tree or as multi-stemmed tree.

A. ginnala. Amur maple. Deciduous shrub or small tree. Stake and train as a single-trunked tree or a multiple-trunked tall shrub.

A. griseum. Paperbark maple. Deciduous tree. Thin to take best advantage of striking winter silhouette of its bare, angling branches.

A. japonicum. Fullmoon maple. Deciduous shrub. Small and slow growing. Best thinned and shaped as shrub.

A. macrophyllum. Bigleaf maple. Deciduous tree. Vigorous grower, needs early staking, training. Too big for most gardens. Roots are greedy and invasive.

A. negundo. Box elder. Deciduous tree. Fast-growing, brittle. When young, prune to form good, strong framework. Thin to keep top open; cut out wind-damaged wood.

SOMETIMES FIR TREES and other vertical conifers form a double leader (two main stems). Cut out the poorer shaped of the two. Make cut at the base.

A. palmatum. Japanese maple. Deciduous shrub or tree. Easy to shape into form and size you want and keep that way. Snip out branches that head in wrong direction; selectively cut back branches to accentuate its habit of growing in planed, layered branches. Dwarf mounding types can be kept low by heading back branches that show tendency to grow upright. Can be trained as multi-stemmed tree.

A. saccharinum. Silver maple. Deciduous tree. Fast growing. Weak wood and narrow crotch angles make it subject to breakage. Thin out branches when young to avoid crowding, retaining best formed, strongest crotches. Also thin top to lessen wind resistance.

ACHILLEA. Yarrow. Perennial. After first bloom, remove stems that have flowered. Cut back to point where fresh growth is coming up. It will bloom again on new growth in late summer or fall.

ACMENA smithii (*Eugenia smithii*). Lilly-Pilly tree. Evergreen large shrub or small tree. Awkward in growth unless trained when young. Prune after dramatic show of berries in winter.

ACOKANTHERA. Evergreen shrub. Avoid poisonous fruits by removing flowers as they fade. Can be espaliered, grown in a tub as small tree, or let range unchecked as handsome, open shrub.

ACROCARPUS fraxinifolius. Deciduous to almost evergreen tree. Somewhat tender; narrow in form. Needs support when young. Cut out branches which detract from its slender shape.

ACROCOMIA. See Palms.

ACTINIDIA. Deciduous vine. Rampant grower; can be pruned heavily if required to shape or to control growth and pattern. Do major pruning while dormant or just as buds begin to swell. Remove some old wood, cutting above buds where you want growth.

ADAM'S NEEDLE. See Yucca.

ADENOCARPUS. Canary Island lupine. Evergreen or semi-evergreen shrub. Can be pruned heavily after flowering if required. Keep faded flowers picked off to prevent seed formation.

AESCULUS. Deciduous trees or large shrubs. Normal training for form when young, very little pruning when mature except to remove dead, diseased wood. Prune in winter or early spring just before new growth begins.

AETHIONEMA. Stonecress. Perennial. Shear stems back after flowers fade.

AFRICAN BOXWOOD. See Myrsine.

AFRICAN LINDEN. See Sparmannia.

ACER PALMATUM 'Dissectum,' a fine-leafed Japanese maple. On mature plants, the only pruning needed is to maintain the clean-cut outlines of the foliage domes.

AFRICAN RED ALDER. See Cunonia.

AFRICAN VIOLET. See Saintpaulia.

AGATHIS robusta. Queensland kauri. Evergreen tree. Remove errant branches while young before they dominate and detract from striking, naturally layered form. Accentuate this form by selectively removing unwanted growth. Also cut off any branches tending to form a double leader.

AGAVE americana. Century plant. Succulent. When 10-15 years old, it sends up flower stalk that grows about a foot daily. If allowed to develop and bloom, plant dies. You can save plant by removing stalk as soon as it appears. Better yet, let it bloom and then propagate by removing and planting some suckers growing around base.

AGONIS. Peppermint tree, Australian willow myrtle, juniper myrtle. Evergreen trees. Pruning depends on form you want. Can be trained as tree or espaliered against a wall. Prune in spring (after danger of frost in cold climate). Freezes to ground in some areas but will come back from stump.

AILANTHUS altissima (*A. glandulosa*). Tree-of-heaven. Deciduous tree. Fast growing with brittle wood; needs selective pruning when young to develop desirable form. Suckers profusely; remove suckers, thin out unwanted wood while dormant to keep in control and to maintain desired form.

AJUGA. Carpet bugle. Perennial. Remove faded flowers. Cut back runners drastically to keep from creeping too far. Replant every 3 or 4 years.

AKEBIA quinata. Fiveleaf akebia. Deciduous vine, evergreen in mild winters. Responds well to heavy pruning but can be controlled with annual cutting back (in spring before growth begins) and by pinching back unwanted growth during growing season. Recovers quickly when cut to ground. For open tracery effect when grown on post or column, cut out all but 2 or 3 basal stems.

ALBIZIA julibrissin. Silk tree. Deciduous tree. Rapid grower to 40 ft. can be held to 10-20 ft. umbrella by heading back. This is the mimosa of the eastern United States. A bit unpredictable in its growth habit. Unpruned, will grow in tiers and usually have several stems. Tends to form branches close to ground if not trained as a tree in its youth by removing branches which are lower than desired. When it is the height you want, top the tree by cutting tip off leader to encourage broader or more umbrella-like crown. Prune in winter or early spring. In winter areas, limit pruning to spring when damage of frost is past.

ALDER BUCKTHORN. See Rhamnus.

ALDER. See Alnus.

ALECTRYON excelsum. Titoki. Evergreen tree. Grows 30-60 ft. high. Can be pruned as tall hedge.

ALLAMANDA cathartica. Evergreen viny shrub or shrubby vine. Will climb to 10 ft. or spread as a shrub, depending on pruning. Pinch during growing season to control growth and shape it to desired form.

ALMOND. Deciduous tree. Requires normal training for the first 2 or 3 seasons in order to form strong framework (see *Training Young Fruit Trees* in the *Pruning Glossary*). Once an almond has become a real tree, you prune it primarily for wood renewal. Almond bears at ends of short spurs which produce for about 5 years, so your pruning objective should be to remove about 1/5 of fruiting wood each season. Also remove dead wood and overcrowded branches as necessary. Rejuvenate older tree by heading branches back to healthy, sound laterals. Almond grows vigorously and young, healthy tree may throw all its energy into vegetative growth which causes it not to start bearing when it should. In this case, stop pruning for a season or two. This will slow heavy growth and bring tree into bearing.

ALMOND, FLOWERING. See Prunus.

ALNUS. Alder. Deciduous trees. Tend to grow multiple trunks; make excellent screening plants. To grow as single-trunked trees, select best young trunk and cut all others down to base. Thin crowns selectively to develop strong framework. They do not require much pruning; when necessary, prune in winter to shape and to remove dead or crossing branches and sucker growth. Roots can be invasive.

ALOYSIA triphylla (*Lippia citriodora*). Lemon verbena. Deciduous or partially evergreen herb-shrub. Pinch during growing season to shape it as you desire. Makes interesting tracery against wall. Thin out old, weak wood before spring growth begins.

ALPINIA speciosa (*A. nutans*). Shell flower, porcelain ginger. Perennial. Remove canes that have flowered to make room for new flowering stems.

ALSOPHILA. See Fern, Tree.

ALSTROEMERIA. Perennial. Cut off ripened foliage and faded flowers to ground level.

ALYSSUM. Perennials. Shear off flower heads after they finish blooming to improve chances of second bloom in the fall. Trimming also helps to keep plants neat and dense by forcing side branches.

AMELANCHIER. Shadblow, shadbush, service berry. Deciduous shrubs or small trees. Prune lightly during winter or just before growth starts in the spring. Look best when allowed to grow naturally with minimum of pruning.

AMPELOPSIS brevipedunculata. Blueberry climber. Deciduous vine. Vigorous grower. Cut back from windows, doors. Cut back and thin out main stems selectively for good spacing. Prune in spring.

AMORPHA. Indigo bush. Deciduous shrub. Flowers on new wood; while dormant, cut out some of oldest wood each year to renew. Will recover if frozen back in colder areas.

AMUR CORK TREE. See Phellodendron.

ANCHUSA capensis. Cape forget-me-not, summer forget-me-not. Biennial. Shear back after first crop of flowers to encourage a second.

ANDROMEDA polifolia. Bog rosemary. Evergreen shrublet. Can be pruned as required to shape after spring bloom.

ANEMOPAEGMA chamberlaynii (*Bignonia chamberlaynii*). Yellow trumpet vine. Evergreen vine. Blooms on new wood. Shorten all shoots in spring to ensure growth of lateral shoots and produce flower buds. Thin growth after bloom and cut weak shoots to ground.

ANGEL'S TRUMPET. See Datura.

ANGOPHORA lanceolata. Gum myrtle. Evergreen tree. Related to eucalyptus and as tough and tolerant. Grows big, needs lots of room. Give it normal training when young. Stake young tree only if it simply cannot stand on its own. As tree matures, prune to shape and to prevent overcrowding of branches. Thin by taking out complete branches back to lateral on main branch. Prune anytime, but best time is late winter, early spring.

ANIGOZANTHUS. Kangaroo paw. Evergreen perennial. Remove dead foliage. Will bloom from late spring to fall if spent flowering spikes are cut to ground. Divide clumps every year or every other year.

ANISACANTHUS thurberi. Desert honeysuckle. Evergreen or deciduous shrub. Looks best when treated as perennial. Cut to ground in winter (if frost doesn't do it) with pruning shears. If frozen, remove dead foliage when new growth appears.

ANNONA cherimola. Cherimoya. Briefly deciduous large shrub or small tree. Very little pruning required except to form well-balanced tree. Overcrowding branches should be removed to provide light to inside growth. Has low-branching habit; remove those below the desired height as tree matures. Good espalier subject.

ANNUALS. An annual is a plant that grows its entire course—from seed to natural death—in one year. Most annuals that you might grow in your garden from seed or nursery plants need little or no pruning during their short but valuable lifetimes. Some, however, do benefit from certain pruning acts. The things you can do are similar to the things you do to the longer-lasting trees, shrubs, and perennials:

1. Pinching tips in early stages of growth makes many lanky or too-open annuals more bushy.

2. Most annuals can benefit from grooming during the peak of their careers. Pick or cut off dead and fading flowers, broken stems, and any branches that spoil the plant's appearance.

3. A few annuals, including petunias, snapdragons, and sweet alyssum, can be cut back hard at the end of what appears to be their complete blooming season, forcing voluminous new growth which in turn will probably produce another cycle of flowers.

ANTHEMIS nobilis. Chamomile. Evergreen perennial. A lawn substitute if mowed or sheared and rolled several times a year to keep low and compact. If not used as lawn, flowering season can be prolonged by removing the faded blooms to prevent the seeds from developing.

ANTHURIUM. Perennial greenhouse or house plant. If plant gets too tall, cut off top 5 or 6 in. of stem and plant this cutting for new plant.

APACHE PLUME. See Fallugia.

APHELANDRA squarrosa. Evergreen house plant. If you keep old flowers picked off, plant will remain colorful for 3-4 months. To make plant bushy and produce more blooms, cut stems back to 1 or 2 pairs of leaves after flowering. A single-stemmed plant will usually produce 2 stems after cutting back. If you pinch tips of these 2 stems when they are a couple of inches long, they will produce 4 new shoots.

APPLE. Deciduous fruit tree. Young tree requires considerable amount of pruning attention to guide it into strong framework (see *Training Young Fruit Trees* in the *Pruning Glossary*).

On mature tree, pruning should be mostly corrective (removal of dead wood, weak limbs). You will also want to thin out new growth on mature tree to encourage development of bearing spurs on older wood and to keep tree desired size. What are bearing spurs and why are they important? Apple trees produce fruit mainly on ends of long-lived spurs, and as a rule require considerably less pruning than some of the other fruit trees. Spurs which bear apples develop from vegetative buds on new shoots. As spurs grow, fruit buds which will produce following season's crop form on the ends. A spur therefore begins producing fruit in its second year. The following spring, the spur

ON YOUNG APPLE TREE, cut A removes weak branch. Branch 2 will grow in length. Cuts B and C subdue branches 3 and 4. On mature tree (with size being maintained), A removes last year's growth; B favors branch 1; C would stimulate replacement wood.

ON YOUNG TREE, cuts at A or A¹ direct growth into uncut branch. B makes branch 1 or 2 more dominant. On old tree, all cuts are to hold back the length.

TWENTY-YEAR-OLD DWARF APPLE espaliered on fence. Fruit bearing laterals off main side branches must be headed back often (up to four times each summer).

BRANCHES 2 AND 3 hang down too much. Apricots will form on spurs at right and along Branch 1 (formed last year).

CUT AT CENTER would make tree more spreading; cut at A would subdue branch 1 so branch 2 could maintain advantage.

puts out a little more growth and sets another terminal fruit bud. Sometimes the spur branches, though this occurs more frequently on pears, which have a similar branching habit. Apple spurs often go through this growing and fruit-setting process over a period as long as 20 years.

APRICOT. Deciduous fruit tree. Unlike apple, pear, or cherry, an apricot tree requires heavy pruning for good fruit production. It bears most fruit on short spurs which form on last year's growth and remain fruitful for about 4 years (see *Bearing Habits* in the *Pruning Glossary*). Pruning should be directed toward conserving enough new growth (which will produce spurs) to replace old, exhausted spurs which should be cut out. To stimulate new, productive growth, cut back older branches to younger, vigorous lateral. For young apricot tree (planting to 4 years old, see *Training Young Fruit Trees* in the *Pruning Glossary*).

APRICOT, JAPANESE FLOWERING. See Prunus.

AQUILEGIA. Columbine. Perennials. Remove faded flowers to encourage longer season of bloom and to help control excessive reseeding. If cut to ground after main bloom period, they may flower again the same season.

ARABIS. Rockcress. Perennial. Cut back enough growth after bloom to remove all seed heads and old flower stalks. Plant will produce new growth, another set of buds, and scattered flowers through summer.

ARALIA chinensis. Chinese angelica. Deciduous shrub-tree. Vertical, slightly spreading habit. Cut out surplus stems at ground level for open effect. Remove diseased or damaged stems if required.

ARALIA, JAPANESE. See Fatsia.

ARALIA, THREADLEAF FALSE. See Dizygotheca.

ARAUCARIA. Monkey puzzle tree, Norfolk Island pine. Evergreen trees. Require very little pruning. If leader is damaged, select best branch immediately below and brace it vertically to take its place.

ARAUJIA sericofera. White bladder flower. Evergreen or partially deciduous vine. Very little pruning necessary. Thin and cut stems for proper spacing, shape.

ARBORVITAE, AMERICAN. See Thuja.

ARBORVITAE, ORIENTAL. See Thuja.

ARBUTUS. Evergreen tree and shrub-tree. Treat all pruning cuts with wound dressing for disease control.

A. menziesii. Madrone. Madroña. Evergreen tree or large shrub. Needs only light pruning to shape. Do this in fall or early spring.

A. unedo. Strawberry tree. Evergreen shrub-tree. Plant has interesting trunk and stem pattern that responds well to selective branch removal, shaping, and training. You can train it easily as single-trunked or multiple-trunked tree, or leave unpruned to form dense hedge. Cut out dead branches anytime; prune to shape in spring before active growth starts.

ARCHONTOPHOENIX. See Palm.

ARCTOSTAPHYLOS. Manzanita. Evergreen shrubs. Range in size from creepers to shrubs and small trees. Control growth and shape by frequent tip-pinching during growing season.

A. columbiana. Hairy manzanita. Naturally assumes an interesting branch pattern. Pinch back while young to prevent legginess. Thin to expose branching pattern you want.

A. densiflora. Vine Hill manzanita. Low growing and spreading. Tip-pinch plant while young to shape.

A. d. 'Howard McMinn.' Mounding spreading growth. Tip-pinch after flowering to make it dense. (Don't pinch tips of prostrate branches.)

A. d. 'Sentinel.' Can be trained as small tree by selecting dominant stem or stems and removing others.

A. edmundsii. Little Sur manzanita. Pinch back while young to encourage bushiness.

A. glandulosa. Eastwood manzanita. Sends up many shoots from woody base. To keep it low, pinch out leaders when soft and young.

A. manzanita. Common manzanita. Thin to expose branching pattern you want. Pinch and head back to prevent legginess.

A. patula. Greenleaf manzanita. Thin out unwanted wood to show off beauty of trunk and branches.

A. stanfordiana. Stanford manzanita. If it becomes too dense, carefully trim out center branches.

A. uva-ursi. Bearberry, kinnikinnick. Ground cover. Pinch tips of vigorous growth to induce branching. Shear back when established to thicken.

ARDISIA. Evergreen shrubs or shrublets. Prune only to control size and spread.

ARECASTRUM romanzoffianum. See Palm.

ARENGA engleri. See Palm.

ARISTOLOCHIA. Deciduous vines. Require little maintenance other than directing twining shoots over area you want to cover. If they become too heavy after several seasons, cut back in the winter and train selected new spring shoots to cover. Respond well to heavy pruning.

ARISTOTELIA racemosa. New Zealand wineberry. Evergreen shrub or small tree. Normal training while young for good branch structure; minimum of pruning required as plant matures.

ARMERIA. Thrift, sea pink. Hardy evergreen perennials. Require little pruning other than clipping off faded flowers and flower stalks.

ARONIA arbutifolia. Red chokeberry. Deciduous shrub. Large, openly branched, upright growth. Prune to encourage branching while young; prune to shape after berries have dropped.

ARROWWOOD. See Viburnum.

ARTEMISIA. Evergreen or deciduous shrubs or woody perennials.

A. absinthium. Common wormwood. Perennial. Woody shrub. In spring, cut it back to within 6 in. of the base to renew.

A. frigida. Fringed wormwood. Perennial. Young plants are compact; to keep their shape, cut back when they become rangy.

A. pycnocephala. Sandhill sage. Shrubby perennial. Remove flower spikes as they open to keep the plant compact.

ARTICHOKE. Perennial vegetable. After each stem has given its last artichoke, it will seem to fold up, and leaves will die back to a degree. This is the signal for you to cut the stem or stalk back to the base.

ARUNDO donax. Giant reed. Perennial. Cut out dead stems and thin occasionally to avoid overcrowded look. Extremely invasive. Plant only where you can control it.

ASH. See Fraxinus.

ASH, MOUNTAIN. See Sorbus.

ASPARAGUS, EDIBLE. Perennial vegetable. When plant turns brown in late fall or early winter, cut stems to ground. In cold winter areas, permit dead stalks to stand until spring before cutting.

ASPARAGUS, ORNAMENTAL. Perennials. Once established, plants need little attention except to remove dead tops when they become noticeable. Remove old stalks at base when brown. Thin stems of vining kinds to prevent tangling. (*A. retrofractus* sheds "needles" on some branches, then grows another

crop; don't be too hasty in cutting out brown, dead-looking stalks.)

ASPEN. See Populus.

ASTER. Perennials. Strong growers are invasive, need root pruning to control.

A. frikartii. Remove faded flowers before they start to go to seed to prolong blooming season. If plants get lanky, or if you want to control their size, cut back to 4 in. from the ground. New growth will come quickly.

A. novae-angliae; A. novi-belgii. Michaelmas daisy. Pinch when young to induce branching; then, when plant is a foot high, cut back hard if you want lower, bushier plant with more flowers. Continue to pinch out new growth, as you would with chrysanthemums. For better formed plant with more flowers, thin out stalks on plant that hasn't been divided for a year or more, leaving only 6-8 stems (most authorities recommend dividing every year in spring). After it finishes blooming, remove faded flowers and cut plant to ground to prevent seeding and growth of inferior new plants. Some early varieties bloom a second time if you cut back after first flowers fade.

ASTILBE. False spiraea, meadow sweet. Perennial. Cut spent flowers to keep plant looking neat and to induce more bloom. In fall, after leaves die, cut stems to ground; new ones will come up in spring. Protect plant in colder areas by not removing dead foliage until spring growth appears.

ATLAS CEDAR. See Cedrus.

ATRIPLEX. Saltbush. Evergreen or deciduous shrubs. Respond well to heavy pruning. Grow as shrubs, windbreaks, clipped hedges.

AUBRIETA deltoidea. Common aubrieta. Perennial. Blooms profusely in spring. To maintain brilliance of separate colors, shear back enough growth after bloom to remove old seed heads but always keep some foliage. Plant will produce new growth, another set of buds, and scattered flowers through summer. Trimming also helps keep plant neat and dense by forcing side branches.

AUCUBA japonica. Japanese aucuba. Evergreen shrub. Few plants are easier to hold in check by pruning. New growth develops quickly; you can prune regularly and hardly notice that shrub has been cut. Shorten plant by cutting back to a pair of buds or to just above leaf joint.

AUSTRALIAN FUCHSIA. See Correa.

AVOCADO (*Persea americana*). Evergreen tree. Normal training while young. Grown primarily for fruit production, this tree should not necessarily be forced into attractive form. Shape varies with variety and is also affected by weight of fruit forcing branches down. Very little pruning should be necessary for mature tree beyond normal removal of weak, damaged wood. (In fact, commercial avocado growers seldom prune tree.) Dead branches and twigs can normally be snapped off with your hands. A continual inside die-back is normal condition as tree matures. Remove dead wood regularly. Bark of avocado is very sensitive to sunlight and sunburns easily so be careful not to remove too much foliage, creating openings through which sunlight can enter and cause damage. Head back upright growth to side branch if you want to keep fruit crop low. (It may be necessary to head back long drooping branches or brace them to prevent their breaking under heavy fruit load.) Best time for any pruning is after harvest.

AZALEA. See Rhododendron.

AZARA microphylla. Evergreen shrub. Can also be trained into single-trunked, small tree. Fan-like, pendulous stems make it natural for espaliering. Responds well to heavy cutting but usually requires only shaping. Prune whenever needed.

BACCHARIS pilularis. Dwarf coyote brush, dwarf chaparral broom. Evergreen shrub. In small plantings prune each year before new growth starts. Cut arching branches and those that grow too tall or out of proportion to rest of plant. Thin out some old wood to rejuvenate. After flowering, remove old flower stems to keep plant looking neat.

BALD CYPRESS. See Taxodium.

BALLOON FLOWER. See Platycodon.

BAMBOO. Giant grasses with woody stems. Large group, includes *Bambusa, Phyllostachys, Pseudosasa.* Major pruning concern with bamboos is to keep them controlled. Once established, running kinds grow fast and spread out of their intended area by invasive, underground roots. All bamboo should be thinned regularly and oldest stems removed to make it easier to clean out old leaves. Beyond this, how you prune depends upon growth habit of your bamboo as well as purpose you have in mind. All bamboos can take a good deal of pruning; control them by thinning and shearing. Best time to do heaviest cutting is during young, rapid growing stage in spring. Bamboos can be divided into 4 general groups: 1) dwarf or low-growing ground cover types; 2) clump bamboos with a fountainlike habit of growth; 3) running bamboos of moderate size and more or less vertical growth; and 4) giant bamboos. To keep dwarf types low and

18" GALVANIZED METAL OR ASBESTOS

ABOVE, BAMBOO SPREADS under a fence, pops up in neighbor's lawn. Below, control method: a subterranean fence.

compact, shear tops back when required; shorten shoots that grow too high. The hardy clump types have widest use in landscaping and can be grown singly, lined up and left unclipped as informal screens, or clipped into hedges and screens. Vertical and giant types can also be planted as groves or used as tall screens and hedges. (On tallest growing kinds you'll have to take out tallest stems to the ground frequently to keep them as low as you want.) An interesting way to prune vertical types is to thin some of the secondary branches back to the main stem. Thinned in this fashion, with half to ⅔ of the leaves removed, bamboo makes an attractive plant with an interesting silhouette. All types—except ground covers—look good when thinned to show off the stems. When cutting stems, take them at or below ground level. When plants get old and dense,

THESE GIANT BAMBOO have had side branches trimmed off half way up. It makes the silhouette more interesting.

cut back heavily; new growth will quickly form a dense mass of foliage farther down. *Root pruning:* before strong rhizomes invade flower and shrubbery beds and lawns, or pop up into driveways and other paved areas, cut them off at edge of bed with sharp spade. Push spade straight down as far as it will go. In some cases you may have to dig a trench and cut down to double depth. You can also plant in containers or use dividers of galvanized sheet metal, cement or redwood set 18 in. deep in ground around plants to keep them in bounds.

BAMBOO, HEAVENLY. See Nandina.

BAMBURANTA. See Hybophrynium.

BANANA. See Musa, Ensete.

BANANA SHRUB. See Michelia.

BAPTISIA australis. False indigo, wild indigo. Perennial. Cut back spent flowers for repeat bloom (unless you want to dry the seed pods for use in winter flower arrangements).

BARBERRY. See Berberis.

BAUHINIA. Evergreen or deciduous trees or half-climbing shrubs.

B. blakeana. Hong Kong orchid tree. Partially deciduous for short period. Train as small tree or allow it to branch at base to form large, multiple-stemmed shrub.

B. galpinii. Red bauhinia. Evergreen to semi-deciduous shrub. Often classed as vine, but may ramble into tree. Prune back heavily after flowering to keep shape; also pinch back tips at any time except during cold weather. If plant is kept rootbound, it will remain more shrublike. Heavy pruning after flowering encourages new growth that bears flowers. These appear in clusters of 2-10 at about every third joint as new growth elongates.

B. variegata. (Commonly sold as *B. purpurea*.) Purple orchid tree. Partially to wholly deciduous. If staked and selectively pruned, can be trained as single-trunked tree 20-35 ft. tall with nearly equal spread. Without pruning and staking, it most often grows as multi-trunked shrub.

BAY, CALIFORNIA. See Umbellularia.

BAYBERRY. See Myrica.

BEAR GRASS. See Xerophyllum.

BEARBERRY. See Arctostaphylos.

BEARD TONGUE. See Penstemon.

BEAR'S BREECH. See Acanthus.

BEAUTY BERRY. See Callicarpa.

BEAUTY BUSH. See Kolkwitzia.

BEECH. See Fagus.

BEAUMONTIA grandiflora. Herald's trumpet, Easter lily vine. Evergreen vine. Thin and head back lightly after flowering to keep in scale, but preserve good proportion of 2 and 3-year-old wood. Flowers on old wood; if you cut back too severely you will reduce the bloom.

BEGONIA. Perennials. Susceptible to stem rot, so when you cut flowers leave about an inch of flower stem on plants. Stub will cure and fall off naturally. This avoids fresh wound on main stem that would be open to infection. Faded flowers and leaves can also cause rot and should be removed. Pinch out growing tips to encourage branching, keep plants compact.

BELLFLOWER. See Campanula.

BELOPERONE guttata (*B. tomentosa*). Shrimp plant. Evergreen shrub. Grows into 3-4 ft. mound but can be kept much lower. To shape plant, pinch continuously in early growth until compact mound of foliage is obtained and then let bloom. To encourage continued bushiness, cut back stems when flower bracts turn black.

BERBERIS. Barberry. Deciduous and evergreen shrubs. Normally require a minimum of pruning beyond what is needed to keep them neat and shaped. They tolerate pruning well; the more vigorous growers can take a lot of cutting back for growth renewal. Left unpruned, some inner branches die and plants become leggy and ratty. Cut oldest wood to within 4-6 in. of ground to renew. Shear hedges whenever required; prune shrubs lightly to shape after bloom and berries have gone. Do renewal pruning before new spring growth starts. Sheared, dense plants are susceptible to scale insects. If this becomes a problem, thin plants and take appropriate control measures.

BERGENIA. Perennial, evergreen except in coldest areas. To keep neat, cut or pull off old faded leaves and remove old flower stalks as they finish blooming. Divide and replant whenever crowns appear crowded. Cut back to ground yearly if you wish to prevent legginess.

BETULA. Birch. Deciduous trees. Birches have a habit of growing branches of equal size from the same point, forming weak, narrow crotches. Remove all but one of these shoots to develop strong frameworks. Need normal staking and training in youth to shape to the forms you want. Thin out crowded growth and do major pruning in winter or very early spring. If pruning is done at other times, trees will tend to bleed. Although this won't hurt them, it can discolor the bark and possibly cause a secondary trunk infection.

BEGONIAS are an exception to the rule: leave a stub when you cut the flowers.

Mature trees require little or no pruning except for removal of weak or damaged wood. On many varieties you also want to remove lower branches to expose the attractive bark.

BIGNONIA. Trumpet vine. Botanists have reclassified plants formerly called *Bignonia*, so that the trumpet vines you knew as *Bignonia* are now placed under other names. Many are still sold under the old names. Since most gardeners still compare one "bignonia" with another when making their selections, we list them below and give the names under which they are described:

B. chamberlaynii. See Anemopaegma.

B. cherere. See Phaedranthus.

B. chinensis. See Campsis.

B. jasminoides. See Pandorea.

B. radicans. See Campsis.

B. speciosa. See Clytostoma.

B. tweediana. See Doxantha.

B. violacea. See Clytostoma.

BIRCH. See Betula.

BIRD OF PARADISE. See Strelitzia.

BITTERSWEET. See Celastrus.

BLACK OLIVE. See Bucida.

BLACKBERRY. If you don't dedicate yourself to your blackberry plants, caring for them as soon as they need care, or if you have only limited space to plant, blackberries can be sheer disaster. Nothing is better than a perfect crop of aromatic Boysens, but nothing is worse than several hundred square feet of canes gone wild, covered with murderous spines and shooting up new runners everywhere.

Among the most popular blackberries are 'Boysen' and 'Thornless Boysen,' with large, aromatic, slightly tart berries; 'Evergreen' and 'Thornless Evergreen,' with heavy crops of large, very firm, sweet berries; 'Himalaya,' an especially thorny, vigorous plant producing jet black, medium-sized berries over a long season; 'Logan' and 'Thornless Logan,' with large, reddish berries that are quite sour and excellent for cooking; 'Nectar,' identical to 'Boysen'; 'Olallie,' with large, shiny black, firm, sweet berries with overtones of wild blackberry flavor; and 'Young' and 'Thornless Young,' which are similar to 'Boysen' but have berries that tend to be a little sweeter and are shiny rather than dull. Other kinds include 'Aurora,' 'Cascade,' 'Marion,' and 'Texas Wonder.'

Blackberries will require some kind of trellis and they need full sun and large amounts of water throughout the growing season. They should not be planted next to a fence, because the fence will block sunlight if it's solid, and because suckers will come up on the neighbor's side. When planting bare-root berries, spread roots and set plant about an inch deeper than it grew in the nursery. Set plants 3 ft. apart, in rows 5 or 6 ft. apart. Cut back the canes to 4-8 in.

Established berries need only a light trim in late winter. (Do heavy pruning at the end of summer after crop has been gathered.) To do light pruning, trim side branches to 12 in. Small, fruit-bearing branches will grow from these.

As soon as last of crop is harvested, you should begin heavy annual pruning. Cut to ground level all canes that have borne fruit. Select up to 16 sturdy canes for next year's production and weave or tie these on the trellis. Cut all weak canes to ground.

SELECTED BLACKBERRY CANES, shown woven onto the trellis at left and tied onto wires at right. Weave or tie selected canes after post-harvest pruning.

BLACK-EYED SUSAN. See Rudbeckia.

BLADDER SENNA. See Colutea.

BLECHNUM (*Lomaria*). Evergreen ferns.
    B. brasiliense. See Fern, Tree.
    B. gibbum. See Fern, Tree.
    B. spicant. See Fern, Hardy.

BLEEDING HEART. See Dicentra.

BLUE BLOSSOM. See Ceanothus.

BLUE DRACAENA. See Cordyline.

BLUE FESCUE. See Festuca.

BLUE MARGUERITE. See Felicia.

BLUEBEARD. See Caryopteris.

BLUEBELL CREEPER, AUSTRALIAN. See Sollya.

BLUEBERRY. Deciduous shrub. Should be pruned annually sometime after leaves fall and before it blooms. Most tend to bear so heavily that fruit size is decreased and growth of plant slows down. It must be thinned so that it will produce fewer, but larger berries. How you prune varies somewhat, depending upon whether your blueberry is low and spreading or upright. Spreading types seldom have multiple stems, upright plants have many stems. In general, cut out weak laterals and twiggy growth, as well as from ¼-⅓ of the least vigorous old wood. Heavy old stems that have lost their vitality may be removed at ground level. To limit fruit production, cut branches with many buds back ½-⅔, and cut fruiting shoots back to 3-5 buds each. Keep first-year plant from bearing by stripping off flowers. On older plant, cut back ends of twigs to point where fruit buds are widely spaced.

BLUEBERRY, BOX. See Vaccinium.

BOG ROSEMARY. See Andromeda.

BOSTON IVY. See Parthenocissus.

BOTTLEBRUSH. See Callistemon.

BOUGAINVILLEA. Evergreen shrubby vines. Vigorous twining growth to 20 ft. or more; can be restrained and kept lower by pruning. Don't be afraid to prune to renew plants' shape or direct growth, then remove weak growth and cut back heavy canes to basal buds. The buds usually grow fast and flower well, whereas weak growth seldom has good flowers. Prune heavily in spring after frost risk is over. First remove any branches killed by frost. Where growth is very thick, remove some laterals completely; others can be cut back, leaving short spurs where they join the main stem. Head back extremely long shoots to bring within bounds. If wall-grown plants, nip back long stems during growing season to produce more flowering wood. Shrubby kinds or heavily-pruned plants make good, self-supporting container shrubs for terrace or patio. Without support and with light corrective pruning, bougainvilleas can make broad, sprawling shrubs or bank and ground covers. When growth of plants used as shrubs or a ground cover is slow, cut back to ground the first or second year. Bougainvilleas are generally pruned more severely (and frequently) in frostfree areas where they are vigorous growers. Too severe pruning in colder regions may result in excessive vegetative growth at expense of flowers. Though tops may be damaged by frost, bougainvilleas usually make a strong comeback if roots have not been hurt.

BOUVARDIA. Evergreen shrubs. Loose, straggly growth habit. Pinch out stem tips on young plants to make them bushier. Cut back after flowering to stimulate new growth, more flowers.

BOX, BOXWOOD. See Buxus.

BOX ELDER. See Acer.

BOX SAND MYRTLE. See Leiophyllum.

BOXWOOD, AFRICAN. See Myrsine.

BOXWOOD, OREGON. See Pachistima.

BRACHYCHITON (*Sterculia*). Evergreen to partly or wholly deciduous trees. Normal guidance and training when young, very little pruning (except for removal of dead, weak wood) required on mature trees.

BRACHYSEMA lanceolatum. Scimitar shrub, Swan River pea shrub. Evergreen. Requires only light pruning. Thin out old, straggly stems in spring.

BRASSAIA actinophylla (*Schefflera actinophylla*). Queensland umbrella tree, octopus tree. Evergreen house plant; outdoor shrub/tree in warmest areas. Good bonsai subject. Rapid growing; cut out tips occasionally to keep from becoming leggy. Leggy stems can be cut almost to ground; they will branch and make a better shaped plant. For screening, plant 2-4 ft. apart and keep tipped to encourage bushiness.

BRAZIL RAINTREE. See Brunfelsia.

BREATH OF HEAVEN. See Coleonema.

BRIDAL WREATH. See Spiraea.

BRISBANE BOX. See Tristania.

BROOM. See Cytisus, Genista, Spartium.

BROUSSONETIA papyrifera. (Has been sold as *Morus papyrifera*.) Paper mulberry. Deciduous tree. Doesn't need much pruning beyond normal training and shaping for framework while young. Remove weak and crossing branches, dead wood in fall and summer. Cut out suckers wherever they appear.

BRUNFELSIA calycina. Brazil raintree. Evergreen shrub. Prune in the spring. Remove straggly growth and wood which detracts from desired shape.
    B. c. floribunda. Yesterday-today-and-tomorrow. Will reach 10 ft. or

more with several stems from the base; may be held as low as 3 ft. by removing tallest canes.

BUCIDA buceras. Black olive; geometry tree. Evergreen or deciduous tree. Prune lightly to keep small and to accentuate plant's geometric branching pattern. Can be trained into handsome bonsai.

BUCKEYE. See Aesculus.

BUCKTHORN. See Rhamnus.

BUCKWHEAT. See Eriogonum.

BUDDLEIA. Butterfly bush. Evergreen or deciduous shrub or small tree.

B. alternifolia. Fountain butterfly bush. Deciduous shrub or small tree. To encourage growth that will produce next season's blossoms, remove some oldest canes after flowering (on large plant take out a third of them) back to bottom two buds (about 4 in. of stem). Can also be trained up into small single or multiple-trunked tree.

B. davidii. Common butterfly bush, summer lilac. Deciduous or semi-evergreen shrub. Unlike *B. alternifolia*, this plant blooms on new wood rather than previous season's wood. So you can prune after flowering or you can wait until spring, after danger of frost is past. In cold climates it will freeze to ground in winter but will send up vigorous new growth from roots when the weather warms. For best appearance, cut to the ground each year after flowering. (In areas where winter frosts come early, wait until spring.)

BUSH ANEMONE. See Carpenteria.

BUSH POPPY. See Dendromecon.

BUTCHER'S BROOM, CLIMBING. See Semele.

BUTIA capitata. See Palm.

BUTTERFLY BUSH. See Buddleia.

BUXUS. Boxwood, box. Evergreen shrubs, small trees. Can be cut back and sheared heavily and they will sprout readily from old wood. Type of pruning will depend upon purpose. Prune anytime from spring to fall, during growing season. Remove dead branches back to live wood.

B. microphylla japonica. Japanese boxwood. Grow slowly to 4-6 ft. informal shrubs if not pruned. Most often clipped as low or medium hedge or shaped into globes, tiers, or pyramids. If hedge grows too tall, lop off practically to ground and let it start over. Best time to do this is just as active growth is beginning in spring so that ugly stubs will soon be concealed by new foliage. To keep the rejuvenated plants compact, start shearing when shoots are 6 in. long.

B. sempervirens. Common boxwood, English boxwood. Most often grown as trimmed hedge, they can also be used as container plants, single shrubs, or topiary forms. Can take any amount of cutting before or after frost. Cut tips of branches on the outside of plants to force new growth on inside to fill in bare areas. Susceptible to a canker-causing fungus which results in dead center branches. These should be removed back to live wood.

CALICO BUSH. See Kalmia.

CALIFORNIA FUCHSIA. See Zauschneria.

CALIFORNIA GERANIUM. See Senecio.

CALLA. See Zantedeschia.

CALLIANDRA. Evergreen shrub.

C. inaequilatera (*C. haematocephala*). Pink powder puff. No heavy pruning should be necessary. Prune immediately after flowering for shape and to encourage new growth and a second flowering. Remove dead and crossing branches by cutting back to good laterals. Once mature, selectively cut some stems to ground each year to renew plant. Makes effective espalier against a wall.

C. tweedii (*C. guildingi*). Trinidad flame bush, Brazilian flame bush. Can be pruned like acacias to open up, thin out, and retain interesting branch pattern. Flower clusters form at branch ends; tip pinch new growth for more branches, blossoms. Cut back overgrown shrub almost to ground or remove entirely and plant new one. Also makes good espalier.

CALLICARPA. Beauty berry. Deciduous shrubs. May freeze to the ground in severe winter, but can be cut to ground in early spring and will come back strong (if roots weren't killed) and produce bloom and berries the same season. Should normally be pruned in late winter or early spring. Heavy spring pruning results in more vigorous growth and heavier fruit set. Take out dead wood, cut old wood back to new growth. Renew each year by cutting stems to ground in early spring.

CALLISTEMON. Bottlebrush. Evergreen shrubs or trees. Left unpruned, plants may become leggy, open, and straggly. By removing dead twigs and heading back selected branches, bottlebrushes can be graceful and will produce an abundance of flower color over long period. Fast growing, easy to train. Quick wall cover as informal espaliers. Several kinds can be trained as small trees. Some can be used in formal clipped hedges or as informal screens or windbreaks. A few can be trained as ground covers.

C. citrinus (*C. lanceolatus*). Lemon bottlebrush. Massive shrub; grows to 10-15 ft. Make cuts in leafy parts of branches; if cut farther back, die-back often results. Train overgrown shrub into multi or single-stemmed tree. Grown as espalier, it will need occasional selective removal of errant growth.

C. salignus. White bottlebrush. Shrub or tree. Train as small shade tree or plant 4-5 ft. apart as hedge.

C. viminalis. Weeping bottlebrush. Shrub or small tree. Rapid grower. Has pendulous branches. Train as tree by staking main stem; thin surplus branches to prevent topheavy growth. Also attractive when allowed to grow naturally with branches sweeping to the ground.

CALOCEDRUS decurrens (*Libocedrus decurrens*). Incense cedar. Evergreen tree. If grown as hedge, plant trees about 6 ft. apart. Clip or shear regularly; branches will remain full to ground. If they become overgrown near house or fence as they mature, remove lower limbs and expose 8-10 ft. of trunk to relieve crowding at ground level. When planted alone and the trunk is not cut back, it will grow as tall, columnar ornamental or shade-producing tree.

CALOCEPHALUS brownii. Cushion bush. Evergreen shrubby perennial. Light pruning keeps the plant in shape. If growth gets too dense, thin it by removing some branches. Cut out dead wood.

CALOTHAMNUS. Net bush. Evergreen shrubs. Prune hard after flowering to keep plants from getting straggly. Generally not attractive in age, showing more wood than foliage.

CALYCANTHUS. Sweet shrub. Deciduous shrubs.

C. floridus. Carolina allspice. Prune after flowering. Take out oldest stems and branches; thin to shape.

C. occidentalis. Spice bush. Can be trained into multi-stemmed small tree. Will grow to 8 ft. or more with widespreading habit, but can be kept smaller and more compact by selective thinning and pinching of errant growth. Thin arching branches in fall.

CAMELLIA. Evergreen shrubs. Among the most adaptable of plants, camellias can be grown as shrubs, trees and standards, and low hedges. Also good subjects for bonsai, dwarfing, and espaliers.
General pruning rules: best time to prune is when the blooms begin to fade, but good results are obtained even if pruning is delayed into summer and fall. Remove spent flowers to prevent seed formation. Remove undesirable growth at any time of year. Whenever possible, make cuts just above scars that mark spots where last year's growth

ended and this year's began. The scars are slightly thickened, somewhat rough areas where bark texture and color change slightly. Cut just above these areas to force 3 or 4 dormant buds into growth, creating bushier shrubs. Common error for gardeners confronted with leggy camellia is to head it back. Such random cutting normally results in only 1 bud being activated beneath the cut. This causes formation of another long, willowy branch, compounding the problem. Start pruning and shaping a camellia when the plant is very young, preferably when only a single stem. Continue to control and shape it throughout its lifetime. Drastic pruning can be kept to a minimum if you tip pinch new growth frequently to keep plant in bounds. Overgrown, unshapely or scraggly camellias are quite tolerant of heavy pruning, except for *C. reticulata*. Most other kinds replace removed wood with new, vigorous growth, provided they have good and healthy root systems.

Some camellias are more vinelike than others and will develop unattractively into leggy, gangly shapes if left to follow their natural bent. To keep them growing straight, stake and then cut to shape and prune them into umbrella forms. If camellias are spreading excessively and growing too close to ground, cut off lowest branches, shorten some downward growing ones, and stake the trunks into upward growing positions.

Pruning container camellias: roots of container-planted camellias should be cut back periodically. A recommended way is to prune ¼ of outer roots each 6 months. With square container, simply shave 1 in. off one side; with round container, take 1 in. off ¼ of the circumference every 6 months. With this control, plant will grow slowly and

TO HELP CAMELLIA grow bushy, make cuts just above point where one year's growth stopped and next began. At left, pencil points to this spot. At right, what you get.

produce bumper crops of blooms season after season. If a container camellia has been allowed to dry out to the stage where its root ball has shrunk from the side, subsequent watering may flow through gap between root ball and container rather than through root ball. In this case, a form of root pruning will be necessary to save plant. This is the procedure to follow:

1. Remove camellia from container and wash off outside inch of soil.

2. Prune destroyed roots and repot plant in fresh humus (as many as half the roots may have been destroyed).

3. Prune top of plant by cutting back to main trunk all the long thin branches of old wood that carry no latent buds. Then cut back to strong laterals the

larger branches that also need to be removed for desired shape. (If plant has lost a great number of leaves during its drought, postpone some top pruning. The injured root system must have leaves to help it grow quickly.)

Pruning overgrown camellias: if your camellia is too big and tall, cut down to size in 2 stages, a year or more apart. Starting in late winter or early spring, just before new growth begins, cut all side branches off main stem except for tuft at top (necessary for plant to nourish itself). At the same time, dig 2 trenches on opposite sides of plant. Replace removed soil with soil mixed with ground bark, peat moss, well-rotted sawdust, or other organic matter. Vigorous new shoots will soon appear along

CUTTING an overgrown camellia down to size. Cut off side branches as shown in second illustration. Dig two trenches. Refill with conditioned soil. A year later, cut trunk above clump of new foliage. Dig and refill two more (third illustration).

bare trunk. Select those needed to form new, lower framework and rub other shoots off. If next year's growth is vigorous and ample enough, cut off old trunk above top branch of new low clump of foliage. (You may prefer to wait another year for the topping back.) Finally, dig and refill 2 more trenches as described on the previous page to complete circle of new soil around the plant.

Disbudding: many varieties of camellias (particularly the Japonicas) set more buds than they can properly mature. Some will drop a high percentage of excess buds of their own accord. Reluctant as a gardener may be to deliberately twist flower buds off his choice camellia, it is recommended procedure in many cases because it results in better flowers at blooming time.

CAMELLIA FLOWER BUD being removed. Skinny bud, upper right, is a leaf bud.

Whether or not to disbud, and to what extent, depends upon variety of camellia as well as effect you desire. Reticulatas set fewer buds than Japonicas and are naturally large flowered, so there is no point in disbudding them. Small-flowered hybrid varieties and Sasanquas set large numbers of buds, but heavy disbudding will spoil the free-flowering quality that is part of their appeal. You should be able to distinguish flower buds from long, slender leaf buds at base of each cluster by midsummer, and you can disbud at that time. Before removing any flower bud, find the narrow, pointed leaf bud — it is often hidden among the flower buds—and be careful not to damage it.

CAMPANULA. Bellflower. Mostly perennial, some biennial, a few annual. Pick old, faded flowers off regularly for prolonged bloom, new growth.

CAMPHOR TREE. See Cinnamomum.

CAMPSIS. Trumpet creeper, trumpet vine. Deciduous vine. Every year in early spring, shorten some branches to 2 or 3 buds and thin out others. Remove dead and weak wood. Remember that blossoms are formed on young new growth, so if you cut off too much wood, you'll reduce flower crop. Pinch vine back frequently during growing season to keep plant bushy and well-foliaged at base. Old plant sometimes becomes topheavy and pulls away from supporting surface unless thinned. Will spread through garden and into neighbors' gardens by suckering roots. Persistent; will grow from piece of root left in soil. Can be trained as big shrub, flowering hedge if branches are shortened after first year's growth.

CANARY BIRD BUSH. See Crotalaria.

CANARY ISLAND DATE PALM. See Phoenix.

CANDLE BUSH. See Cassia.

CANDYTUFT. See Iberis.

CANNA. Tuberous rootstock. After first frost, cut off all leaf stalks and dig up the rootstalks. In warm, frost-free areas cannas may be left in ground during winter. They will remain green during large part of year. Old stalks should be cut to ground.

CANTUA buxifolia. Magic flower, sacred flower of the Incas. Evergreen shrub. Scraggly, open growth. Thin after flowering to shape.

CAPE FORGET-ME-NOT. See Anchusa.

CAPE FUCHSIA. See Phygelius.

CAPE HONEYSUCKLE. See Tecomaria.

CAPE PLUMBAGO. See Plumbago.

CARAGANA arborescens. Siberian peashrub. Deciduous shrub or small tree. With severe pruning, you can keep it any height you want. In fact, the more you prune, the denser the growth. Pruning also helps curb leggy tendency. When trained to grow as small tree, it will reach 18 or 20 ft. with 12-ft. spread. Prune after flowering, trim off blooms as soon as they fade and before seeds ripen and scatter; you'll avoid later nuisance of many volunteer seedlings. Use as windbreak, clipped hedge, cover for wildlife. Attractive small tree.

CARICA papaya. Papaya. Evergreen tree or greenhouse plant. If cut back to 2 or 3 ft. from ground, the normally straight, branchless trunk will send out side shoots that thicken and bear fruit. Keep only 2 or 3 of these side shoots; if you let all develop, fruits will be small.

CARISSA grandiflora. Natal plum. Evergreen shrub. Can be heavily pruned and may be trained as clipped hedge,

NATAL PLUM held in good shape. Wild branch at upper right should be removed.

espalier, or ground cover, or grown as single shrub. Beware of spiny stems. Naturally sprawling, but young plant can be trained to open-form shrub by cutting off low-growing stems and encouraging balanced framework of branches. Shape by pruning and pinching unwanted growth often. Older shrub may send out erratic shoots, making the plant lopsided. Cut these off as they appear, to bring the plant back into balance. Pruning in spring will not interfere with fruit and flower production. Do not prune after September where there is danger of frost. Important: remove old twiggy or dead growth. Thin some old wood yearly or plant becomes very woody. Plant can be restrained to 3-5 ft. with annual pruning.

CARMEL CREEPER. See Ceanothus.

CARNATION. See Dianthus.

CAROB. See Ceratonia.

CAROLINA ALLSPICE. See Calycanthus.

CAROLINA JESSAMINE. See Gelsemium.

CAROLINA LAUREL CHERRY. See Prunus.

CARPENTERIA californica. Bush anemone. Evergreen shrub. Prune after flowering to restrain growth or shape. Because leaves tend to discolor in cold weather, many faded leaves and branchlets make plant look somewhat untidy during winter and early spring. Trim these off as soon as frosts are past, or wait for new foliage to hide them.

CARPET BUGLE. See Ajuga.

CARPINUS. Hornbean. Deciduous trees. Need little pruning, but respond well to heavy pruning. Adaptable; can be trained and clipped into large or small hedges or screens if desired.

CARROT WOOD. See Cupaniopsis.

CARYA illinoinensis (*Carya pecan*). Pecan. Deciduous tree. Needs only normal early training and guidance. Prune mature tree only to shape or to remove dead, weak wood.

CARYOPTERIS. Bluebeard. Deciduous shrubs. Will freeze back in colder areas. Cut frost-damaged tops back in spring. New growth will come quickly when weather warms. In areas where they don't freeze back, cut back to ground in early spring to keep them compact and encourage strong new growth and better bloom.

CARYOTA. See Palm.

CASIMIROA edulis. White sapote. Evergreen or erratically briefly deciduous tree. Unpruned, it will reach 30 ft. in height, with an equal spread, but you can keep the tree lower by selectively thinning out and heading back branches that grow higher than you want. Normally branches almost to ground, but you can train it as umbrella-shaped shade tree by pinching out terminal buds to encourage lateral branching and by removing lower branches as the young tree spreads out. Thinning in spring may reduce crop during main bearing season, but it stimulates the tree into producing a second crop and stretches the bearing season to 4 or 5 months.

CASSIA. Senna. Evergreen, partially evergreen, or deciduous shrubs, trees. You prune all of them after flowering, though some are pruned more severely than others.
  C. alata. Candle bush. Deciduous shrub. Prune freely after flowering.
  C. artemisioides. Feathery cassia. Evergreen shrub. Prune this plant lightly after flowering. Stems tend to be long and sprawly unless the plant is kept trimmed.
  C. bicapsularis. Evergreen shrub. Prune hard after flowering.
  C. corymbosa. Flowery senna. Large evergreen shrub. Prune hard after flowering.
  C. excelsa (*C. carnaval*). Crown of gold tree. Partially evergreen tree. Fast growing; prune hard after flowering.
  C. nairobensis. This one is a stump sprouter and should be cut back regularly. To induce longer bloom period, remove flowering stems one at a time, as soon as blossoms fade.
  C. splendida. Golden wonder senna. Evergreen shrub. This name has been applied to a number of cassias of varying growth habits. All require much thinning after flowering.
  C. surattensis (*C. glauca*). Evergreen shrub. Does not need to be pruned heavily; grows fast to 6-8 ft. and spreads wider.

  C. tomentosa. Woolly senna. Evergreen shrub. Vigorous, rank growth; prune hard after flowering.

CASTANEA. Chestnut. Deciduous trees. Give normal training and guidance for forms and strong frameworks when young. Need only corrective pruning when mature. Some are susceptible to a fungus; remove blighted parts completely if they appear.

CASTANOPSIS. Chinquapin. Evergreen trees and shrubs. Little care after established, though they respond well to pruning.
  C. chrysophylla. Giant chinquapin. Tree or shrubby tree. Adaptable, can be trained and pruned from start into desired form.
  C. c. minor. Golden chinquapin. Shrubby, very adaptable to pruning. Makes good, dense hedge.
  C. sempervirens. Bush chinquapin, Sierra chinquapin. Shrub to 8 ft. Grows naturally in thickets, useful as low, ground-covering shrub. Can be kept under 8 ft. by cutting out upright growth.

CASTOR BEAN. See Ricinus.

CASUARINA. Beefwood, she-oak. Evergreen trees. Give young trees normal training, then prune only if required to shape. Thin out all center branches if necessary to get air and light inside. Can be pruned anytime.

CAT'S CLAW. See Doxantha.

CATALINA CHERRY. See Prunus.

CATALINA IRONWOOD. See Lyonothamnus.

CATALPA. Deciduous tree. Catalpas branch close to the ground. If you're growing one to live under, train a 10-12 ft. whip to produce trunk of desired height before heading it back to force branching. Do major pruning during dormant season.
  C. bignonioides. Common catalpa. Train as above to get tree tall enough to walk under. Needs very little pruning thereafter, except to remove dead, damaged wood. Can be pollarded very much like sycamore (see *Pruning Glossary*).
  C. b. 'Nana.' (Almost always sold as *C. bungei*.) Umbrella catalpa. This variety is grafted 6-7 ft. from ground to form dense, umbrella-like head. Cut it back annually to old wood to keep in scale, retain its tight formal outline. Winter form after pruning is nothing more than a bare stick with switches on the end.
  C. speciosa. Western catalpa. Train and selectively prune tall trunk and umbrella-shaped crown.

CATHA edulis. Khat. Evergreen shrub. Start pinching and pruning early to

shape it. Can grow as high as 20 ft. but can be kept from 3-8 ft. high by selectively thinning and heading back upright growth. Effective when trained as espalier.

CATMINT. See Nepeta.

CATNIP. See Nepeta.

CEANOTHUS. Wild lilac. Mostly evergreen shrubs, small trees, or ground covers (a few are deciduous). Prune after flowering. Shape during growing season with frequent pinching out of undesirable, errant growth. Best to avoid drastic, annual pruning because heavy pruning of some species leads to fungus attack, with resulting dieback and possible loss of plant. Try to limit pruning and thinning cuts to branches no thicker than a pencil. (Do not prune in rainy, wet weather, as the fungus is spread by rain.) You should, of course, cut out diseased wood by cutting well back into healthy tissue. Treat these pruning cuts with a wound dressing, disinfect your pruning tools, and discard cuttings in an area where they cannot infect healthy plants.
  C. arboreus. Feltleaf ceanothus. Large shrub or small tree. Prune lightly but frequently to shape.
  C. a. 'Ray Hartman.' Big shrub or small tree. Easily shaped into single or multi-stemmed tree. Severe pruning will inhibit flowering for a year.
  C. cyaneus 'Sierra Blue.' Shrub. Has neat erect form and ability to stand clipping. Useful as hedges and high screens. Can be shaped lightly into attractive informal screen.
  C. delilianus. Deciduous shrub. Flowers on new wood, looks best with annual pruning in late winter or early spring. Shorten main branches back 12-18 in. and cut secondary branches back to 2-6 buds.
  C. gloriosus. Point Reyes ceanothus. Ground cover. You can keep plant flat and as low as 8 in. if you pinch out tips of upright shoots.
  C. 'Gloire de Versailles.' Deciduous shrub. Prune as you would *C. delilianus* (above). Can also be trained against wall where space is at a premium.
  C. griseus horizontalis. Carmel creeper. Ground cover. In its natural environment, Carmel creeper is kept low and spreading by coastal winds. In garden environment, prune as follows to get effect you want: for low spreading effect, thin and cut back as often as necessary branches that tend to grow upright. For more upright, bushy plant, do less shortening and thinning of stronger growing branches. Heaviest pruning should be done in late summer just before new growth starts in fall. This rampant grower may tend to get leggy with age. Prune to shape with

DEODAR CEDARS in situation at left needed side pruning to keep them slim enough. To do this side pruning, cut branches back to top-of-branch shoots like the one the man is holding in his left hand in the picture at right.

frequent pinching out of unwanted growth.

C. impressus. Santa Barbara ceanothus. Shrub. Pinch growing tips frequently to induce bushiness, prevent legginess.

C. i. 'Mountain Haze.' Shrub. Responds well to clipping and pruning.

C. 'Julia Phelps.' Shrub. Pinch to shape when young. Prune lightly after bloom. Can be trained as big screen planting, or single shrub.

C. 'Mary Lake.' High ground cover. Prune lightly when young. Trailing branches take root; pull them out to control.

C. prostratus. Squaw carpet, Mahala mat. Ground cover. Forms dense mat that spreads by rooting branches. Prune only as needed to control.

C. pumilus. Low shrub, ground cover. Habit and pruning requirements same as *C. prostratus*.

C. thyrsiflorus. Blue blossom. Shrub or small tree. Variable in growth. Pinch to shape when young.

C. t. repens. Creeping blue blossom. Ground cover. Keep it flat by pinching back upright growth.

CEDAR. See Cedrus.

CEDAR, INCENSE. See Calocedrus.

CEDAR, WESTERN RED. See Thuja.

CEDRELA. Deciduous or evergreen trees. Normal training for shape and to form good branch structure when young; a minimum of pruning as trees mature.

CEDRUS. Cedar. Evergreen trees.

C. atlantica. Atlas cedar. Needs very little pruning. On young tree, branches may often appear to get too long and heavy. This may sometimes be corrected by pinching or cutting back the tips, but don't be in too much of a hurry to do this. As the tree matures, what first appeared to be an ungainly form often turns out to be shapely. Branches occasionally mat together, cutting out light and air circulation from body of tree, resulting in dieback. Thin out by cutting selected, unwanted branches back to trunk.

C. deodara. Deodar cedar. Most gardeners will want to plant this tree in area large enough for natural growth to display its grace and charm. However, annual pruning in late spring will keep shape you want. To control spread of tree, cut new growth of side branches halfway back in late spring. This will make tree more dense. Keep this naturally tall-growing tree as low as 4-6 ft. by cutting leader back each year and taping a suitable side branch into vertical position as new tip. Will also tolerate shearing.

C. libani. Cedar of Lebanon. Slow growing. Pruning should be kept to minimum.

CELASTRUS. Bittersweet. Deciduous vines. Vigorous, rampant vines capable of strangling young trees if not checked. Will become tangled mass of intertwining branches unless pruned on a regular basis. Cut out fruiting branches in winter, pinch out tips of vigorous branches during the summer. Old plants can be renewed by cutting them to ground.

CELTIS. Hackberry. Deciduous trees. Normal training for good form and structure while young. Need only thinning, removal of unwanted wood when mature.

CENTRANTHUS ruber (*Valeriana rubra*). Jupiter's beard, red valerian, gate lilac. Perennial. Cut off old flowering stems to shape plant and prolong bloom.

CENTURY PLANT. See Agave.

CEPHALOTAXUS harringtonia. Korean yew. Evergreen tree. Shrubby and slow growing. Useful as hedge or screen. Very little pruning required except to shape it in form desired.

CERASTIUM tomentosum. Snow-in-summer. Perennial. How far it spreads or hangs down is up to you. Clip back or pull out whenever it goes too far. In desert gardens, don't shear heavily during the hot season. After flowers turn brown, you have three choices: shear back tops with hedge shears, leaving plant clean of dead flowers but shorn of its usual softness; pull dead flowers out of their sockets individually or by the handful (though a tedious and slow job, this keeps the attractive mounding form intact); or just ignore the dead flowers. In a couple of months the foliage mass will grow enough to swallow them up. Looks shabby in cold winters, but revives rapidly in spring.

CERATONIA siliqua. Carob, St. John's bread. Evergreen large shrub or tree. Tends to branch low to the ground. Easily trained to form high crown by heading trunk at about 7 ft., forcing side branches at that point. Though it can stand heavy pruning and reshaping, drastic cutting isn't necessary if you thin and shape regularly each winter from the start. Allowed to grow naturally, it maintains a bushy form with branches to ground. Often multi-stemmed. Use this way as a big hedge, informal or trimmed. Train it as a compact hedge by topping stems low and letting it spread.

CERATOSTIGMA plumbaginoides. (Often sold as *Plumbago larpentae*.) Dwarf plumbago. Perennial ground cover. Cut declining top growth to the ground after flowering.

CERCIDIPHYLLUM japonicum. Katsura tree. Deciduous tree. Slow growing. May form multiple trunks. For a slender, more upright tree, remove all but one of the multiple trunks. Give normal training and guidance when young; very little pruning required when established.

CERCIDIUM. Palo verde. Deciduous trees. Only require pruning necessary to shape them. Watch out for sharp spines.

CERCIS. Redbud. Deciduous shrubs or trees. Confine pruning to removal of dead and brittle branches that may be broken by wind and cutting out any off-balance growth. To keep tops trained to canopy shapes, cut upright branches back to good laterals. Remove branches that compete with leaders but never cut leaders.

CERCOCARPUS. Mountain-mahogany. Evergreen or partially deciduous tall shrubs or small trees. Will take heavy pruning. To keep them the form you choose, heavy pruning may be necessary. Can be trained as dense screening plants or as trees. Old straggly plants can be cut back to ground to renew.

CEREUS peruvianus. Cactus. Corrective pruning is all that is normally required.

CESTRUM. Evergreen shrubs. May freeze back in heavy frosts. Wait until after spring growth starts to prune out frost-damaged wood. Fast growing, inclined to be rangy and topheavy unless frequently pruned. Nip back growing tips consistently for compactness and cut back severely after flowering or fruiting.

C. nocturnum. Night jessamine. Cut flowering (new) wood back to about 6 in. immediately after bloom. This will usually bring on new growth and flowering in fall.

CHAENOMELES. (Some formerly called *Cydonia*.) Flowering quince. Deciduous shrubs. Left alone, quince can grow into a thicket, their flowers nearly hidden by the tangles. Start training them as young shrubs. Select main branches as skeletons of plants and remove the rest. On older or neglected quince, remove weak branches, suckers, and crossed limbs. Shorten strong branches you wish to keep. Because flowering quince blooms on wood that is one or more years old, they are one of the few spring-flowering shrubs you can prune in winter that will still produce flowers. With an eye to maintaining their delicate, open symmetry, cut back new growth at least ⅓, thin out weak or crossing branches, and remove suckers. Reclaim old bushes gradually over a period of several seasons by cutting out oldest wood. Many gardeners like to prune in the tight bud season in winter, using cut branches for indoor arrangements. The new growth that follows will bear next year's flowers.

Plants also respond well to consistent summer pruning to divert growing strength into main branches and into formation of next year's flowers. Each summer, as soon as your shrubs have made most of their new growth, cut back by half on the main shoots and trim laterals back to 2 or 3 leaves. Slow down subsequent growth by rationing late summer water and keep fertilization to a minimum.

CHAMAECYPARIS. False cypress. Evergreen trees, shrubs, and shrublets. Stimulate new growth, control size and shape by pinching branch tips.

C. lawsoniana. Lawson cypress, Port Orford cedar. Normally grows to more than 60 ft. Can be topped and be held at 10 ft. As a hedge plant, it takes shearing very well. Shear in early spring and later as needed.

C. l. 'Forsteckensis.' Forsteck cypress. Makes a dense, informal hedge.

C. obtusa. Hinoki false cypress. Splendid bonsai subject. Prune to shape.

C. o. 'Crippsii.' Conical growth to 30 ft. but can be kept lower by pruning. Effective when pruned by spacing branches at various levels.

C. pisifera (*Retinospora pisifera*). Sawara false cypress. Head back or shear heavily to force new growth, hide dead foliage on inner branches.

C. p. 'Plumosa.' Plume false cypress. Leave it unpruned as tree or carefully prune it into big shrub. Remove lower branches which die or lose vigor. Can also be sheared to shape it.

C. p. 'Plumosa Aurea.' Prune hard by pinching tips to restrain growth, promote density.

C. p. 'Squarrosa.' Moss cypress. Should be thinned out as it ages to give more character.

CHAMAEDOREA. See Palm.

CHAMAELAUCIUM uncinatum. (Sometimes sold as *C. ciliatum*.) Geraldton waxflower. Evergreen shrub. Cut freely for arrangements or cut back after flowering to maintain a better balanced shape.

CHAMAEROPS humilis. See Palm.

CHAMOMILE. See Anthemis.

CHASTE TREE. See Vitex.

THREAD SAWARA FALSE CYPRESS (Chamaecyparis pisifera 'Filifera'), like other varieties of Sawara cypress, can be clipped and opened out into layered mounds.

CHERRY. Deciduous fruit tree. Young cherry trees tend to grow long, pendulous branches without properly placed laterals. As trees develop, new growth should be pinched or headed back to encourage proper branching. Mature cherries bear fruit on short spurs which have a productive life of 10-12 years or more (see *Bearing Habits of Fruit Trees* in the *Pruning Glossary*). These spurs grow very slowly, and because of their longevity, mature cherry trees require less pruning than other deciduous fruit trees. About all that is required is removal of dead or weak wood. Take out no more than 10 percent of oldest wood each season. Another good way to prune is to pinch soft tips of new growth in summer.

CHERRY, BRUSH. See Syzygium.

CHERRY, CATALINA. See Prunus.

CHERRY, FLOWERING. See Prunus.

CHESTNUT. See Castanea.

CHILEAN JASMINE. See Mandevilla.

CHILOPSIS linearis. Desert willow. Deciduous large shrub or small tree. Tends to be ragged and undisciplined; needs some heading back and thinning out to keep it in shape.

CHIMONANTHUS praecox (*C. fragrans, Meratia praecox*). Wintersweet. Deciduous shrub. Thrives on pruning. Cut branches back to good lateral or promising bud during bloom or right afterwards (or you can cut branches in bud to force into flower indoors). Like most other spring flowering plants, wintersweet bears its flowers on 1-yr.-old wood. Thorough pruning, as described above, will stimulate new growth during spring and summer and produce more flowers next season. After it reaches 8-10 ft., you can make a small, multiple-trunked tree out of it by cutting weakest trunks to the ground and removing the twiggy growth from bottoms of trunks that remain.

CHINA FIR. See Cunninghamia.

CHINA-BERRY. See Melia.

CHINESE ANGELICA. See Aralia.

CHINESE BELLFLOWER. See Abutilon.

CHINESE LANTERN. See Abutilon.

CHINESE PISTACHE. See Pistacia.

CHINESE TALLOW TREE. See Sapium.

CHINESE WITCH HAZEL. See Hamamelis.

CHINQUAPIN. See Castanopsis.

CHIONANTHUS. Fringe tree. Deciduous trees. Use as slow-growing, airy shrubs or attractive small trees. Once established in forms you want they don't require much pruning. Thin as needed to control size. Cut some of oldest stems to ground (if trained as shrubs) to renew. Prune after bloom, as flowers are borne on tips of branches. Heading back in winter and spring will reduce bloom.

CHIRANTHODENDRON pentadactylon (*C. platanoides*). Monkey hand tree. Evergreen tree. Fast growth means brittle wood and undisciplined habit. Needs regular thinning out and heading back for bushiness. Tree tends to be topheavy and may fall over in a strong windstorm. To prevent this, keep branches thinned out to let wind pass through.

CHLOROPHYTUM comosum (*C. capense*). Spider plant. Evergreen perennial. To keep it in bounds, when used as a ground cover, remove the long, arching flower stems before they take root in adjacent garden bed.

CHOISYA ternata. Mexican orange. Evergreen shrub. A fast grower, it will respond well to any amount of pruning. Prune after flowering and pinch tips throughout growing season as required to shape. Thinning out older branches in center of plant encourages production of new wood. Cut freely for decoration when in bloom. After blooming, remove spent flowers but don't shear. Older, very woody plant benefits from severe cutting back and will sprout from the stump.

CHOKEBERRY, RED. See Aronia.

CHORISIA speciosa. Floss silk tree. Evergreen to briefly deciduous tree. Prune as required to shape.

CHORIZEMA. Flame pea. Evergreen shrubs. Keep plants bushy and free blooming by cutting back heavily after they flower.

CHRISTMAS BERRY. See Heteromeles.

CHRYSALIDOCARPUS lutescens. See Palm.

CHRYSANTHEMUM. Annuals, perennials. Procedure for cutting plants back after bloom in fall depends on whether or not you live in frost-free area. In cold winter areas, let plants fade after flowering. Then cut back in stages by first removing faded flowers, then top half of stems, and finally remaining stalks to within 8 in. of ground. This gradual cutting back helps to minimize shock to plants. Before late fall or early winter, all plants should have been cut down and ready for lifting and storing. If you live in a mild climate (and soil is well-drained) you can cut plants back to ground after bloom and leave roots in ground.

Chrysanthemums need growth control. Allowed to grow unchecked, they'll

TREE CHRYSANTHEMUM. Lower shoots removed in spring, tops pinched 4 times.

be sprawling by blooming time. For sturdy plants and big flowers, pinch them frequently, beginning at planting time by removing tips of new plants. Select 1-4 lateral shoots which will form continued growth. Continue pinching all summer, nipping top pair of leaves on every shoot that reaches 5 in. On some early-blooming cushion varieties, or in coldest regions, pinching should be stopped in mid-August. Stake plants to keep them upright. To produce big, showy blooms, disbud by removing all flower buds except for 1 (or 2) in each cluster. If you want masses of color, leave buds alone.

TO DISBUD CHRYSANTHEMUM, remove all buds except two shown. When the end bud is bigger, remove the other one.

C. balsamita. Costmary. A weedy perennial. Spreads rapidly, pull up rooted stems to thin. Keep it at 8-10 in. by pruning back vigorously. Or, just cut back the leggy stems to encourage attractive basal leaves.

C. coccineum (*Pyrethrum roseum*). Painted daisy, pyrethrum. Bushy perennial. Early bloomer. If cut to ground after bloom, may flower again in late summer.

C. frutescens. Marguerite, Paris daisy. Perennial. Start pinching or cutting back marguerite as soon as small plant is set out to make it branch. Keep it up through summer. If left alone, it frequently takes on lopsided shape and becomes woody. Then if you cut back very hard, it may never recover, for marguerite can't withstand shock of heavy trimming. Blooms almost all year if protected from frost and if you pick off faded flowers. Keep healthy and productive by pruning lightly at frequent intervals. Remember to cut green wood only; you can kill plant by cutting into hard wood since it seldom produces new growth. (This is especially true in hot climates.)

C. maximum. Shasta daisy. Perennial. Commercial growers cut plants back after peak bloom period in spring to get another flush of new growth and second crop of blooms. Home gardeners preferring continuous bloom should keep old flowers picked off regularly. In mild areas this will result in year-around bloom; in colder areas, it will keep plant blooming from early spring until killing frosts.

CHRYSOLARIX amabilis (*Pseudolarix amabilis, P. kaempferi*). Golden larch. Deciduous conifer. Slow growing, needs only normal training while young, very little pruning later. Young plant is good bonsai or container plant.

CIBOTIUM. See Fern, Tree.

CIGAR PLANT. See Cuphea.

CINNAMOMUM camphora. Camphor tree. Evergreen tree. Slow to moderate growth, needs only early training, little pruning later. Subject to root rot, causing twigs and branches to show brownish discoloration. Cut out damaged wood.

CINQUEFOIL. See Potentilla.

CISSUS. Evergreen vines. Climb by tendrils. Outdoors in mild climates, prune as needed to avoid tangling or overgrowth and to remove dead or damaged wood. If you grow them as house plants, tip-pinch to control stem length and promote branching.

CISTUS. Rockrose. Evergreen shrubs. Generally, rockroses tend to resent heavy pruning (though there are instances where drastically pruned plants came back as vigorously as before). Happily, their form and growth make heavy pruning generally unnecessary. If you want to give plants a neater appearance, remove a few branches at a time, enabling these to start new growth before you cut back other branches. All branches should have some foliage left, or they may not grow again. Rockroses can be kept in bounds either by constantly pinching back or by a light annual pruning right after flowering. Some gardeners don't prune at all, preferring

to let the plants grow naturally in tumbled masses. But you may find it necessary to remove dead wood occasionally.

CITRUS. Evergreen trees and shrubs. As a group, these do not require as much pruning as deciduous fruit trees. Citrus fruits are borne at ends of current season's growth. It's not necessary, therefore, to prune for large amounts of wood removal. Pruning requirements vary within the group and are also somewhat determined by whether you are growing your citrus as an ornamental or for fruit production (it's probably a compromise in most home gardens). Specific pruning directions for citrus forms that need them are given at the end of this section.

When young, all citrus must be pruned and shaped for form. Some vigorous growers will send out branches unevenly beyond the mass of the tree. If you want even growth (in youth as well as maturity), cut shoots way back to a good lateral or to main branches at any time. Constantly pinch back tips of any new growth that threatens to take off alone. Most citrus growers strive for compact, bushy trees.

PRUNING TO REINVIGORATE OLD CITRUS TREES
As orange and lemon trees get older, they tend to lose vigor, fill up with dead wood, and produce less and less new growth capable of good fruit production. This is the time to prune them all severely to encourage new growth and better fruit production. Here are some things you can do:

Topping: Cut out top limbs that keep light from lower branches. Removing 2 or 3 limbs each year won't reduce crop.

Brushing out: Remove dead wood; this lets more light through the branches and forces some growth all over tree.

Hedging: Cut back side branches of tree 1-3 ft. This opens up tree and increases new growth. In frost-free areas, these jobs can be done in January. Wait until all danger of frost is past in inland and desert areas.

PRUNING DWARF CITRUS
Same general pruning rules apply to dwarf citrus, except that they require less pruning per tree than normal-sized plant. But here too you may want to renew an old plant and develop stronger, lower, more compact branch

THESE WERE LANKY, overgrown tangerine plants. Cut back to 12-inch stubs in March.

BY MID-JULY, new growth forms a leafy canopy 2 feet tall. No crop for several years.

'EUREKA' LEMON trained as an espalier. To remain presentable, it needs regular pinching of vertical growth and occasional thinning of branchlets and twigs.

framework. To do that, prune severely. If you have healthy plant with sound root system, you can expect normal growth response to this renewal pruning, just as in other varieties.

Your approach can be drastic, cutting all trunks back to 12-in. stubs (do this only in spring, after danger of frost is past); or you can accomplish the same thing gradually and maintain more attractive, leafy plant. To accomplish this, prune successively in spring, summer, and fall, removing about ⅓ of the plant each time. Whichever method you use, follow-up care—especially during first 2 years after pruning—is extremely important. A few weeks after pruning, closely spaced new shoots appear along stems, mostly toward the tips. Remove up to ½ of these; those you keep should be rather evenly spaced along the stems. Cut off any new growth from below bud union. Later, cut off a few more fastest growing shoots. To force remaining new growth to branch out, prune back tips when about 8 in. long. The resulting new branches should be tipped back, in turn, after they've grown about 8 in. long. At the same time, remove crowded branches; too-dense growth shades center of plant and restricts future flower and fruit production. Citrus pruned this heavily won't produce crop for 2 or 3 years.

BARK PROTECTION ON PRUNED CITRUS

To protect newly-exposed bark from sunburning, either coat it with white protective paint (often called "tree white") or build cloth-covered wood frame to shade plant from hot afternoon sun. Because of drastic reduction in size of plant, it requires much less water.

PRUNING ORNAMENTAL CITRUS

Generally, if you are growing your citrus mainly for appearance, prune them lightly as you would other broadleafed evergreens, removing wood that detracts from plant's shape and encouraging growth in direction you want it to take. Remove dead, damaged wood, too. But if you want good fruit production — especially with lemons — you'll have to prune more in the manner of the commercial growers. One obvious difference (apparent when you look at a commercial grove) is that producers usually leave lower branches on citrus even if they touch ground. Most of fruit crop comes on lower branches and it is easier to pick down there. Then too, lower branches filter out light necessary for weeds, so there are fewer of them to hoe.

Because citrus trees are sensitive to

sunburn, you should avoid making large openings in the leaf canopy. Delay pruning out frost damaged wood until danger of frost is past. Then cut back gradually until you come to live, green wood. The object is to prune out first live bud and leave next lower one to develop.

LEMONS

Lemons generally have a more scraggly, undisciplined growth habit than other citrus fruits and must be pruned more heavily to be kept under control. Lemons also respond much better to pruning cuts and produce new wood more readily. Young nursery tree should be headed back to about 3 ft. and 3 or 4 laterals selected. Head these back quite severely to balance top with reduced root system. As tree matures, encourage a few more well spaced laterals and strive for strong, compact structure. A vigorous young lemon tree usually produces fair crop of strong growing, upright suckers each year. They emerge from trunk and run vertically up center of tree. Most of them should be snapped off. If tree has gaps in branch structure, however, you can turn a sucker into new scaffold branch quite simply. A sucker of the right age is limber enough to bend without snapping off if you grasp it about a foot above point where it joins trunk. Slowly bend it in large arc toward the ground. Ordinarily, it will stay in desired position after you release it. If it's a bit too old, it might spring back; if it does, weight it with a small stone. New lateral shoots will grow out along top of arc to fill the gap in tree. The awkward growth habit typical of lemons often results in long, pendulous branches carrying foliage at very end. These should be cut back severely to encourage fruiting shoots closer toward center of tree.

ORANGES

Once established, oranges require very little pruning beyond the removal of dead, crowded, twiggy growth. But they do require careful early training and pruning to help them establish strong framework. Starting with young nursery tree, head back central leader (to about 3 ft.) as with the lemon, but head back laterals only lightly. In first 2 or 3 years, aim for strong framework with upright branches, keeping in mind that weight of foliage and fruit will bend branches down. Allow lower branches to remain on young tree, removing gradually to get clean trunk to height you want. As tree matures, remaining lower limbs will droop; keep the lowest high enough so that they clear ground.

Sour orange, Seville orange (Citrus aurantium). These have dense and bushy growth and can be trained as trees, container plants, or (with heavy clipping and pruning) attractive hedges.

GRAPEFRUIT AND OTHER CITRUS

Prune as you do oranges: train to strong framework when young; very little pruning later.

CLADRASTIS lutea. Yellow wood. Deciduous tree. Pruning is important, especially when tree is young. Occasionally in early summer shorten side branches that tend to spread widely. This shortening will also force a strong leading shoot. For a taller trunk, remove lower branches while tree is still young. Prune mature tree as required after bloom.

CLEMATIS. Deciduous, evergreen vines, sprawling perennials. When and how you prune depend upon time of flowering. Clematis fall into three general groups: spring flowering; summer flowering; and those that flower in spring and then again in summer. The first group flowers on wood formed the previous season, the second blooms on new wood formed since spring growth started, and the third group flowers on year-old wood in spring and on new wood in summer. Prune those that flower only in spring severely just after flowering. This will give the wood that will bear next spring's flowers the longest possible time to develop. You have two choices with those that bloom in summer. You can cut back after flowering in the fall, or you can wait until the buds swell in early spring. Cut to within 6-12 in. of the ground or to 2-3 buds for the first 2 or 3 years. Cut older plants to 2 ft. or less. Those types blooming both in spring and summer should have flowered portions pruned immediately after spring bloom; then prune in fall or early spring to remove unruly or excessive growth. These basic techniques apply to all types: if you want a low plant with a maximum number of flowers, prune just above the first joint of the previous season's growth. For a higher vine, train the first leader to the height you want, and then cut back the side branches each year. Always leave one joint of previous year's growth on side branches. You can train clematis in many ways: on wire mesh frames in containers, on a fence or wall as a handsome tracery, twining up a tree, around a deck support or lamp post, or draping down a partly shaded bank.

C. armandii. Evergreen clematis. This evergreen vine blooms in spring, needs constant pruning after flowering to prevent tangling and buildup of dead thatch on inner parts of vine. Keep and tie up

CLEMATIS ARMANDII in bloom. Prune this vine after the flower drop.

stems you want, and cut out all others. Frequent pinching will hold the foliage to eye level. Normally makes a dense, heavy growth, but you can train it to produce a sharply defined outline. Cut out brown die-back.

C. chrysocoma. Deciduous vine. Blooms in spring on old wood, later blooms in summer from new wood.

C. 'Crimson King.' Flowers in early spring, again in summer.

C. davidiana. See *C. heracleifolia davidiana.*

C. dioscoreifolia (*C. paniculata*). Sweet autumn clematis. Blooms in late

summer and fall. After bloom or in early spring, prune year's growth to 1 or 2 buds.

C. 'Duchess of Edinburgh.' Blooms in early spring, again in summer.

C. 'Ernest Markham.' Blooms in summer only.

C. 'Gypsy Queen.' Blooms in summer/fall only.

C. 'Hagley Hybrid.' Blooms in summer only.

C. heracleifolia davidiana. Blooms in summer only.

C. integrifolia. Flowers in June-July. Prune after bloom.

C. jackmanii. All flower in summer on new wood and do well with severe pruning in early spring as buds begin to swell. Freezes to ground in cold winter areas. Can climb to 20 ft. in a single summer but is easily kept to 6 ft. by pruning.

C. lanuginosa. Blooms on old wood in spring, new wood in summer. After first flush of flowers, cut back flowered portions promptly for another crop later in summer. Then in early spring, prune lightly, removing only dead or weak growth.

C. 'Lasurstern.' Blooms in spring and again in summer.

C. lawsoniana. Spring and summer blooms.

C. 'Lord Neville.' Flowers in spring and summer.

C. macropetala. Downy clematis. Blooms in early spring, followed by

TWO VARIETIES of deciduous clematis. 'Ramona' at left and C. lawsoniana 'Henri' at right. Both bloom spring and summer, need same kind of pruning at same time.

showy seed clusters, so delay your pruning until they fade. Then to remove dead, weak wood prune lightly in early spring as buds begin to swell.

C. 'Mme. Baron-Veillard.' Blooms in summer only.

C. montana. Anemone clematis. Flowers in early spring on old wood so it can be heavily thinned and cut back immediately after flowering to rejuvenate or to reduce size. A vigorous grower, it has a habit of climbing quickly to the top of its support and then growing into an untidy tangle. To avoid this, start training vine to grow horizontally when still young. If an old vine seems hopelessly tangled, a good time to prune it is early spring, as soon as swelling buds indicate which stems are living, which dead. Cut out all dead wood, as well as poor, weak canes or stalks. (If stems are badly tangled, cut out dead wood in short sections rather than tugging at the whole stem.)

C. m. 'Rubens.' Less vigorous than above. Prune lightly after spring bloom.

C. m. 'Tetrarose.' More vigorous than above. Prune after spring bloom.

C. 'Mrs. Cholmondeley.' Vigorous, blooms in summer only.

C. 'Nelly Moser.' Blooms in spring and summer. Use where you want light tracery.

C. 'Ramona.' Spring and summer blooming.

C. 'Susan P. Emory.' Blooms both spring and summer.

C. tangutica. Golden clematis. Blooms in summer. After bloom, or in early spring, prune year's growth to 1 or 2 buds.

C. texensis. Scarlet clematis. Blooms in summer only.

C. 'The President.' Blooms in spring and summer.

C. viticella. Blooms in summer only.

CLERODENDRUM. Glorybower. Evergreen or deciduous shrubs, trees, or vines.

C. bungei (*C. foetidum*). Cashmere bouquet. Evergreen shrub. Rapid grower, suckers readily. Thin and head back thoroughly in spring and pinch back through the growing season to keep compact. Will form thicket if not restrained. Remove suckers when they appear. Reset plant anywhere you need more shrubs.

C. thomsoniae (*C. balfouri*). Bleeding heart glorybower. Evergreen shrubby vine. Thin and head back heavily after bloom to keep a dense, shrubby plant and to produce more flowers next year.

C. trichotomum. Harlequin glorybower. Deciduous shrub-tree. You may prune after flowering, but this will remove showy fruit. To enjoy both, delay pruning until plant becomes dormant.

Keep it as a shrub by heading back and by removing tall branches. To train as tree, cut off all but strongest shoot you want to develop as main trunk. Remove suckers as they appear.

CLETHRA. Deciduous shrub and evergreen tree.

C. alnifolia. Summersweet, sweet pepperbush. Deciduous shrub. Has naturally upright habit, which fits it for hedging. But clipping results in twiggy growth at expense of pleasing natural form and flowers. Cut out overgrown old growth to renew. Prune to shape while dormant.

C. arborea. Lily-of-the-valley tree. Evergreen tree. Small, moderate rate of growth. Requires only normal training while young for form and structure and very little pruning, though it will tolerate it. If damaged or frozen back, it will grow from old wood or from the roots.

CLEYERA japonica (*Eurya ochnacea*). Evergreen shrub. Similar to camellia in pruning requirements. Needs training and shaping when young to develop into desired form. Continue to shape as it matures with selective cutting and pinching back.

CLIANTHUS puniceus. Parrot-beak. Evergreen, shrublike vine. After bloom, cut out dead wood and thin out and cut back older canes and weak branches. This will encourage strong growth for next season's bloom. Train either as vine on walls, fences, or trellises or as a tall shrub or standard.

CLIFF ROSE. See Cowania.

CLIVIA miniata. Kaffir lily. Evergreen perennial with tuberous roots. Cut off dead outside leaves; remove old flower stalks to prevent fruit from forming.

CLYTOSTOMA callistegioides (*Bignonia violacea, B. speciosa*). Violet trumpet vine. Evergreen. Strong, clambering grower. Stems need some support and training in direction you want. Blooms in spring and summer; prune after each flowering to control growth, prevent tangling.

COBAEA scandens. Cup-and-saucer-vine. Perennial. Vigorous growth to 25 ft. or more if not trimmed. Start pinching back plant when 6 in. tall to make it bushy.

COCCOLOBIS uvifera. Sea grape, seaside plum. Evergreen shrub. Very adaptable. Can be trained to single trunk, planted in row to provide effective windbreak, or espaliered. To get good espalier, start with very young plant, fasten branches in design you want, and trim off stray whips that break desired pattern.

COCCULUS laurifolius. Evergreen shrub or small tree. Makes a good informal espalier. Needs frequent pruning to keep it in bounds because it wants to grow as high as 20 ft., spreading as wide. Early thinning as plant develops will prevent legginess. Don't head back; instead, thin entire branches to main trunk. Regular selective reduction of new and old growth (except main structural members) will produce healthier, greener foliage. Will respond to pruning rapidly if growing in rich soil. It can be staked and trained as a single trunked, umbrella-shaped tree.

COFFEA arabica. Coffee. Evergreen house or patio plant, outdoor shrub. Prune to shape when young; corrective pruning as necessary as plant matures.

COFFEEBERRY. See Rhamnus.

COLEONEMA and DIOSMA. Breath of heaven. Evergreen shrubs. Trim back lightly with hedge shears each year after main bloom to keep plants compact. Limit severe pruning to old plants that have had no attention. To renew neglected, old plants, thin out straggly or dead growth and cut plants back about half way. Plants don't always recover from this heavy pruning.

COLEUS blumei. Coleus. Perennial. Left alone, coleus becomes tall and leggy topped with spikes of pale blue flowers. For compact growth and luxuriant foliage, pinch out growing tips regularly during summer to encourage branching. Remove flower buds to keep plant growing vigorously.

COLOCASIA esculenta (*Caladium esculentum*). Taro, elephant's ear. Perennial with tuberous roots. Remove old leaves when they begin to yellow. Cut frost-damaged stalks to ground in spring after danger of frost is past.

COLUMBINE. See Aquilegia.

COLUTEA. Bladder senna. Shrub. Cut back to the ground each year in spring after last frost. This promotes new growth. For a larger plant, remove weak wood and cut other stems back halfway.

COMAROSTAPHYLIS diversifolia. Summer holly. Evergreen shrub or small tree. Train as dense, compact shrub by pinching back growing tips; or form small tree by removing lower limbs.

COMMON TANSY. See Tanacetum.

CONVOLVULUS. Evergreen shrub, evergreen perennial, and an annual.

C. cneorum. Bush morning glory. Evergreen shrub. Rapid growing. Thin and head back thoroughly in late winter to renew plant; pinch tips of new growth. Can get leggy if left alone.

C. mauritanicus. Ground morning glory. Evergreen perennial. Trim back in late winter to keep from getting woody. Pinch tips during the growing season.

COPROSMA. Evergreen shrubs. All respond well to heavy pruning, shaping.

C. kirkii. If ground cover plantings get too high or too uneven, cut them back with hedge shears. Late spring or early summer is a good time to do it.

C. repens (*C. baueri*). Mirror plant. A fairly fast grower that will take all the pruning you want to give it. An open, straggly shrub if neglected but a beautiful plant when cared for. Two prunings a year should be sufficient to keep it dense and at height you want. Take out some stems to the base; cut others back to lateral you want to retain. Where shrub receives ocean wind, little pruning is necessary. Use as hedge, screen, wall shrub, informal espalier.

CORAL BELLS. See Heuchera.

CORAL BERRY. See Symphoricarpos.

CORAL TREE. See Erythrina.

CORDYLINE. Evergreen palmlike shrubs or trees. (Often sold as *Dracaena*.)

C. australis (*Dracaena australis*). Will grow into 20-30 ft. tree, rather stiff like Joshua tree. For more graceful plant, head back when young to force multiple trunks or plant in clumps, cutting a few back to ground each year until all develop multiple trunks.

C. indivisa. Blue dracaena. Removal of lower leaves as they die is only pruning requirement.

C. stricta. Will grow to 15 ft. but can be kept lower by cutting tall canes to ground. New canes will replace them. Long cuttings will root quickly if you stick them into ground.

C. terminalis. Ti. Cut back to encourage branching. Will survive even when chopped to ground. Start new plants with cut portions.

COREOPSIS. Annual and perennial. Prolong bloom on all types by removing old flowers. Cut perennial types back to ground when they finish blooming in fall.

CORNUS. Dogwood. Deciduous shrub or tree. Tree forms require only normal shaping and training for structure when young and very little pruning later. Prune lightly if required to maintain shape, removing dead and weak wood in spring after flowering. (If bleeding occurs, prune as required in winter or early spring.) Shrub forms generally require more pruning than trees.

DOGWOOD in winter. Left branch ends in 3 flower buds, right in 3 leaf buds.

C. alba. Tatarian dogwood; and **C. a. 'Sibirica.'** Siberian dogwood. Shrubs. In cold-winter areas, the blood red, bare twigs are very colorful. New wood is brightest, so cut some of older wood back to side branches in spring to force new growth.

C. controversa. Giant dogwood. Tree. Lower branches often sweep ground. Trim them off if you want to use as shade tree to sit under or as street tree to walk under.

C. florida. Flowering dogwood, Eastern dogwood. Tree. Lowest branches often sweep ground, giving natural protection. In cold winter areas, don't prune off these low branches. If they don't branch low naturally, they may need special care during coldest weather when morning sun can crack and split frozen bark. Protect with shrubs planted around it or place evergreen boughs against the east side of tree trunks. Unprotected bark, in defense, may send out leafy sucker shoots. If you remove these suckers, the bark may crack and die.

C. f. 'Welchii.' Tricolor dogwood. You can let it grow as a big shrub with foliage to the ground or train it into tree form.

C. mas. Cornelian cherry. Shrub or tree. Grows naturally as airy, twiggy shrub but can be pruned high to form small, finely branched tree.

COCCULUS LAURIFOLIUS shading this patio was planted as shrub 12 years earlier. Skeleton made showy by pruning. Inside wires support lower branches.

C. nuttallii. Pacific dogwood, Western dogwood. Give only routine training while young because this tree reacts unfavorably to pruning. If protecting trees or shrubbery don't shade trunk, tree tends to send out suckers on sunny side. Pruning these off may cause sunscorched bark of tree to split, inviting insects and diseases which can eventually damage and kill the tree. Protect from bark injury by planting a buffer strip of shrubbery around its base.

C. sanguinea. Bloodtwig dogwood. Shrub. Grows as many-stemmed shrub. Remove oldest stems at ground in spring to produce new red branches and twigs for winter color.

C. stolonifera. Redtwig dogwood, red-osier dogwood. Shrub. Remove oldest, darkest stems to ground in early spring to encourage fresh new ones and to hold plant in check. Cut back if it gets too tall. Spreads rapidly by underground stems and from tip layering (see *Pruning Glossary*). To control, use a space to cut off roots that have gone too far. Cut off branches that touch ground.

COROKIA. Evergreen shrubs. Naturally picturesque plants. You don't normally have to prune them to achieve this effect, except occasionally when upright stems develop in the center of plants. Cut these out as they appear in order to keep plants in proper balance.

CORONILLA varia. Crown vetch. Perennial. Tenacious ground cover that goes dormant and looks ratty during coldest weather unless it is covered with snow. Mow it in spring to get lush green summer cover.

CORREA. Australian fuchsia. Evergreen shrubs. Prune very lightly after flowers have faded to keep the shrubs compact and the size you want. Pinch back regularly to keep from spreading. Since they don't sprout readily from old wood, they should not be given hard pruning.

CORTADERIA selloana. Pampas grass. Evergreen giant ornamental grass. Difficult to prune because its leaves are sharp and cut your hands easily, but it must be cut back from time to time to keep it under control. Cut off fluffy plumes before they go to seed because they get messy. Most efficient way to control it is to burn it to the ground periodically if you are in an area where this can be done. If burning is not permitted, shear it to ground.

CORYLOPSIS. Winter hazel. Deciduous shrubs. Slow growing, rather open structures, and delicate branching patterns. Little pruning required; thin and shape as necessary after bloom.

CORYLUS. Filbert, hazelnut. Deciduous shrubs or small trees. Need only early training or shaping. If necessary, thin by cutting selected stems at bases when dormant. If trained as a tree, select best trunk and remove its side branches to desired height. Also remove suckers as they appear.

CORYNOCARPUS laevigatus. New Zealand laurel. Evergreen shrub or small tree. Will withstand heavy pruning though seldom required. Slow growing, keeps attractive form for years. Older specimens can grow as high as 30 or 40 ft., but you can control height by thinning and heading back selectively. Small orange fruits are extremely poisonous.

COSTMARY. See Chrysanthemum.

COTINUS coggygria (*Rhus cotinus*). Smoke tree. Deciduous. Thin lightly when dormant to eliminate overly dense growth or dead wood. Can be trained as a multi or single-trunked tree or shrub.

COTONEASTER. Evergreen, semi-deciduous, and deciduous shrubs. These range all the way from ground covers to upright small shrubs to taller shrubs and trees of fountainlike growth with graceful, arching branches. Vigorous growers, they all respond well to pruning though they don't normally require much beyond shaping and removing branches that have carried berries—cut them just above an unberried side branch. (Cutting the berries for indoor decoration is usually enough pruning.) For deciduous types, major pruning is normally done in winter or early spring. Evergreen types should be pruned just before new growth begins. Cotoneasters all need elbow room. To avoid having to prune severely and frequently, choose a type that will fit your space. Some medium and tall growers can be sheared, but they look best when allowed to maintain natural fountain shapes. Prune only to enhance graceful arch of branches. Keep low growers looking young by cutting out portion of oldest wood each year. Prune ground covers to remove dead or awkward branches. Don't plant where branch ends need shearing (near a walk or drive) because

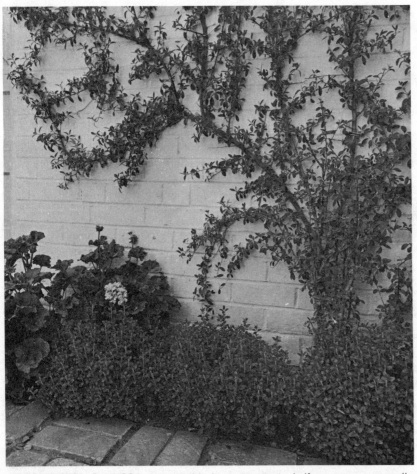

COTONEASTER PANNOSA—a type that is evergreen to half-evergreen—normally grows as a 10 by 10 foot shrub. This one has been fastened to wall and pruned often.

stubbed branches are unattractive. Neglected shrubs can be cut back heavily to renew. New vigorous growth sprouts readily from old wood. If a neglected shrub has become a brambly eyesore, transform it into a gnarled, picturesque tree with a pruning saw. Lop off branches that grow out between ground level and shoulder height to reveal pleasing trunk lines hidden under excess branch growth. Cotoneasters are susceptible to fireblight. Examine them carefully as soon as buds begin to expand in spring; dead branches may indicate the disease in areas where it's a problem. Prune out dead branches to lessen chance of infecting new growth. Sterilize pruning tools.

C. parneyi. Evergreen. Cotoneaster, red clusterberry. (Plants sold under this name are usually *C. lactea*.) This hardy shrub will endure heavy pruning, responding with vigorous growth from old wood. Such severe treatment should be necessary only when periodic pruning has been neglected. Heavy pruning will cost you one crop of berries. Holds its foliage near the ground, a characteristic that makes it good as free-standing shrub or hedge, or even as espalier or shrub for container. It is one of the few plants that can be woven through a chain link fence. If you wish, you can confine pruning to removal of berried branches for display indoors. Remove branches at point just above a lateral. When there are no such side branches, cut just above ground level. Through such heading back and thinning, you can preserve the over-all character of the shrub and keep it a profusely berrying plant. It has such flexible branches that you can lead it into any pattern you want. You can espalier it, training the branches by fastening them to wires strung between nails driven in the wall. Or use it as a ground cover. Start with small plants that show a low, spreading growth habit. Set 3-4 ft. apart, peg branches to the ground with inverted U made of wire. To make a standard, select a plant with a vertical stem. Keep it staked for 2-4 years. When stem reaches 3-4 ft., pinch out tip to force branching. Grow as clipped hedge. By pruning you can control it at any height up to about 6 ft. If let grow naturally, it forms a graceful 6-ft. high shrub.

COTTONWOOD. See Populus.

COWANIA mexicana stansburiana. Cliff rose. Evergreen shrub. Trim off some branches and straggly growth to show off smoky pink trunk bark. Prune as required to shape after flowering and fruiting.

COYOTE BRUSH, DWARF. See Baccharis.

CRABAPPLE, FLOWERING. See Malus.

CRABAPPLE, FRUITING. See Apple.

CRANBERRY, HIGHBUSH. See Viburnum.

CRANBERRY, MOUNTAIN. See Vaccinium.

CRAPE MYRTLE. See Lagerstroemia.

CRASSULA. Succulents including jade plant. Can be easily pruned and shaped, but they grow slowly and retain their shape many years without excessive pruning. Some pruning may be necessary to prevent plants from becoming topheavy and falling over or to bring symmetry to lopsided plants. Remove growth at any time to control shape and height and for use in flower arrangements. Remove whole stems, making cuts cleanly just above a node.

JADE PLANT (Crassula) with many side branches removed to show its good bones.

CRATAEGUS. Hawthorn. Deciduous trees. Require very little pruning. They are much prettier if you don't interfere with the natural, dense growth. Some types have a tendency to grow tops that are too dense. An annual thinning will minimize the danger of being uprooted by wind. Beyond this, restrict pruning to removal of suckers from trunk and around the base and thinning excess twiggy growth. Never tip back shoots. For a hedge, start with young unbranched trees planted 3 ft. apart. Kept trimmed, they will grow into a dense, somewhat thorny flowering hedge. Keeping them closely clipped means that you sacrifice some flowers, but there will be bloom if you wait to prune until after flowering. Susceptible to fireblight in some areas. Cut out blighted branches well below dead part; wash pruning tools with disinfectant between each cut.

CREAM BUSH. See Holodiscus.

CREEPING FIG. See Ficus.

CRINODENDRON patagua (*C. dependens, Tricuspidaria dependens*). Lily-of-the-valley tree. Evergreen tree. Needs early training and shaping to make an attractive tree. Left on its own, it tends to become shrubby. Keep a single-trunk tree clean of extra growth. Thin out brushy growth toward the center; remove branches that tend to hang down.

CROTALARIA agatiflora. Canary bird bush. Evergreen shrub. Fast, rank grower, not particularly attractive unless thinned and pruned consistently. Criss-cross growth needs continued pruning and cleaning out. Prune heavily about 3 times during the growing season: after the heavy fall blooming period, prior to late spring growth, and again in midsummer. In coldest areas, frost does some of the pruning. Cut out freeze-damaged wood. New growth will sprout from stump.

CROWN OF GOLD TREE. See Cassia.

CROWN VETCH. See Coronilla.

CRYPTOCARYA rubra. Evergreen tree. Grows with multiple trunks but can be trained and pruned to single trunk. Easily restrained as a small tree or in the confined space of a container.

CRYPTOMERIA japonica. Japanese cryptomeria. Evergreen tree. Needs very little pruning—just the removal of errant branches.

C. j. 'Elegans.' Plume cedar, plume cryptomeria. Can be pruned for oriental effect by taking out some branches to give a tiered look, or by leaving clusters of foliage on tips of branches in a pompon effect.

CUNNINGHAMIA lanceolata. China fir. Evergreen tree. Responds well to pruning, though all that is required is normal training and guidance and removal of dead branches. Remove suckers that form at base.

CUNONIA capensis. African red alder. Evergreen large shrub or small tree. Buy as tree form or as dense shrub. By thinning and heading back selectively on regular basis, you can hold plant to about 6 ft.

CUP FLOWER. See Nierembergia.

CUP-AND-SAUCER VINE. See Cobaea.

CUP-OF-GOLD VINE. See Solandra.

CUPANIOPSIS anacardioides (*Cupania anacardioides*). Carrot wood, tuckeroo. Evergreen tree. Prune to enhance structure, remove excess branches. Never stub back; always cut to a side branch. Interesting when trained as multi-stemmed tree.

CUPHEA ignea. Cigar plant. Perennial. Cut back after flowering to encourage more bloom. Tends to sprawl, but you can keep it relatively compact by pinching out growing tips. Cut older plant back severely in late fall, early spring.

CUPRESSOCYPARIS leylandii. Evergreen tree. Grows extremely fast. Responds well to light or heavy pruning as needed.

CUPRESSUS. Cypress. Evergreen trees.

C. forbesii. Tecate cypress. Very fast growing. Thin out some of top to keep from becoming topheavy for size of its root system. Can be trained and pruned as hedge.

C. glabra. (Often sold as *C. arizonica.*) Smooth Arizona cypress. Fast grower. Train it as tree or tall screen.

C. macrocarpa. Monterey cypress. Grows naturally into picturesque form. Little pruning required except to remove dead wood.

C. sempervirens. Italian cypress. Branches often pull away from main body of plant. Don't attempt to tie them back in place. Cut branch off a little inside of where it breaks away from column. This will force side growth to fill in bare area and maintain a sturdy plant. For formal hedging, you can shear it lightly anytime.

CURRANT. Deciduous shrub. Currants bear at the base of year-old wood and on spurs on 2 and 3-year wood. Prune while dormant so that you keep balance of 1, 2, and 3-year canes. Prune out older canes and weak growth.

CURRANT, INDIAN. See Symphoricarpos.

CURRANT, ORNAMENTAL. See Ribes.

CUSHION BUSH. See Calocephalus.

CYPERUS alternifolius and C. papyrus. Umbrella plant, papyrus. Perennials. Pruning these tropicals is a matter of grooming and control. Clean up at least twice a year. Cut back overgrown and brown flower heads at base of long stems. To keep plants from spreading, chop off above ground the basal stems that keep spreading out. What is left will sprout and make more compact plants. Prune out overripe foliage down to bases before active growth in spring. Unless these stems are cut down, they turn brown and make clump look ugly, messy, and overcrowded. In colder areas, frost may cut them down to ground. New growth will appear in spring.

CYPRESS. See Cupressus.

CYPRESS, BALD. See Taxodium.

CYPRESS, FALSE. See Chamaecyparis.

CYTISUS, GENISTA, SPARTIUM. Brooms. Evergreen or deciduous shrubs and shrublets. To grow brooms successfully, prune right after flowering every year. If you cut brooms all the way back into old wood, the limbs will probably die; however, there have been cases where some types have come back from the root crown after being pruned to the ground. Old plants that have become coarse and leggy from neglect cannot be made trim and vigorous again. It's best to discard them and start with new ones. Each spring, cut off all flowering wood and up to half new vegetative wood. If you remove spent flowers before they have a chance to set seeds, you will minimize haphazard volunteer seeding and spreading. In colder areas, unpruned brooms can be damaged by snow. Once the weight of snow has pinned limbs to the ground, they will have a stiff and somewhat awkward shape when they rise again. You will find the same condition if children or pets play in them.

DAHLIA. Perennial grown from tuberous roots. Bushes, summer hedges, screens and low borders. When tall-growing dahlias are 4-5 in. high, thin in spring to strongest shoot or 2 shoots (make cuttings of removed ones). When plants reach 8-12 in. and 3 or 4 sets of leaves have formed, pick off tips just above the topmost pair of leaves. This procedure, known as "crowning-out," will encourage side branching and produce

FOR BUSHY DAHLIAS, pinch out tips. Initial growth response shown below.

rounder, bushier plants with well-distributed blossoms. Without pinching, dahlias tend to become lanky and topheavy, having all their flowers at the top. For even bushier plants, tips of subsequent laterals can also be pinched out.

Disbudding: You will get the best possible flowers if you remove surplus flower buds on decorative types—normally there are 3 buds at the tip of each branch. (Many types such as Tom Thumb need no disbudding.) In early morning or evening, buds are brittle and snap off with a flick of your finger. When they are the size of small peas, snap off 2 buds at the sides of the tip so that terminal bud will get benefit of plant's energy and reach maximum development. At the next node below the terminal bud, 2 other buds will develop. Snap these off, too. By the time

TO MAKE BIGGER dahlia flowers, disbud 2 outer flower buds. Middle one benefits.

terminal bud has matured and bloomed, flowers on lower laterals will be showing color. Repeat disbudding as buds emerge. If you don't crown-out and disbud dahlias, they will form one large bloom at top of plants and increasingly shorter stems on lower side branches.

Cutting flowers: Cut dahlias only after flowers are fully open (buds don't develop well after being cut). For a second batch of flowers, cut stems that have flowered back to one joint on the main stalk.

Fall cutback: When dahlia tops have been cut by frost or have died down, cut tops to 4 in., lift the clumps of tubers, and store in a cool, dry place until time to divide and plant in the spring.

D. imperialis. Tree dahlia. Cut back to ground in fall after bloom or after frost kills it. Grows each year from permanent roots.

DAIS cotinifolia. Pompon tree. Briefly deciduous. Form may be a bit gross, but you can improve it markedly by pruning unwanted, erratic growth to reveal some of its branching form. Naturally multiple trunked, it looks best trained to single trunk.

DAISY, MICHAELMAS. See Aster.

DAISY, TRANSVAAL. See Gerbera.

DAISY BUSH. See Olearia.

DALEA spinosa. Smoke tree. Deciduous tree. Prune only to shape as required.

DAPHNE. Evergreen and deciduous shrubs. Daphnes can withstand severe pruning, but they seldom need it except to reshape plants. (*D. mezereum,* February daphne, may not bloom again for a year after pruning.) Daphnes can be pruned whenever their shoots get out of bounds, but normal procedure is to prune during and after bloom. A good way to shape plants is by cutting small clusters of flowers to wear during the flowering season (late winter). If you want big cut branches, make cuts just above growth buds, or small shoots. Cutting to outward facing buds results in spreading plants; cutting to inside facing buds will tend to produce erect plants. Daphnes can also be cut in bud and brought indoors for forcing into bloom.

DATE PALM. See Phoenix.

DATURA. Angel's trumpet. Evergreen shrubs. Strong, vigorous growth and soft wood make it necessary to trim, shape, and clean out shrubs at least once a season. Do serious pruning in early spring, after last frost. Cut back branches to 1 or 2 buds.

DAUBENTONIA tripetii. Scarlet wisteria tree. Deciduous shrub or small tree. Prune severely in early spring. Thin and shorten side branches to stubs. Blooms from May through summer. Pods that follow blossoms should be removed to prolong flowering. Often trained to flat-topped standard tree on 6-ft. trunk.

DAVIDIA involucrata. Dove tree. Deciduous. Prune plant lightly to maintain desired shape. Remove crossing, rubbing branches; dead or diseased wood. Prune after flowering, leaving no stubs; remove entire twig or branch back to base. Wounds are susceptible to disease, rot. Treat cuts ½ in. or wider with wound dressing (see *Pruning Glossary*).

DAYLILY. See Hemerocallis.

DELPHINIUM. Perennials, biennials, annuals. When new shoots develop in spring, remove all but 2 or 3 strongest (you may leave more on older, better established plants). When first large flower spikes finish blooming, cut stalks to within 6 or 8 in. of ground. Leave stubs of old stalks until new shoots from bases are several inches high and then remove them. New shoots will bloom in late summer and early fall. Blooms will continue to come all summer if you cut off faded flower stalks.

D. cheilanthum. Sturdy, bushy perennial. Should be treated a bit differently, for many flowering stems branch off main stalk. When all flowers have faded, cut plant to ground, and new growth will shoot up.

DENDROMECON. Bush poppy. Evergreen shrubs. Will withstand almost any amount of pruning, though light and infrequent pruning to remove dead wood and renew old wood is all that is normally required. Cut off long shoot growths to prevent legginess. Do major pruning after bloom. Cut *D. rigida* back to 2 ft. after flowering.

DEODAR CEDAR. See Cedrus.

DESERT CANDLE. See Eremurus.

DESERT HONEYSUCKLE. See Anisacanthus.

DESERT WILLOW. See Chilopsis.

DEUTZIA. Deciduous flowering shrubs. Respond well to heavy pruning right after bloom. Thin twiggy growths any time. Some pruning while plants are blooming will provide good display of color for the house. Cut flowering branches back to strong side branches of new growth. Cut oldest stems of low and medium growing kinds to ground to force new shoots. Prune tall-growing kinds severely by cutting back wood that has flowered (cut to outward facing side branches). It's good practice to prune deutzias before the flowers are all gone. New growth will start well out on blooming branches, and by the time growth starts, you'll need a steely heart to cut away all the wood you should. Cut flowering branches far back into center of plants. Later in summer, tip back the new growth if necessary. Cut back unwanted shoots and suckers that emerge from ground around plants.

DIANELLA tasmanica. Perennial. Groom by removing shabby leaves and dead fruiting stalks.

DIANTHUS. Carnation, pink. Perennials, biennials, annuals. For long bloom, shear off spent flowers frequently. Cut plants back to about half-size in fall to encourage new bottom growth and keep from becoming straggly.

D. caryophyllus. Carnation, clove pink. Perennial. For large flowers, leave only terminal bloom on each stem. Pinch out all other buds down to fifth joint, below which new flowering stems will develop. Do not disbud if you want lots of flowers. Carnations tend to become straggly when permitted to grow at will. Pinching will reward you with bushy plants. When cuttings are about 7 joints high, nip out growing tips to encourage side branching. Pinch out growing tips on side shoots if they get out of line. (Don't pinch out top growth later or you'll remove current season's flowers.) When you cut blooms for arrangements, take flowers with long stems, cutting back to main stalk.

D. 'Beatrix.' Perennial. Give full year to become established and trim foliage

back halfway in late fall to keep plant full and shapely.

D. chinensis. Chinese pink, rainbow pink. Biennial or short-lived perennial. Pick off faded flowers along with bases to prolong bloom.

D. 'Little Joe.' Perennial. Will bloom from May to November if dead blooms are removed.

D. 'Rose Bowl.' Perennial. Blooms almost continually if spent blooms are removed regularly.

DICENTRA. Bleeding heart. Perennials. Cut back after flowering for second growth and sometimes repeat bloom.

DICKSONIA. See Fern, Tree.

DIEFFENBACHIA. Dumb cane. Evergreen indoor foliage plant. When plant gets tall, it loses most lower leaves, so you may want to start new plant by rooting cuttings in water. Or you can cut the old plant back to size by air-layering (see *Pruning Glossary*).

DIGITALIS purpurea. Common foxglove. Biennial, sometimes perennial. After first flowering, cut main spike. If all cultural conditions are to the plant's liking, side shoots will then develop and bloom in summer.

DIMORPHOTHECA ecklonis. See Osteospermum.

DIOSMA. See Coleonema.

DIPLACUS. Shrubby monkey flower. Shrubby perennial or evergreen shrub or shrublet. If pruned after first flowering, will bloom again in fall. Prune also in spring before new growth starts.

DIPLOPAPPUS filifolius (*Aster fruticosus*). Shrub aster. Evergreen shrub. Bushy, densely branched. Shear off dead flowers after bloom, then thin by taking out whole branches and dead weak wood.

DISTICTIS. Evergreen vines.

D. laxiflora (*D. lactiflora, D. cinerea*). Vanilla trumpet vine. More restrained than most trumpet vines, requiring less pruning.

D. 'Rivers.' (Sometimes labeled *D. riversii*.) Royal trumpet vine. Much more vigorous and needs heavy pruning.

DISTYLIUM racemosum. Evergreen shrub. Resembles Japanese privet (*Ligustrum japonicum*). Can tolerate heavy pruning or shearing. Can be trained either as dense clipped screen or as espaliered wall plant. Prune any time in milder areas, but wait until spring in colder parts of country.

DIZYGOTHECA elegantissima. (Often sold as *Aralia elegantissima*.) Threadleaf false aralia. House plant (juvenile stage); evergreen garden shrub (mature form). In subtropical areas, gardeners who grow it as landscape plant usually cut it back every year or so in spring to keep delicate juvenile leaves coming along. Can become small tree with 10-12-ft. spread if not pruned severely. If plant has several trunks, train them to grow at staggered heights by cutting back tallest one to base each year or so. A single shoot will sprout quickly from trunk base beneath the cut and grow straight up. This pruning method puts foliage along whole trunk rather than just at top of long bare stem. It also keeps lacy juvenile leaves coming. Unpruned plant eventually develops coarser, thicker, mature leaves.

DODONAEA viscosa. Hop bush, hopseed bush. Evergreen shrub. Left on its own, it will become an attractive, informal, leafy wall, needing only occasional thinning and pinching back of errant growth. Can also be sheared into neat, compact, formal hedge, or trained as espalier. Fast growing, with many upright stems, it can be trained as a tree by cutting out all but a single stem. In this case, keep well staked and remove side shoots up to desired height of clear trunk when they appear on main stem.

DOGWOOD. See Cornus.

DOLICHOS lignnosus. Australian pea vine. Perennial twining vine. Evergreen in mild winters. Vigorous, rapid grower that must be cut back if it gets out of control. If overgrown or freeze damaged, cut back to ground in spring and start over with new growth.

DOMBEYA wallichii. Evergreen shrub. Fast growth means brittle wood and undisciplined habit. Needs regular thinning out and heading back for bushiness. Faded flower clusters tend to hang on and look untidy unless removed. Can be espaliered or trained over arbors to display flowers.

DORONICUM. Leopards bane. Perennial. If you cut back flower stalks as soon as blooms have faded, you encourage second flowering.

DOUGLAS FIR. See Pseudotsuga.

DOVE TREE. See Davidia.

DOVYALIS caffra (*Aberia caffra*). Kei apple. Evergreen shrub. Thin out some stems and head others back annually to keep to size you wish. Can be kept anywhere from 1-8 or 10 ft. high and as little as 12 in. wide. If pampered with water and fertilizer, it will grow taller and rangier, requiring pruning back of straggly branches.

DOXANTHA unguis-cati. Cat's claw, yellow trumpet vine. Partly deciduous vine. Prune hard after bloom to keep in bounds. Remove all old and weak shoots, cut back some stems nearly to

ground to stimulate new growth lower down. Control size by pinching new growth during growing season.

DRACAENA draco. Dragon tree. Evergreen foliage plant. Clusters of flowers form at branch ends. After blossoms drop, stemmy clusters remain. Trim off to keep plant neat. Strip off dead leaves.

DRAGON TREE. See Dracaena.

DRIMYS winteri. Winter's bark. Evergreen tree. Usually multi-stemmed but easily trained to single trunk. May require pruning for shape from time to time to maintain pleasing symmetry of outline.

DUCHESNEA indica. Indian mock strawberry. Perennial. Grows rapidly as a ground cover, can become a nuisance if neglected. Shear surface and trim edges to keep under control.

DUMB CANE. See Dieffenbachia.

DURANTA. Evergreen shrubs. Need continual thinning and pruning to keep under control. Remove to ground (or to strong unflowered laterals) all branches that have produced berries. Tip pruning should be avoided, for it will result in bushy growth just below cuts.

DUSTY MILLER. See Senecio.

EASTER LILY VINE. See Beaumontia.

ECHEVERIA. Succulents. All the pruning that the low, squatty types (represented mostly by plant called hen and chicks) need is to have old, dead leaf rosettes and flower stalks removed. With tall kinds, your concern will be what to do with them when they get leggy. It's simple. Just cut off the top and insert its stem into sand. The big cutting will form new roots. Then new growth will sprout from the base.

ECHINACEA purpurea (*Rudbeckia purpurea*). Purple coneflower. Perennial. Cut to the ground after bloom.

ECHIUM fastuosum. Pride of Madeira. Shrubby perennial. After each spike finishes blooming, cut stalk off a few inches down in foliage. Lightly trim plant to keep bushy. If you cut back too hard, it may not survive. If, on the other hand, you don't do any cutting or pinching, the plant's vigor soon turns it into bizarre, tree-like shrub.

ELAEAGNUS. Deciduous and evergreen large shrubs or small trees. All are tough, grow fast (when young), and typically can exist a lifetime with no pruning at all. Pruning becomes necessary when the plants get too big or—infrequently—when they get an ugly shape. When you must prune, plant will respond well to selective branch removal

and cutting back. Prune at any time of year. Plants can be shaped and pruned like bonsai.

E. angustifolia. Russian olive. Small deciduous tree. Varies greatly in growth habit. In selecting one look for form you want; otherwise you'll have to do a lot of training and shaping. Should be pruned at least every 2 or 3 years. Limbs that have grown too long may break from wind or the weight of snow; cut these back. Tree can be trained as clipped or informal hedge or screen or grown as well-groomed tree.

E. fruitlandii. Fruitland silverberry. Evergreen shrub. Much like *E. pungens*. Grows dense, full, firm, and tough. Natural shape is good when given plenty of room. Excellent for large bank planting. Best grown naturally or sheared as a thickly foliaged screen.

E. pungens. Silverberry. Large evergreen shrub. Naturally sprawling, it will take any amount of pruning and direction you give it. By encouraging angular nature of stems, you can make picturesque container plant. Can be trained as small tree completely clothed in foliage or directed toward a more formal small standard. Clipped, makes an excellent hedge. With pinching and heading back of errant growth, it will form flat wall cover, either full foliaged or with open pattern of spiny branches and shimmery leaves.

ELDERBERRY. See Sambucus.

ELEPHANT'S EAR. See Colocasia.

ELEPHANT'S FOOD. See Portulacaria.

ELM. See Ulmus.

EMPRESS TREE. See Paulownia.

ENGLISH LAUREL. See Prunus.

ENKIANTHUS. Deciduous shrubs. Prune only to remove dead or broken branches. Short spurs tend to develop along stems of old plants, detracting from their interesting, angular forms. Keep these spurs snipped off.

ENSETE. Big, palm-like perennials. Evergreen in mild areas, die back in winter and regrow in spring in colder climates.

E. ventricosum (*Musa ensete*). Abyssinian banana. When older, bottom leaves begin to droop and turn yellow. Cut off at base using sharp steel knife. After flowering, plant dies to roots. Cut stalk off at base so that new growth will sprout.

EPAULETTE TREE. See Pterostyrax.

EPIDENDRUM. Epiphytic or terrestrial orchids. Flower on new growth. To keep new blooms coming all year, cut flowering stems back to within 1 or 2 nodes of ground after flowers have faded. Besides more flower stems, you'll get more compact growth. This applies to reed-stemmed terrestrial species only. Some epidendrums have pseudobulbs and need no pruning.

EPIMEDIUM. Perennials. In early spring, after danger of frost is past, cut off old foliage to make room for new growth.

EQUISETUM hyemale. Horsetail. Perennial. Can get out of hand so fast that it should be grown in concrete or metal-lined container. In the garden, you'll have to chop back invasive roots and shoots. Cut oldest canes to base as they begin to fall over and become messy.

ERANTHEMUM nervosum. (Sometimes sold as *E. pulchellum.*) Evergreen shrub. Pinch back stem tips 2 or 3 times early in growing season to keep plant compact and encourage more flower production. Cut leggy plant to ground to stimulate fresh new growth.

EREMURUS. Foxtail lily, desert candle. Perennials. Cut flower stalks to base as soon as last blooms fade. If allowed to set seed, plants are usually weakened and may not bloom for several years.

ERIOBOTRYA japonica. Loquat. Evergreen tree. Can tolerate any amount of pruning or none at all. Normally seen as single or multi-stemmed tree and espalier. It can be trained to hedge form. Trained as espalier, branches are quite rigid and need firm tying. Left to grow naturally, tree becomes compact and round. For maximum fruit, prune to admit light. Prune in spring before new growth starts. Thin fruit some to reduce chances of fruit-laden branches breaking in storms.

Susceptible to fireblight in some areas. Watch for it as buds begin to expand; dead branches may indicate the disease. If leaves and stems blacken from the top downward, prune back 12 in. or more into healthy wood. Discard prunings (burn them if possible) and sterilize shears between cuts.

ERIOGONUM. Wild buckwheat. Annuals, perennials, shrubs. You can do some pruning to shape if you start when plants are young. If they've had no attention and have become straggly, better replace them.

ERYTHEA. See Palm.

ERYTHRINA. Coral tree. Mostly deciduous (some nearly evergreen) trees or shrubs. Can be pruned at any time of the year, since they don't have a true dormant period. The important thing is to distinguish old wood from new wood, and to know if the kind of coral tree you are pruning blooms on new or old wood. It's wise to prune before new growth starts, because pruning then doesn't weaken the tree and because then you can direct new growth where

you want it to go. Most corals look best with multiple trunks or 2 or 3 low trunklike branches.

E. bidwillii. Deciduous shrub. Closely related to *E. crista-galli*, and you can prune it in the same way—hard, before new growth begins.

E. caffra. Kaffirboom coral tree. Briefly deciduous. One of the really big corals, it almost never needs pruning except to eliminate branches that grow too low. A pruning can actually stop tree from blooming for several years. It takes that long for branches to get old enough to produce blooms. The tree's shape is naturally that of a spreading horizontal tree.

E. coralloides. Naked coral tree. Deciduous. Blooms before any leaves show in spring, so its bare structure is important. Left alone, it can get pretty scraggly, with branches going every which way (sometimes even in circles). Properly pruned, it can be open, airy, and architectural. Prune so that most remaining branches are horizontal and spreading. Prune by removing whole branches, not by tipping the ends. Flowering happens at the tips. You may need to do some pruning every year.

E. crista-galli. Cockspur coral tree. Deciduous shrub or tree. Can have as many as 3 distinct flowering periods, spring through fall. Cut back old flower stems and deadened branch-ends after each wave of bloom. This stimulates new growth, resulting in another good crop of blooms.

E. humeana. Natal coral tree. Deciduous, sometimes evergreen. Blooms off and on all summer, so unless you must shape the tree don't cut off anything except dead flower spikes.

ESCALLONIA. Evergreen shrubs. Vigorous growers, they can stand any amount of pruning or shaping. They tend to get woody and rangy if not pruned. After bloom, remove about a third of old wood to ground, snip back leggy stems, and cut off old seed clusters that hang on long after flowering. Escallonias look best if you don't clip them closely, but even if you trim them as formal hedge you'll get some flowers because they grow on new wood. You can train the taller growing forms into trees; as the plants age, trunk structures become more interesting. Tip pinch smaller kinds to keep them compact.

EUCALYPTUS. Evergreen trees and shrubs. Though eucalypts can take heavy pruning, they generally don't require much. Most can live a lifetime with no pruning. However, many kinds do grow extremely fast and may need some early training. The trunk of a young tree you select at a nursery should be sturdy enough not to need staking. If it isn't, bend it down to the ground, making an arch. Hold the trunk in this arched position by wiring to a rock or a short stake. New sprouts will then grow from the base and a new trunk, probably huskier than the original, will develop. About a year later cut off the old, arched trunk.

There are about 150 different kinds of eucalyptus grown in the milder parts of the Western and Southwestern United States. They can be grouped broadly into three forms: the mallees, or shrubby, multi-trunk species; the medium or intermediate size with single trunk or many trunks; and the tall, single trunk forest trees.

The mallees—the shrubby forms—are usually best left alone. They'll normally form dense clumps on their own

---

EUCALYPTUS GROWTH TYPES

The commonly grown eucalyptus species can be divided into the following groups:

Mallee	Intermediate	Forest Tree
E. caesia	E. cinerea	E. calophylla
E. eremophila	E. cloeziana	E. camaldulensis
E. erythronema	E. erythrocorys	E. citriodora
E. grossa	E. ficifolia	E. cladocalyx
E. kruseana	E. forrestiana	E. cornuta
E. macrocarpa	E. lehmannii	E. globulus
E. orbifolia	E. leucoxylon	E. globulus 'Compacta'
E. orpetii	E. leucoxylon macrocarpa 'Rosea'	E. gunnii
E. preissiana	E. linearis	E. maculata
E. pyriformis	E. macrandra	E. maculosa
E. rhodantha	E. megacornuta	E. melliodora
E. tetraptera	E. microtheca	E. nicholii
	E. niphophila	E. pauciflora
	E. perriniana	E. robusta
	E. platypus	E. rudis
	E. polyanthemos	E. saligna
	E. pulverulenta	E. sideroxylon
	E. spathulata	E. viminalis
	E. stellulata	
	E. torquata	

and pruning may make them look awkward. If you have a mallee with rangy, leggy stems, you can cut it to the ground to force multiple shoots and shrubby growth from the ground. Later, select 3 to 5 of the strongest new shoots for the framework and cut out the rest.

Medium or intermediate size types like *E. lehmannii* can grow either as single or multiple trunk trees. If you need to encourage a single trunk, cut off side shoots (but not immediately after planting—leave them on for a while, to help nourish the tree). If you need to encourage a multi-trunk, cut off the top at 2 ft. if there are plenty of side shoots beneath. Or bend it to the ground as described on page 39 and start over with the new sprouts.

Tall, forest type, single trunk eucalypts seldom need pruning, except to train in the early stages as outlined on page 39. At times on any big single trunk species, you (or a commercial tree pruning man wearing safety equipment) may have to cut out storm damaged or weak wood.

Mature tree types that have grown too tall are often cut back to stumps. They have a great capacity for regrowth and will respond by sprouting several new trunks. With proper shaping and training, you have one or several new, smaller trees in just a few seasons.

If pruning is necessary, the best time to do it is spring and summer (after bloom where flowers are important). If possible, cut back to just above a side branch or bud. If you can't find a promising growth point, cut right into a smooth trunk; if the plant is established, new growth will break out beneath the cut. Later, remove all excess new branches—keep only those that are mechanically well placed.

AN INTERMEDIATE eucalyptus—E. lehmannii, grown with single trunk, high branches. Left unpruned, this type usually has several trunks and its branches sweep the ground.

HABIT typical of mallee eucalyptus, this is E. rhodantha. Up to this stage, it needs no pruning. Later, if it eats up too much space, cut longest branches to bases.

THE MOST FAMOUS of forest types, blue gum (E. globulus). This one, at Stanford University, had been cut to stump (10 feet above cyclists' heads) 50 years earlier.

EUONYMUS. Evergreen or deciduous shrubs, evergreen vines, ground covers. They all withstand heavy pruning (any time in mild areas, in spring after danger of frost is past in colder climates). The type of pruning and training you do depends on plant type and how you're using it.

E. alata. Winged euonymus. Deciduous shrub. Slow growth, dense, twiggy. Prune for form in early spring, much as you would lilac.

E. fortunei. (Formerly *E. radicans acuta.*) Evergreen vine or shrub. This versatile plant will grow as a vine, attaching itself with minimum of assistance if given wall to climb on or tumble over. Without some kind of support to climb, it doesn't send out long vining stems but instead becomes low growing, bushy, mounded shrub. Keep top growth cut to train as ground cover. It can take heavy pruning but seldom needs it once established. Cut dead wood back to healthy growth and shape in spring. On variegated form, cut out all-green shoots. As plant gets older, trim out some center stems occasionally.

E. japonica. Evergreen euonymus. Evergreen shrub. Upright growth to 8-10 ft., can be held lower by pruning or shearing. Older shrubs make attractive trees if you thin to reveal curving trunks, angled stems. After you have formed it into tree you want, pinch back tip growth to keep it compact. If plant is too compact and dense in wet areas, it may mildew badly. To prevent this, thin growth in center of plant.

E. kiautschovica (*E. patens*). Evergreen shrub. Spreading shrub; lower branches will sometimes root in moist soil. Can be trained as hedge, screen, sheared formal plant, espalier.

EUPHORBIA. Spurge. Shrubs, subshrubs, perennials.

E. biglandulosa. Evergreen perennial or subshrub. Stems die back after seeds set and should be removed. New ones come up to take their places.

E. epithymoides. Cut back to ground in fall in areas where winters are not severe enough to cause normal dieback.

E. pulcherrima. Poinsettia. Evergreen or deciduous shrub. Poinsettia must be pruned heavily in spring after bloom so that it will make rapid comeback and produce strong framework for following winter's flowers. It should not be pruned at any other time of year. Pruning is usually done in April or May, but the best time will depend upon your climate as well as when you want show of color to be at peak. If show of color is premature, peaking before Christmas holidays, you pruned too early. Delay pruning next time, even if plant begins to look straggly and spindly. Cut plant almost all the way back, leaving 2 or 3 buds or leaf scars at base of each stem

EUONYMUS JAPONICA needs clipping twice a year to keep neat tree shape.

to produce growth for following season. Keep stump as compact as possible. If growth is very crowded, it may be necessary to remove some large stems to base. Sufficient new growth will come from rest of stump to make up for loss of older stems. (You can start a supply of new plants by making cuttings from stems you cut off.) As new growth

CUT POINSETTIAS back hard. Stubs on stump have 2 or 3 leaf scars each.

proceeds, pinch back growing tips to encourage bushiness. This will produce more flowers.

To care for Christmas gift plants: when leaves fall in late winter or early spring, cut stems back to 2 or 3 buds, withhold water, and store in cool place. When danger of frost is past (or in late spring), set pots in sun outside. Train as they grow by pinching, as described above.

EUROPEAN BEECH. See Fagus.

EUROPEAN MOUNTAIN ASH. See Sorbus.

EUROPEAN PLUM. See Plum.

EURYA emarginata. Evergreen shrub. Slow growing, spreading, but easily kept at 3-4 ft. and compact by pruning back to bud or side branch. Can be trained to almost any shape. Natural for miniature espalier effect.

EURYOPS. Shrubby evergreen perennials. Keep old blooms picked off, prune to keep neat after flowering.

EVERGREEN PEAR. See Pyrus.

EVODIA hupehensis. Hupeh evodia. Deciduous tree. Rapid grower when young; prune to shape as required. Branches are brittle. Thin out some to minimize snow, sleet, and wind damage.

EXOCHORDA. Pearl bush. Deciduous shrubs. Generally pruning after bloom is required only to control size and form. Head branches back occasionally if you want more bushiness.

FAGUS sylvatica. European beech. Deciduous tree. Requires only normal training while young. Will grow naturally into conical-shaped tree with branches almost to ground. If you want standing or sitting room under it, remove lower branches.

FALLUGIA paradoxa. Apache plume. Partially evergreen shrub. In fall when fruits have turned to seed, prune back wood produced during current season.

FALSE CYPRESS. See Chamaecyparis.

FALSE DRAGON-HEAD. See Physostegia.

FALSE INDIGO. See Baptisia.

FALSE SPIRAEA. See Astilbe.

FATSHEDERA lizei. Evergreen vine, shrub, ground cover. This hybrid between *Fatsia japonica* and *Hedera helix* comes from nursery both as a single and multi-stalked plant. It can be trained as a shrub, as a small tree, as a vine, as a ground cover, shaped into a pillar, potted as a container plant, or strung out as an espalier. A rampant plant, it has an erratic growth pattern that can get out of control, but can be shaped if you are persistent. Pinch tip growth to force side branching. If plant gets away from you, cut it back to the ground; it will regrow quickly. If you want to use it as a ground cover, cut back vertical growth every 2-3 weeks during growing season. Fatshedera tends to become unruly foliage mass unless you constantly pinch and cut back to keep it controlled.

FATSIA japonica (*Aralia sieboldii, A. japonica*). Japanese aralia. Evergreen shrub. Responds well to severe pruning, but once established it requires little care. Established plant often suckers freely. You can remove them or keep 1 or 2 as new main stems. Old, tired, spindly plant can be cut back to about 6 in. in spring. Rush of new growth will come from stub. For bigger, lustier leaves, cut flowers off as soon as they appear. Attractive when trained and trimmed as single-stemmed tree.

FEATHER BUSH. See Lysiloma.

FEIJOA sellowiana. Pineapple guava. Evergreen shrub or small tree. Normally a many-stemmed shrub. However, it can take any amount of pruning and can be held at almost any height and trained to grow in almost any shape: espalier, screen, hedge, small tree. If you want to train to tree form, select good single trunk specimen at nursery. As it grows, remove all secondary stems at ground level and thin out crossing branches. Control top growth by pinching back tips of branches you wish to retard.

Will usually recover nicely if killed back by frost. Do major pruning in late spring after new growth begins.

Tree also has exceptional potential as multi-stemmed specimen. Allow to grow naturally as shrub with many trunks for 2-3 years (depending on location and culture). Then start training by selectively removing base growth, leaving from 2-5 trunks desired for tree form; questionable trunks can be removed later on. Annually raise open area 9-12 in. and selectively prune upper growth.

FELICIA amelloides (*F. aethiopica, Agathaea coelestis*). Blue marguerite. Shrubby perennial. Vigorous and likely to overgrow and look ragged; trim severely for cut flowers and prune back hard in late summer to encourage new blooming wood. Keep seed heads removed to prolong bloom.

FERN, HARDY. Perennial plants. All ferns look best well groomed. Cut back old or unattractive fronds after new growth has started in spring. Ferns make root growth in the fall and need old fronds for food reserves at that time. (Fronds also form protective mulch for spring growth.) After new growth is well started and danger of frost is past,

cut off old fronds right at soil line. (Be careful not to injure new growth.) If well protected, maidenhair and sword ferns respond well to cutting back to ground level in spring—just before new growth starts. If ferns should revert (throw plain fronds from plants that normally have crested or finely divided fronds), cut mavericks off close to plants. (Root disturbance can cause plants to revert.)

FERN PINE. See Podocarpus.

FERN, TENDER OR EXOTIC. Perennials. Tender ferns grown indoors need only grooming to keep them looking good. Grooming includes removing dead or damaged fronds when they appear and dividing plant when surplus crowns or an excess of creeping stems give plant a crowded look. Where exotic ferns grow out of doors in mild-winter climates, delay removing fronds and trimming until spring (see Fern, Hardy).

FERN, TREE. Perennials. Groom by cutting off dead or unsightly fronds near the trunk, leaving a short stub. They are usually the oldest fronds, growing from farthest down on the trunk. In Australian tree fern (*Alsophila cooperi, A. australis*) stubs will eventually drop off, leaving a smooth trunk with attractive diamond patterning. With others, stubs will remain a long time, giving a rugged, shaggy look.

FESCUE. See Festuca.

FESTUCA ovina 'Glauca' (*F. glauca*). Blue fescue. Ornamental grass. Necessary to trim festuca back almost to ground (2-3 in.) each year to prevent it from getting shaggy and to encourage new growth. In late spring or early summer when it starts to go to seed, give plant a close haircut. Easiest tool to use for few plants is pruning shears; hedge shears are best for larger numbers of plants. (A power rotary mower with blades set 2 in. high will work on extensive area.) Trimmed grass will look shabby and stubby for few weeks; then it will put out fresh, new spiky growth in typical blue fescue color.

CUT TO 2"-3"

NEW GROWTH IN A FEW WEEKS

FESTUCA before and after its late spring haircut. This shearing keeps it fresh.

FICUS. Ornamental figs. Evergreen or deciduous trees, vines, shrubs, house plants. These take wide variety of shapes and sizes, most tolerating pruning well. Prune anytime except when approaching cold weather could harm tender new growth. (They will usually recover nicely from frost damage, though.) Wait until weather warms and danger of frost is past to prune frozen, winter damaged wood from plants.

F. benjamina. Weeping Chinese banyan. Evergreen tree, house plant. Can be damaged by frost in marginal areas but recovers quickly as weather warms. Tolerates pruning well. You can easily keep it confined to container, for it is easiest of group to keep pruned to small size.

Tree has good potential for multi-stem use. Follow same procedure as described for *Feijoa sellowiana*.

F. elastica. Rubber plant. Evergreen shrub or tree, house plant. Can be pruned whenever necessary to shape. If potted plant gets too tall and leggy, cut off top and select side branch to form new main shoot. Or you can air layer top section (see *Pruning Glossary*) to get new plant.

F. e. 'Variegata' (*F. doescheri*). Pruning procedure is same as above.

F. lyrata (*F. pandurata*). Fiddleleaf fig. Evergreen tree or large shrub, house plant. Vertical growth habit; can be trained as vine. To increase branching, pinch back tips when plant is young. Air layers easily (see *Pruning Glossary*).

F. pumila (*F. repens*). Creeping fig. Evergreen vine, house plant. Cut back to ground soon after planting to make new growth that will take off fast. Once it begins to climb, there is almost no limit to size of this vine and area it will cover. Unless restrained, it can in time envelop a 3 or 4-story building. If you use it on a house, cut it to ground every few years. Or control by removing fruiting stems from time to time as they form. Roots are invasive, have to be pruned to be contained. *F. p. 'Minima'* is not as invasive but should be watched.

F. retusa. Indian laurel fig. Evergreen tree. Serves well as patio or street tree. Excellent for training into multi-stemmed, canopy form. With regular care, will provide good shade, throwing interesting shade and light patterns. Slim trunk supporting massive crown may be concealed by lower trailing branches if these are not trimmed off regularly. You can keep it more shrublike or train it as formal hedge.

F. r. nitida. Tolerates pruning well at any time of year. You can form it to almost any size or shape you want. Well suited to formal shearing. An attractive house plant if given a lot of pruning and shaping. Also good in multi-stem, canopy form.

F. roxburghii. Briefly deciduous. Usually takes form of large spreading shrub. Must be kept under control by pruning because it is so vigorous it can take over an entire planting area. If large overgrown plant is cut back to 5-ft.-high stem, new leaves will soon fill it out. Best time to prune is summer, early fall. (Don't prune any later than September in areas where there is danger of frost.)

FIG, EDIBLE. Deciduous tree. Vigorous plant, fig can take a good deal of pruning without appreciably reducing fruit crop. It can also grow an appreciable fruit crop every year with no pruning at all. An understanding of the fig's bearing habit will help you to prune it correctly when necessary. It normally bears two crops of fruit each year—first in early summer, next in late summer. The first crop is always carried on last year's wood; the second crop is carried farther out on branches, on new wood grown during summer after harvest of the first crop. On unpruned tree, figs form farther and farther out on branches or on new laterals.

Method of pruning a fig will vary somewhat depending upon whether you're pruning for looks or for fruit crop. If growing a fig for looks and you don't care how big it gets, let grow naturally except for removing ugly branches. If growing a fig for looks and you wish to control size, select branches for most attractive placement and prune out others. Do heaviest pruning in winter and then lightly prune vigorous growth 2 or 3 times during summer to keep plant presentable.

For best fruit, prune to encourage formation of new wood. Retain young side branches that break from main trunk and train as part of framework. Some light summer pruning will be necessary to keep plant in bounds. Avoid heavy cutting between fruit crops because this not only seriously reduces second fruit crop but also removes wood that will carry next season's first crop. Pinch back runaway shoots any time.

To espalier a fig, plant bare-root plant as close as possible to support, cutting main stem back to where you want first side branches to form. As laterals break from the main stem, support those you want to keep and remove all others. This diverts all growth into basic framework.

FIG, ORNAMENTAL. See Ficus.

FILBERT. See Corylus.

FIR. See Abies.

FIR, DOUGLAS. See Pseudotsuga.

FIRETHORN. See Pyracantha.

FIREWHEEL TREE. See Stenocarpus.

FIRMIANA plantanifolia (*F. simplex*). Chinese parasol tree. Deciduous tree. Slow growing. When tree is dormant, thin out branches as necessary to get good branch spacing, good form.

FITTONIA verschaffeltii. Fittonia. Evergreen house plant. Pinch back to encourage branching and to keep the plant low.

FLAME BUSH, TRINIDAD OR BRAZILIAN. See Calliandra.

FLAME PEA. See Chorizema.

FLAME TREE. See Brachychiton.

FLAME TREE, CHINESE. See Koelreuteria.

FLAME VINE. See Pyrostegia.

FLANNEL BUSH. See Fremontodendron.

FLAX, NEW ZEALAND. See Phormium.

FLOWERING MAPLE. See Abutilon.

FLOWERING QUINCE. See Chaenomeles.

FORSYTHIA. Deciduous shrubs. Most bushes need no trimming during the first few seasons in your garden. When they reach the size you wish to maintain, take out a third of stems as soon as shrubs finish blooming. If they have 6 major stems, remove two each spring, at the same time cutting out weak or crowded growth. To maintain plant's graceful form, remove old, woody branches at ground. Don't head back because it will force brush of suckers from the cuts. You can, of course, start pruning while plants are flowering and use branches for indoor arrangements. Well-budded branches can be forced into bloom several weeks early indoors. If you have old, neglected, overgrown shrub, you can cut it to within 6 in. of ground in early spring. This will sacrifice a season's flowers.

FORSYTHIA, WHITE. See Abeliophyllum.

FORTNIGHT LILY. See Moraea.

FOTHERGILLA. Deciduous shrubs. To preserve plants' natural grace, an occasional thinning in center of shrubs may be necessary. Cut unwanted stems to ground. This pruning is best done in winter, when plants are dormant. You may also prune, if required, after flowering in spring.

FOUNTAIN GRASS. See Pennisetum.

FOXGLOVE, COMMON. See Digitalis.

FOXTAIL LILY. See Eremurus.

FRAGRANT SNOWBELL. See Styrax.

FRANKLINIA alatamaha (*Gordonia alatamaha*). Deciduous tree. Normal training while young. Prune while dormant to remove dead, weak wood.

FRAXINUS. Ash. Deciduous trees (*F. uhdei* is semi-evergreen, holds leaves all winter in mild areas). These are fast growers, requiring some attention during their early years to shape into trees you want, Remove lower side branches to get clean, single trunks and then head back laterals you want to keep to promote branching and to form the desirable rounded, dense tops. Cut out any long, whippy, lanky branches that tend to throw trees off balance. Mature trees that have been well trained while young will require little pruning beyond the removal of dead, damaged wood. Shamel ash (*F. uhdei*) and Modesto ash (*F. velutina* 'Modesto') tend to form deep, V-shaped crotches that are weak and likely to split under stress of windstorm. Prevent these weak formations by literally "nipping them in the bud."

TO PREVENT deep V-shaped crotches (as shown by dotted lines) on Shamel and Modesto Ash, remove upper buds.

One-year-old twigs form two pairs of buds at each node. The top pair are primary buds, the ones that form narrow crotches. Only if you pinch these off will you stimulate dormant lower, or secondary, buds into growth. These lower branches will grow at much wider (and stronger) angle from main branch. If branches do develop from primary buds, these can still be removed after 1 or 2 seasons of growth to stimulate secondary bud into growth.

FREMONTODENDRON (*Fremontia*). Flannel bush. Evergreen shrubs or small trees. Fast growers; will get rangy if not pinched and pruned regularly from the start. Respond well to heavy pruning right after flowering.

FRINGE TREE. See Chionanthus.

FUCHSIA. Evergreen to deciduous shrubs or shrublets. Fuchsias should be pruned when most dormant—November to February. Pruning may force the development of tender new shoots, though, so if you live in areas subject to frost in winter, postpone pruning until danger of frost is past. (To protect plants in winter areas, you can prune

FUCHSIAS IN POTS need annual pruning of tops and roots to bring about lots of fresh growth in one summer. Here go the old tops (to pot edge) on this one.

PRUNING COMPLETED, much old soil has been removed. Here comes new soil.

FUCHSIA STANDARD (manufactured branch holder), ready to be pruned.

THE BRANCHES at left have been cut back. Ones at right will be next.

COMPLETE. It's San Francisco pruning (less in Seattle, more in San Diego).

BUSH FUCHSIA, ready to be pruned in late winter. This also in San Francisco.

LEFT BRANCH and center branch have been cut back far enough.

FINISHED PLANT, cut back to enough skeleton for the next year's growth.

back in fall and mulch ground heavily.) Many fuchsias in older gardens have gone unpruned for years, but these plants get a little larger each year and ultimately most get too big (and maybe too rangy) to be attractive any longer. Because they bloom on new wood, fuchsias can be cut back severely. Some fuchsia growers cut all the way back to one node on past summer's growth; more cautious pruners make cuts just above second node. In cold winter areas where plants are to be stored, prune lightly, remove leaves and twiggy growth before bringing in. Then in spring cut out any broken branches. Cut hanging basket types back to perimeter of container. Frequently pinch back tips as new growth sprouts to develop better branching, bushier growth, and more flowers. If you want spectacular show of color for some special occasion in summer or fall, continue to pinch until about 6 weeks before the date you're aiming at, and then let flower buds develop and bloom.

FUCHSIA, AUSTRALIAN. See Correa.

FUCHSIA, CALIFORNIA. See Zauschneria.

FUCHSIA, CAPE. See Phygelius.

GAILLARDIA aristata. Perennial. Nip off faded blossoms every few days to prolong flowering.

GAMOLEPIS chrysanthemoides. Evergreen shrub. Regular pinching and pruning during blooming season will control untidy, leggy tendencies and also insure summer-through-winter show of flowers. Plant usually grows from 2-4 ft. high with as much as 3-4 ft. spread but can be kept lower with constant pruning and shaping. Can also be used as clipped hedge.

GARDENIA. Evergreen shrubs. Require little or no pruning. But to maintain vigorous growth, you should remove weak wood and thin out some shoots when plants are in bloom. Plants are easily reshaped, if necessary, by careful thinning. For best flower production, hold plants to about 30 in. Remove old flower clusters as they fade. When plants become old and straggly, cut oldest, weakest stems back to 6 or 8 in. from ground before spring growth begins. This will stimulate new growth from base. Remove more of oldest wood during following season to renew plants gradually.

GARRYA. Silktassel. Evergreen shrubs. Can be trained as small trees. Respond well to pruning and shaping. Because some tend to become rangy, you'll have to trim to keep them neat. Remove old tassels after flowering.

AUSTRALIAN WILLOW (Geijera), showing the adolescent form you should aim for in your early pruning – like a compromise between a willow and a eucalyptus.

GAULTHERIA shallon. Salal. Evergreen shrub. Only neglected plant needs pruning. Can be pruned at any time of the year, but best time is spring, when old growth looks shaggy and new growth is just starting. Do not shear it but prune back each branch, as you would a rose, to just above a leaf node. In this way, a planting that has become thin or leggy through neglect can be restored to its thick, lustrous best. Cut freely for use in house. Foliage stays green a long time in arrangements.

GAURA lindheimeri. Gaura. Perennial. Blossoms drop off cleanly when spent, but seed-bearing spikes should be cut.

GAZANIA. Perennials. Shear overgrown or weary-looking plants back heavily in early spring to stimulate fresh new growth (fertilizer and water are also required).

GEIJERA parviflora. Australian willow, wilga. Evergreen tree. Prune this graceful tree only enough to correct form.

GELSEMIUM sempervirens. Carolina jessamine. Evergreen vine. Tolerates heavy pruning when necessary to control. If vine gets top-heavy, cut back severely. Usually well-behaved, its stems

seldom get thick and woody and are easy to prune and shape. Used in some areas as a ground cover, kept to a height of about 3 ft. by pruning and trimming back vertical growth. Do most pruning and thinning immediately after flowering.

GENISTA. See Cytisus.

GEOMETRY TREE. See Bucida.

GERALDTON WAXFLOWER. See Chamaelaucium.

GERANIUM. For common geranium, ivy geranium, Lady Washington or Martha Washington geranium, and scented geraniums see *Pelargonium*.

The true geraniums are hardy perennials for borders or rock gardens. They require no more than grooming and occasional division when clumps become crowded and blooms drop off.

GERBERA jamesonii. Transvaal daisy. Perennial. When you pick flowers for the house, cut stems at base or pull stems off as you would those of rhubarb. Stubs of cut stems remaining on plant have sharp points that can cause painful cuts. Keep dead leaves and flowers picked off plant.

GERMANDER. See Teucrium.

GEUM. Perennials. Keep dead flowers picked off to prolong bloom. If cut back after spring bloom, they will flower again in fall.

GIANT REED. See Arundo.

GINGER LILY. See Hedychium.

GINKGO biloba. Maidenhair tree. Deciduous tree. Graceful, slow growing. Needs early staking and training, very little pruning afterwards except to remove dead, weak, or damaged wood. Tree sometimes produces upward-growing shoots which are parallel with central leader. Remove back to lateral or to branch they grew on.

GLADIOLUS. Corm. Cut gladiolus flower stalks about where 3rd and 4th leaves cross stem, making sure you leave at least 4 or 5 leaves on plant. These are vital for manufacture of next season's corms. Cut leaves off only after they have turned brown and you have harvested corms.

GLAUCIUM flavum. Yellow horned poppy. Perennial or biennial. Cut back each year to new basal leaves when healthy and growing. This encourages new growth.

GLEDITSIA triacanthos. Honey locust. Deciduous tree. Will withstand heavy pruning and shaping. Stake and train young tree to get basic branch pattern you want. Large spikes and thorns on trunk and branches can be hazard to children and gardeners. Remove these spikes as soon as they appear. Thin crowded branches. 'Sunburst' variety has tendency to grow unruly branches. Head back to produce better balanced tree.

GLORIOSA DAISY. See Rudbeckia.

A YOUNG 'Sunburst' honey locust (Gleditsia) that's been pruned to best form.

GLORYBOWER. See Clerodendrum.

GOATNUT. See Simmondsia.

GOLDEN LARCH. See Chrysolarix.

GOLDEN TRUMPET TREE. See Tabebuia.

GOLDENCHAIN TREE. See Laburnum.

GOLDENRAIN TREE. See Koelreuteria.

GOOSEBERRY. See Ribes.

GRAPE. Deciduous vine. You can't let a grape vine run wild. A badly trained, badly pruned vine will tangle, tend to get mildew, always bear disappointing crops of fruit—and never grow into anything that's much to look at.

If you want a neatly trained vine as well as good fruit production, best way to prune is usually one of two methods shown on the next page, depending on which kind of grape you have planted. The sketches take you through a grape vine's first 4 years, from planting to maturity. Devote the first 3 years to training the vine. After it has matured, treat it the same way each pruning season (December 1 to March 1).

To be sure of large, good-flavored grapes, you have to thin out some of crop each year. Until the vine matures, never let more than half a dozen bunches develop; cut off rest as soon as fruit forms. After maturity, let about half the bunches develop.

WHICH PRUNING METHOD?

How to prune depends on the variety of grape. One of the two methods is called spur pruning and the other long-cane pruning. If you follow either system or if you train a vine on an arbor, do the same thing for the first year and a half: always start out by following the 3 steps you see illustrated below.

Spur pruning. This method works for most European grape varieties except 'Thompson Seedless'; use it, for example, for 'Cardinal,' 'Muscat,' 'Perlette,' 'Red Malaga,' 'Ribier,' 'Tokay,' and the California wine varieties. The sketches show the vine trained on a simple wire support. You can train a vine like this on top of a fence or similar structure.

Long-cane pruning. Use this method for 'Thompson Seedless' and for most

STARTING A GRAPE VINE ... PLANTING TO SECOND SPRING

At planting time

Soak roots if dry. Cut plant back to three buds, trim roots to 6 inches. Bury whole thing except top two buds. Water. Mound light soil over top (buds grow through).

First winter after planting

Time to start training and pruning. Until now object has been to let plant sprawl, develop strong roots. Cut off all but strongest cane. Cut that to three buds. Tie.

Second spring

New shoots grew from buds left after pruning. When shoots are a foot long, select most vigorous to serve as a permanent trunk, cut off others. Tie to stake loosely.

This is spur pruning

Second summer
When main shoot reaches foot above wire, cut it back even with wire. When top two buds sprout, train shoots horizontally. Tie each one to wire about foot from tip.

Second winter
Cut off all branches from two main side arms (don't injure bud at base of each branch). You aren't pruning for fruit yet. The object is to develop a strong framework.

Third winter
Now begin pruning for fruit production. First cut out all weak and crowded branches. Then select strong canes 6 to 10 inches apart; cut each one back to two-bud spur.

**Fourth winter...
and after**
Two canes grew from last winter's spurs and had fruit. Cut off outer cane at base. Shorten one closest to trunk to two buds. Repeat process each winter from now on.

This is long-cane pruning

Second summer
Pinch out tip of stem a foot above the top wire. Let side shoots grow on upper third of plant; cut off shoots on bottom two-thirds. Tie vine near the top and at the middle.

Second winter
Cut off stem right through bud just above wire. Remove side branches below midpoint. Above, remove all but two to four side shoots; cut back to the two-bud spurs.

Third winter
Last winter's spurs now long branches. Cut two as fruiting canes (leave 8 to 12 buds). Train in fan shape. Cut two to four as two-bud spurs. Cut off the other canes.

**Fourth winter...
and after**
Cut off old fruiting canes. Each spur sent out two shoots; cut upper as fruiting cane (8 to 12 buds), lower as spur. Keep 4 to 6 spurs, and the same number of canes.

This is how you train a grape vine on an arbor

Second summer
Unlike above methods, don't stop stem. When tip of it reaches top of support, tie down over corner. Encourage stem to grow long by pinching back side shoots.

**Second winter...
and following spring**
Cut back main stem to pencil-sized wood. Cut off side branches. In spring, when new shoots are 6 inches long, thin to foot apart. When 18 inches, tie down at midpoint.

Third winter ... and after
Spur-pruned varieties: Cut back shoots to two buds. Next year, prune as in drawing at top right of this page. Long-cane pruning: Alternate spurs with fruiting canes (8 to 12 buds). Next year, cut off canes; prune spurs as in middle right. With both methods, you can leave strong canes about 4 feet long every 3 feet to become part of the permanent framework.

American grapes (for example, 'Concord,' 'Delaware,' 'Niagara,' 'Pierce'). These kinds don't produce much fruit when cut back to short spurs. They bear most of their fruit from buds farther out on the canes (the part that's cut off when branches are spur-pruned). Train them on the same type of structures as spur-pruned vines.

Arbors. If led in the right direction, almost any grape can climb up and over an arbor. Spend the first few years getting the vine to cover the structure, then prune annually using the method (spur or long-cane) that's best for the variety.

GRAPE, EVERGREEN. See Rhoicissus.

GRAPE, OREGON. See Mahonia.

GRAPEFRUIT. See Citrus.

GREVILLEA robusta. Silk oak. Evergreen tree. Branches tend to be brittle and subject to wind damage. Head tree back hard at planting time to strengthen framework. Then prune it lightly each year after flowering. Avoid heavy pruning; if cut too severely, wood may fail to heal properly. Young plant can be pruned and confined in tub for few years.

GREWIA caffra. Lavender starflower. Evergreen shrub. Fast growing and sprawling, it takes kindly to pruning and is easily kept under control. Pinch back tips regularly to make dense. Tends to form natural espalier if given some support. Can also be used as clipped hedge or screen, as ground cover (prune out upright growth), trained and staked as single-trunked tree, or tied and trained to cover arbor or trellis. After first heavy bloom, prune to keep new flowering wood coming into continued bloom through autumn, then prune again after flowering.

GRISELINIA littoralis. Evergreen shrub. Neat, compact, and well-groomed. Only pruning it needs is heading back each year to encourage dense branching habit. Good espalier subject.

GUAVA, STRAWBERRY. See Psidium.

GUM. See Eucalyptus.

GUM, SWEET. See Liquidambar.

GUNNERA. Perennial. Improve appearance of plant by cutting leaves to base each winter. In cold winter areas, leaves die back completely in winter; elsewhere, old leaves remain green for more than one year.

GYMNOCLADUS dioica. Kentucky coffee tree. Deciduous tree. Often naturally grows with 3 or 4 upright main stems from trunk into narrow, round-headed tree. Young tree needs normal staking and training; mature tree requires little pruning aside from removal of weak and damaged wood.

GYPSOPHILA. Annuals, perennials. To prolong bloom, cut back flowering stems before seed clusters form. Cut back to ground in fall after main bloom period ends.

HACKBERRY. See Celtis.

HAKEA. Evergreen shrubs, trees. Pinching tips while young will promote bushier growth. Can be trained into tree forms but should not be sheared, for they will not recover quickly.

HALESIA carolina (*H. tetraptera*). Snowdrop tree, silver bell. Deciduous tree. Prune to single stem when young unless you want to let it grow as a large shrub. If pruned to fork at 4 or 5 ft. height, it will form attractive structure. Once established, very little pruning will be required. Do any necessary pruning after bloom period.

HALIMIUM. Evergreen shrublets. Shear plants back after spring flowering to encourage fall bloom.

HAMAMELIS mollis. Chinese witch hazel. Deciduous tree or shrub. Prune lightly in winter to keep open branch pattern. You can do this when you cut flowers for indoors. Will eventually grow into 12-15-ft-high shrub. Can be kept small by heading unwanted growth back to side branches. New growth can be promoted by cutting out oldest wood.

HARDENBERGIA. Evergreen shrubby vines. Pinch back during growing season to shape. Cut back after blooming to prevent tangling. Remove old, weak growths to keep from getting leggy.

HARPEPHYLLUM caffrum. Kaffir plum. Evergreen tree. Easy to train while young. New growth can be erratic, but with patience, stems and branches can be shaped into almost any form. Tends to have dense head, but tree can be opened up by thinning out inside branches. Can be pruned into many interesting shapes. Recovers quickly from damage of pruning and freezing.

HAWTHORN. See Crataegus.

HAZELNUT. See Corylus.

HEAVENLY BAMBOO. See Nandina.

HEBE. Evergreen shrubs. Prune after blooming, shortening flowering branches considerably to keep plants compact and bushy. Flowering branches can be cut to ground each year after they fade. Plants withstand heavy pruning, sprout readily from old wood.

HEDERA. Ivy. Evergreen woody vines. May be pruned as lightly or as heavily as you wish at almost any time of year, though pruning should be avoided in late fall and winter because regrowth is very slow then. Most ivy ground covers need trimming around edges with hedge shears, machete, or sharp spade 2 or 3 times a year. Ivy on fences and walls need shearing or trimming 2-3 times a year. (If you are trying to retain pattern effect, you will have to trim every time pattern gets out of line—as often as every 2 weeks.)

Overgrown leggy beds can be mowed with a heavy-duty rotary power mower or cut back with hedge shears. Do this in spring so new growth will quickly cover the bald look. If you want clusters of berries on your English ivy (*Hedera helix*) in winter, direct some of it to upright growth and allow it to go its own way. It will ultimately produce stiff-branched clusters of small, ivory green flowers in fall. Tiny berries that follow will last well into winter and lend themselves to holiday decorating.

HEDYCHIUM. Ginger lily. Perennials. After bloom, remove old flower stems. As soon as cold weather approaches, plants become shabby looking and should be cut back to ground. Forms that die down to ground each year can be treated much like cannas: cut stems back to ground after frosts in spring.

HELENIUM autumnale. Common sneezeweed. Perennial. Pinch back tips of all shoots until mid-June to keep plants compact and to produce more bloom. Trim off faded blossoms to encourage more blooms.

HELIANTHEMUM nummularium. Sunrose. Evergreen shrublets. In cold sections, helianthemums will die back to roots almost every winter. They will come back in spring. Remove dead portions in early spring. In less severe winters, leaves will die but stems will grow new leaves again. Shear plants back after they bloom in spring and early summer to encourage fall bloom. Occasionally nip off seed pods to encourage scattering of blooms into late fall.

HELICHRYSUM petiolatum (*Gnaphalium lanatum*). Shrubby perennial. In mild winter areas, prune plant back occasionally to keep it tidy. In colder areas, plant is apt to be cut back by frost, so prune to remove dead wood only after weather warms in spring. If you cut back a helichrysum too severely, you may lose it.

HELIOTROPE. See Heliotropium.

HELIOTROPIUM arborescens (*H. peruvianum*). Common heliotrope. Perennial. To make plant bushy, pinch back tip growth when stems are 4-5 in. high.

With this early pinching, the rather sprawling, bushy plant can be kept below 18 in. Trimming off some stems when removing faded flowers keeps plant compact and at the same time encourages new crop of blossoms.

HELLEBORE. See Helleborus.

HELLEBORUS. Hellebore. Perennial. When flowering season is over, new growth comes from roots. Cut off all dead or dying leaves near ground (don't pull them off) only after you can see new foliage starting. After that, avoid cutting the foliage; it's needed to manufacture food for next flower crop.

HEMEROCALLIS. Daylily. Perennial, evergreen and deciduous. Snap off faded flowers daily, cut back severely after bloom to stimulate plant and make lots of new growth. Remove dead foliage on deciduous varieties in late winter or early spring before new growth appears. Can be transplanted successfully by trimming off broken and bruised roots and about ⅔ of the top growth.

HEMLOCK. See Tsuga.

HERALD'S TRUMPET. See Beaumontia.

HETEROMELES arbutifolia (*Photinia arbutifolia*). Toyon, Christmas berry, California holly. Evergreen shrub or small tree. Will stand any amount of pruning to keep it low or to prevent loose straggly growth. Even a plant cut back to ground will sprout up from roots. Can be pruned and trained to spread out over bank, to form informal hedge, or to grow as a small, single-trunked tree. If trimmed to produce abundance of year-old wood, it will produce more berries. Since it is susceptible to fireblight, as soon as buds begin to expand in spring, look it over for dead branches indicating disease. Cut these out to lessen chance of infecting new growth. Sterilize pruning tools after cutting any diseased wood.

HEUCHERA sanguinea. Coral bells. Perennial. Requires little care beyond removal of spent flowers by snapping off stems at base. If cut to ground after main bloom, it may bloom again same year.

HIBBERTIA scandens (*H. volubilis*). Guinea gold vine. Evergreen twining vine. Needs little pruning. Keep stems from tangling and cut out frost-damaged wood in spring. If vine gets topheavy, cut back a few of the oldest stems to force out new, lower growth.

HIBISCUS. Perennials, deciduous, and evergreen shrubs.
  H. huegelii. Blue hibiscus. Evergreen shrub. Needs only occasional pinching or pruning to keep compact. Do it after danger of frost is past.
  H. moscheutos. Perennial hibiscus, rose-mallow. Perennial. Each fall after flowering, cut plant to within 3 in. of ground.
  H. rosa-sinensis. Chinese hibiscus, tropical hibiscus. Evergreen shrub. Should not be pruned in winter (except in tropical climates) because chilly weather slows it down and lowers its vitality. After weather warms, don't be afraid to prune old wood severely, for showy flowers are produced on new wood. Young plants seldom need pruning, but nipping growing tips of branches will help to increase flowering wood. Progressively cut back old shrubs with unproductive, woody branches: starting in spring, cut out 1 or 2 oldest stems. Do this once a month until August. Do not shear shrub like a hedge. Instead, cut few forward branches, not all same height. When these have leafed out, treat back growth the same way. Continued pruning throughout growing season will encourage more branching and will control size of plant so you won't need to prune as drastically following season. Don't prune after mid-September in areas where there is danger of freezing because new growth is susceptible to frost. Good management program includes yearly removal of one or more old branches and cutting back from ⅓-⅔ of last season's growth. This encourages new shoots, leafage low down on plant, and more bloom. Strong growers ('Agnes Galt,' 'Kona,' 'San Diego Red,' 'White Wings') must be pruned severely every spring

'AGNES GALT' hibiscus (plants 6 feet apart) make hedge 3 feet deep, 7 feet high.

PRUNE SHRUB-FORM hibiscus as shown with dark lines above. Response below.

or they will become thick-trunked, sprawling and so high you won't be able to see flowers carried at ends of branches. Best procedure is to remove crossing or conflicting branches, leaving strongest and those providing best framework. Cut rank growth back severely and remove some laterals, particularly those growing toward inside of plant. Leave about 3-6 well-placed laterals on each main branch and cut them back to 2 or 3 buds. Pruning should start as growth begins in spring. If frost blackened foliage during the winter, or if the weather was so cold that the plant stopped growing and producing flowers, cut stems back to about 6 in. from ground.
  H. syriacus. Rose of Sharon, shrub althaea. Deciduous shrub. Needs only light pruning to shape; for bigger flowers, though, prune more severely, cutting back in winter previous season's growth to 2 buds.

HIGHBUSH CRANBERRY. See Viburnum.

HIPPOCREPIS comosa. Perennial ground cover. If used as lawn substitute, mow once a year, just after flowers fade.

HOHERIA. Evergreen tree and deciduous tree or shrub. Can be trained as single or multiple-stemmed plant. Only light pruning required once form has been established. Prune after flowering.

HOLLY. See Ilex.

HOLLY, CALIFORNIA. See Heteromeles.

HOLLY, COSTA RICAN. See Olmediella.

HOLLY, GUATEMALAN. See Olmediella.

HOLLY, SUMMER. See Comarostaphylis.

HOLLYLEAF CHERRY. See Prunus.

HOLLYLEAF SWEETSPIRE. See Itea.

HOLODISCUS discolor. Cream bush, ocean spray. Deciduous shrub. Can get ragged, needs pruning to be kept neat. Do major pruning after bloom—prune longest branches back to laterals. Also, remove all seed clusters. In spring, prune off any freeze-damaged portions.

HOMOLANTHUS populifolius. Queensland poplar. Evergreen or semi-evergreen small tree. To train as a full-sized tree, cut off lower branches when young (do it in winter). When mature, remove lower branches if necessary, and cut off straggling upper limbs. Thin out heavy top growth to keep the tree's shape attractive. Remove dead wood and suckers.

HONEY BELL. See Mahernia.

HONEY BUSH. See Melianthus.

HONEY LOCUST. See Gleditsia.

HONEYSUCKLE. See Lonicera.

HOP BUSH. See Dodonaea.

HOP, COMMON. See Humulus.

HOPSEED BUSH. See Dodonaea.

HORNBEAM. See Carpinus.

HORSECHESTNUT. See Aesculus.

HORSETAIL. See Equisetum.

HOSTA (*Funkia*). Plantain lily. Perennials. All forms go dormant in winter. Shear leaves off after they turn brown and remove old flower stalks. New, fresh-looking leaves begin to grow from perennial roots in early spring.

HOWEIA. See Palm.

HUCKLEBERRY. See Vaccinium.

HUMMINGBIRD FLOWER. See Zauschneria.

HUMULUS lupulus. Common hop. Perennial vine. Cut stems to ground after frost turns them brown. Regrowth comes from ground the following spring. Twining stems should be trained by hand in June and July.

HYACINTH SHRUB. See Xanthoceras.

HYBOPHRYNIUM brauneanum (*Bamburanta arnoldiana*). Bamburanta. Perennial. Thin or divide when clumps get too thick. In most cases, old stalks should be cut to ground when their leaves become shabby. Also remove old flower stalks.

HYDRANGEA. Deciduous shrubs, vines. Though all forms are deciduous, many hold their leaves throughout the year where winters are mild. The various kinds of hydrangeas make two kinds of flower heads—the full, round heads and the kind where big flowers form only around the edge. The latter are called "lace cap" hydrangeas. Remove their flowers as soon as they have bloomed. This allows for next year's growth by keeping them from going to seed. Hydrangeas can also be cut back each year to point just above bases of previous year's growth. For plants that have not bloomed well, try removing spent flowers to help force remaining buds. Cut stems just above round pair of leaves below flower heads.

H. anomala petiolaris (*H. petiolaris*). Climbing hydrangea. Deciduous vine. Only pruning normally required is shortening of new growth that sometimes swings out from wall in summer and may loosen vine from its support. Left unpruned, climbing hydrangea can cover jumbled rockery.

H. arborescens. Smooth hydrangea. Deciduous shrubs. Need heavy pruning in spring. Remove crowded and dead stems; head back live wood to 2 or 3 buds to stimulate new growth.

H. macrophylla (*H. hortensia, H. opuloides, H. otaksa*). Bigleaf hydrangea, garden hydrangea. Deciduous shrubs. Strong, rank growers that should be pruned heavily as flowers fade. Cut stems back to strong laterals or promising buds. In early spring remove frost-damaged wood and thin out half of oldest woody stems by cutting them to the ground. Stems that bloomed last season should be cut back to within 2 pairs of buds from ground level. When neglected, plants tend to become woody

CUT HYDRANGEA BRANCHES when flowers fade. Notice that some branches will flower next year (save them).

or stubby; prune to ground and let them start over. (Winter damage to buds may cause plants to produce foliage but no flowers. If this happens, prune in summer after normal flowering time and *do not* prune following winter or spring.)

H. paniculata 'Grandiflora.' Pee gee hydrangea. Deciduous shrub or small standard tree. Can grow high and wide but can also be kept as a 3 or 4-ft. hedge by pruning. For fewer but larger flower clusters, prune heavily in early spring, heading back year-old wood to 3 or 4 spurs. If trained to one stem, cut back to 2 or 3 growth buds on well-placed branches.

H. quercifolia. Oakleaf hydrangea. Deciduous shrub. If pruned to ground each spring, makes compact, 3-ft. shrub. Thinned to well-spaced branches, makes distinguished container plant.

HYMENOSPORUM flavum. Sweetshade. Evergreen small tree or large shrub. Early training is necessary, for branches spread out in almost equal threes, creating weak crotches that are likely to split. Thin out weak branches and prune to space out remaining branches. Strengthen branches by frequent pinching and shortening. When planted in small groves, tree grows well without staking or pruning.

HYPERICUM. St. Johnswort. Shrubs and perennials, evergreen or semi-evergreen. Will respond well to heavy pruning during dormant season or in spring when new growth begins. Remove crowded, weak, dead branches; cut others back to 2 or 3 buds. If neglected, plants will become straggly, twiggy, and untidy. Cut back severely to give them room to produce new growth.

H. calycinum. Aaron's beard, creeping St. Johnswort. Evergreen shrub, ground cover (semi-deciduous where winters are cold). Spreads by means of underground runners and fills in quickly. So vigorous you often have to chop back the underground runners with sharp spade. To thicken, shear or mow off tops at least every 2 or 3 years while most dormant.

H. 'Sungold.' Twiggy, rounded shrub. Little pruning required other than removing oldest wood every 2 or 3 years to rejuvenate.

IBERIS. Candytuft. Annuals, perennials. For neat appearance, remove spent flower clusters by shearing lightly after flowering to stimulate new growth.

I. sempervirens. Evergreen candytuft. Perennial. Planted close together, they make solid, rather formal miniature hedge or ground cover you can keep low with heavy annual shearing.

ICE PLANT. Succulent perennials, sub-shrubs, or annuals. Chop or shear expanding edges or burgeoning tops as necessary to keep the planting under control.

Lampranthus. Cut back lightly after bloom to eliminate fruit capsules, encourage new leafy growth.

ILEX. Holly. Evergreen shrubs or trees. All types will withstand heavy pruning any time of the year, and can be used as sheared hedges, topiary, bonsai, shrubs, or trees. One of best times to prune berried hollies is during Christmas season so that you may use berried greens indoors (only female plants have berries). When they grow large, they tend to droop to the ground and root, creating an impenetrable jungle underneath. Best to remove branches up a bit on trunks, high enough so that drooping branches do not touch ground. Important to have enough clearance to get rake underneath to keep them cleaned out. When cutting back holly, do not leave leafless stubs.

I. altaclarensis 'Wilsonii' (*I. wilsonii*). Wilson holly. Shrub or tree. Fast, strong grower, can be shaped as standard tree, espalier, shrub, screen, or clipped hedge. Regular pruning of shrub type will keep it bushy and increase amount of berry wood. May grow to 20 ft., but can be kept as low as 6 or 8 ft. tall with annual prunings.

I. aquifolium. English holly, Christmas holly. Shrubs, trees. Will take great deal of cutting, thinning, or shearing. If young trees develop two main trunks, remove one to avoid danger of splitting.

WILSON HOLLY. Longish branches, upper left and right, ready to be headed back.

To give shrubs solid compact look, pinch tips of new growth back in spring to force branching. (Remember, however, that dense growth tends to increase scale insect problems, and that unfruited tips of last season's growth produce berries for coming year.) When cutting holly for decorations, consider each branch tip—whether 3 in. or 20 in. long—a holly spray. Make cuts to enhance regular form of trees, rather than being concerned with size of sprays.

I. cornuta 'Burfordii.' Burford holly. Shrub or small tree. Not a fast grower so it doesn't require as much attention as English holly. But it also needs occasional thinning and pruning to keep it in shape.

I. c. 'Rotunda.' Dwarf Chinese holly. Because of compact habit and slow growth, you'll find little need for pruning. Makes excellent low, trimmed hedge.

I. crenata. Japanese holly. Shrub. Left alone, shrub becomes rather tall, slim, densely-foliaged spire. However, it can be trained and shaped by pruning to almost any form you want. In Japan it is used frequently for topiary. Naturally neat and low growing, it can be kept even lower.

I. c. 'Convexa.' (Often sold as *I. c. bullata.*) Plant has a pleasing shape whether it's clipped or left to grow naturally. Trimmed, looks like boxwood. Will grow to 6 ft. but can be kept lower by pruning.

I. c. 'Helleri.' Dwarf. Makes excellent low trimmed hedge with minimum of pruning. Attractive left unpruned.

I. c. 'Microphylla.' Capable of growing to tree size. It can be kept to 2-4 ft. by cutting back or even shearing like hedge.

I. pernyi. Shrub or small tree. May grow to height of 20 ft., becoming open and gangly as it matures, but form is easily controlled by pruning.

IMPATIENS oliveri. Oliver's snapweed, poor man's rhododendron. Perennial. In colder areas, frost kills to ground; it will grow again in spring. Where frost does not kill it, you can cut it to the ground in fall for new growth in spring.

INCENSE CEDAR. See Calocedrus.

INDIA DEVIL TREE. See Rauwolfia.

INDIAN CURRANT. See Symphoricarpos.

INDIAN LAUREL FIG. See Ficus.

INDIAN MOCK STRAWBERRY. See Duchesnea.

INDIGO BUSH. See Amorpha.

INDIGO, FALSE. See Baptisia.

IOCHROMA cyaneum (*I. lanceolatum, I. purpureum, I. tubulosum*). Evergreen

shrub. Prune it hard after bloom. Softwooded, it looks best espaliered or tied up against wall. Take out some oldest shoots to ground annually.

IPOMOEA. Morning glory. Vining perennials. Train on fence, trellis, or use as ground cover. Cut to ground annually in fall. New growth will appear in spring.

IRIS. Bulbs, rhizomes. Dormant plants, with dead outside leaves and yellowed leaf tips, are unsightly and serve as winter hiding place for insects, snails, and slugs. Remove old leaves to prepare for next year's blooms. Plants that retain good, green foliage generally should not be cut back.

ITALIAN BUCKTHORN. See Rhamnus.

ITEA ilicifolia. Hollyleaf sweetspire. Evergreen shrub or small tree. Graceful, open shrub, requires only minimum of pruning for shaping, removal of dead wood. Normally grows to about 10 ft. but can easily be kept to 4 or 5 ft. with occasional thinning.

IVY. See Hedera.

IVY, BOSTON. See Parthenocissus.

IVY GERANIUM. See Pelargonium.

JACARANDA acutifolia (*J. mimosaefolia*). Jacaranda. Deciduous to semi-evergreen tree. Very adaptable, can be trained to single or multiple-trunked plant. Once you have the form you want, little pruning is necessary beyond light heading back and cleaning out small inner branches that have died back. In cases where tree is frozen badly, a number of shoots will develop at base of trunk. For single-stemmed tree, select most vigorous shoot and encourage it. For clump-type tree, select 3 or 4 of strongest shoots. To convert a single-trunked tree into a multi-trunked one, lop off trunk 2 ft. or less above ground. New branches will break below cut, and tree can be trained to 3 or 4 main trunks. Pinch out growing tips every 3 ft. or so to force more branching. If tree gets rangy, cut it back.

JACOBINIA carnea. Brazilian plume flower. Evergreen shrub. In colder climates, cut back to ground each fall, or frost will do it for you. (You can, of course, grow it in container and bring indoors in winter.) In milder areas, grow as evergreen shrub, cutting back every 2 or 3 years to keep neat. Heavy pruning just as plant starts to grow in spring results in more vigorous, compact growth and a better crop of flowers. As plant grows pinch developing stems once or twice to increase the number of branching stems.

JADE PLANT. See Crassula.

JAPANESE ARALIA. See Fatsia.

JAPANESE KNOTWEED. See Polygonum.

JAPANESE PAGODA TREE. See Sophora.

JAPANESE SPURGE. See Pachysandra.

JASMINE. See Jasminum.

JASMINE, CHILEAN. See Mandevilla.

JASMINE, STAR. See Trachelospermum.

JASMINUM. Jasmine. Evergreen or deciduous shrubs or vines. All jasmines need frequent pinching, thinning, and shaping to control growth.

J. grandiflorum (*J. officinale grandiflorum*). Spanish jasmine. Semi-evergreen to deciduous vine. Can be pruned and trained as a vine or as a shrub.

J. humile. Italian jasmine. Evergreen shrub or vine. Erect willowy shoots form tall, arching shrub. Can be trained as vine.

J. magnificum. See *J. nitidum*.

J. mesnyi (*J. primulinum*). Primrose jasmine. Evergreen shrub. Long, arching branches form 6-10 ft. shrub. Will grow taller if trained against wall.

J. multiflorum. (Often sold as *J. gracillimum*.) Pinwheel jasmine. Evergreen shrub or vine. Will get bare and leggy if not headed back regularly to force bushiness.

J. nitidum. (Often sold as *J. magnificum*.) Angelwing jasmine. Evergreen or semi-deciduous vine. Versatile, very receptive to training. If planted 3-5 ft.

apart and left to grow as it likes, will make good, solid ground cover in couple of years. Trained up trellis or wall, it weaves stems into screen of solid green. By pinching or clipping straying branches, you can turn it into handsome low-growing shrub.

J. nudiflorum. Winter jasmine. Deciduous viny shrub. Prune hard by thinning ⅓ of wood each year after bloom. This keeps the plant in bounds and forces new flowering growth. An easy way to keep it in bounds is to consistently pick twiggy side branches before buds bloom and bring them indoors (they last well in water).

J. officinale. Common white jasmine, poet's jasmine. Semi-evergreen to deciduous twining vine. Very fast growing; it often rambles to over 50 ft. if not controlled. Requires constant shaping and heading back during growing season.

J. parkeri. Dwarf jasmine. Evergreen shrub. Normally low-tufted plant with many twiggy branches. Keep it lower and more spreading as ground cover by shearing tops after bloom.

J. polyanthum. Evergreen vine. Head back and thin branches each year after bloom.

J. sambac. Arabian jasmine. Evergreen shrub. Will get bare and leggy if not headed back regularly to force bushiness.

JERUSALEM SAGE. See Phlomis.

JERUSALEM THORN. See Parkinsonia.

JESSAMINE, CAROLINA. See Gelsemium.

JESSAMINE, ORANGE. See Murraya.

JETBEAD. See Rhodotypos.

JOHNNY-JUMP-UP. See Viola.

JOJOBA. See Simmondsia.

JUGLANS. See Walnut.

JUJUBE, CHINESE. See Zizyphus.

JUNIPER. See Juniperus.

JUNIPER MYRTLE. See Agonis.

JUNIPERUS. Juniper. Evergreen shrubs and trees. Junipers respond well to pruning. If they look straggly or lopsided, prune to improve the shape before new growth starts. Shrub types can be developed into thick, well-shaped plants by cutting tips of branches back to first fork (or farther if more drastic measures are required) each spring. Upper branches on low growing junipers tend to block off light and air from weaker ones below. To prevent this, cut back and thin out some of top growth in late spring or early summer. Take entire branches where possible, always making cuts to enhance beauty of shrubs. Good time to cut back junipers that have outgrown their allotted space is just before Christmas holidays when you can use the greenery for decorations. Tree forms generally require less pruning than the lower growing junipers. Sometimes it's better to replace junipers which have outgrown their space than pruning them way back.

The preceding general advice applies to all junipers. Following are several forms for which some specific pruning or training information will be useful.

J. chinensis 'Pfitzeriana Aurea.' Golden pfitzer juniper. Has interestingly irregular outline that can be emphasized with selective pruning. Fast growing, needs to be pruned regularly.

J. c. 'Torulosa.' Hollywood juniper. twisted juniper. One of easiest conifers to train. Prune or shape in any direction. Looks awkward when young because of flexible branches; needs support for several years and can then be left to go its own way. To control shape, thin out selected branches in spring or fall. Never shear it. Pruning to encourage greater density tends to increase plant's susceptibility to twig blight.

J. horizontalis. Prostrata juniper. Can take espalier form against wall if supported and trained. Thin, do not chop back.

J. scopulorum. Silver king juniper, Rocky Mountain juniper, Western red cedar. Withstands heavy pruning, needs occasional trimming for symmetrical form. Prune moderately from the start for dense, compact shrub.

J. virginiana. Red cedar juniper, Eastern red cedar. Tree. Sometimes

STAR JASMINE plants held up in place against wall by copper wires spray-painted black. The plants are pruned to 3 inches from the wall.

HOLLYWOOD JUNIPER (J. C. 'Torulosa') needs little pruning; just heading back.

'SILVER SPREADER' JUNIPER (ground cover form of J. virginiana) also needs little pruning – just remove big upper branches to let light through to lower ones.

ROCKY MOUNTAIN JUNIPER having side branches cut to keep it symmetrical.

sheared, but best to train and prune as tree. Seldom requires much pruning, but size and form can be controlled by cutting back new growth in late spring or early summer.

JUPITER'S BEARD. See Centranthus.

KADSURA japonica. Scarlet kadsura. Twining evergreen vine. Fast growing. With support can be trained against wall or fence or on trellis; without support it sprawls over ground. Start training while young to keep it from becoming tangled mass. Prune to thin and shape in early spring.

KAFFIR LILY. See Clivia.

KAFFIR PLUM. See Harpephyllum.

KALMIA latifolia. Mountain laurel, calico bush. Evergreen shrub. Like rhododendrons, kalmia will respond well to heavy pruning but seldom needs it. Some gardeners feel that faded flower heads weaken plant and should be removed. If you think they look untidy and want to remove them, shear off, being especially careful not to cut into growth buds at the base of leaves. If you injure them, you may not get flowers next year. Generally prune plant after flowering. Cut some oldest stems to ground to encourage new growth.

KATSURA TREE. See Cercidiphyllum.

KEI APPLE. See Dovyalis.

KENTUCKY COFFEE TREE. See Gymnocladus.

KERRIA japonica. Deciduous shrub. Responds well to heavy pruning. Cut back old growth that has flowered to ground, along with dead or weak wood. For loose, open shrub, remove as many as half of old canes at ground level as soon as flowers fade. This will encourage new shoots.

KHAT. See Catha.

KINNIKINNICK. See Arctostaphylos.

KIWI. See Actinidia.

KLEINIA. Succulents. Keep unattractive flowers cut off to preserve foliage quality.

KNIPHOFIA uvaria (*Tritoma uvaria*). Red-hot poker, torch-lily, poker plant. Perennial. Remove flower spikes after bloom and cut old leaves off at base in fall. New leaves will replace them.

KOELREUTERIA. Chinese flame tree, goldenrain tree. Deciduous trees. Normal staking and training for shape while young, very little annual pruning afterward. You may want to cut off fat, papery capsules after they turn brown and unsightly, at the same time selectively remove extra growth to maintain open, graceful forms.

KOLKWITZIA amabilis. Beauty bush. Deciduous shrub. If adequate room to grow in, plant shouldn't require heavy pruning. However, like deutzia, it responds well to heavy pruning right after bloom. Still, some gardeners enjoy silver brown, bristly fruits for winter interest and do not prune at that time, letting fruits develop and then removing them in spring. To keep from getting too large and to renew, cut some oldest canes to ground each spring.

KOREAN SPICE VIBURNUM. See Viburnum.

KOREAN YEW. See Cephalotaxus.

LABURNUM. Goldenchain tree. Deciduous tree or large shrub. Prune right after bloom. To train as tree, take off side shoots along trunk. To train into bushy, low-branching shrub, head back to trunk to force new growth low on plant. To renew vigor of this fast-growing, comparatively short-lived tree, some gardeners prune drastically by cutting back to basic skeleton of branches. Plants must be pruned regularly to keep them tidy. Remove seed pods because they are poisonous, untidy, and also because heavy crop of pods drains strength from plants.

LAGERSTROEMIA indica. Crape myrtle. Deciduous shrub or tree. Needs overall, heavy pruning after leaves drop to encourage new wood that will produce next season's flowers. Flower production will tend to be disappointing if it is left unpruned, though it has beautiful natural form that is especially attractive in winter. To prune large shrub or tree, cut back new growth 12-18 in. from tip, removing whole branches where necessary for shape and symmetry. Cut out sucker growth and flower clusters, too. With dwarf shrub form, remove spent flower clusters and prune out small twiggy growth. You can train it as a small, vase-shaped tree to display attractive trunk and branch pattern.

LAGUNARIA patersonii. Primrose tree, cow itch tree. Evergreen tree. Needs no pruning aside from removal of dead or damaged wood. If injured when young, tree has tendency to sucker. Remove the suckers. If frost damaged, wait until new growth begins before taking out frozen wood. Avoid contact with juice from cut stems and branches; it causes skin reaction, itching.

LAMB'S EARS. See Stachys.

LANTANA. Evergreen and deciduous vining shrubs. Tend to build up high, leafless underbrush, a potential fire hazard. To avoid this, prune hard each year in spring to remove dead wood. New growth breaks readily from old wood and from stumps. Remove leggy growth at any time during growing season to encourage compact habit. If damaged by frost, wait until spring to cut plants back. They will recover rapidly after weather warms.

LAPAGERIA rosea. Chilean bellflower. Evergreen vine. Slender stems need training to desired shape. Very little pruning required beyond that. Cut out weak, straggly growth to encourage strong, healthy wood. Blooms spring through fall.

LARCH. See Larix.

LARIX. See Chrysolarix.

LATHYRUS. Sweet pea. Annual vines or bushlike, perennial vines. Pinch back

PINCH BACK TIPS of young sweet pea vines like this to make them grow bushy.

tips when 4-5 in. tall to make vines bushier. For longer bloom, do not allow to go to seed. Cut flowers often and remove all seed pods. If neglected, will eventually make tangled mound of stems, tendrils, leaves, and flowers. When they reach this stage, simply cut off at ground level stems you wish to discourage.

LAUREL, CALIFORNIA. See Umbellularia.

LAUREL, EVERGREEN. See Prunus.

LAUREL, MOUNTAIN. See Kalmia.

LAUREL, NEW ZEALAND. See Corynocarpus.

LAUREL, SIERRA. See Leucothoe.

LAURUSTINUS. See Viburnum.

LAVANDULA. Lavender. Evergreen shrubs or subshrubs. All forms, even dwarf, require pruning to keep them bushy and in good health. After bloom, cut off all flowering stems at base. (If you intend to dry the flowers, pick them as they begin to open. At that time, concentration of fragrance is highest.) If there is danger of frost and plants were not pruned immediately after flowering, wait until spring. Fall pruning induces tender growth that will freeze, disfiguring the plants. If neglected, lavenders develop gnarled, silver gray trunks from which topheavy head of silvery foliage tumbles toward ground. Bushes neglected for any length of time can never be restored to former appearance. In this case, it is best to take cuttings and replace old woody plants with young ones.

LAVENDER. See Lavandula.

LAVENDER COTTON. See Santolina.

LAVENDER STARFLOWER. See Grewia.

LEIOPHYLLUM buxifolium. Box sand myrtle. Evergreen shrub. Neat, compact, slow growth to 2 ft. Prune it lightly as you would an evergreen azalea.

LEMON. See Citrus.

LEMON VERBENA. See Aloysia.

LEONOTIS leonurus. Lion's tail. Perennial. Cut back to ground each year after it flowers in mild winter climates, or as new spring growth begins in colder areas. Plant produces many stems from base and will grow 5-6 ft. high, even when trimmed back. Tends to be shrubby but striking if kept well-groomed.

LEOPARD'S BANE. See Doronicum.

LEPTOSPERMUM. Tea tree. Evergreen shrubs or small trees. Though they require little pruning, all types can take some surface shearing. When you do prune, cut back only to side branches, leaving some foliage. Never cut into bare wood. Thin occasionally to maintain foliage on inner parts of plants. Instead of cutting branches to conform to set pattern, let them show you the way they want to grow. Some develop very irregular and interesting shapes. Trees have same potential for multi-stem use as described for *Feijoa sellowiana.*

L. laevigatum. Australian tea tree. Large shrub or small tree. To grow as small tree, select and train main branches early. Some specimens need some thinning and heading back, especially when young. Others don't. Several planted close together will make thick natural screen or clipped hedge, not developing visible branching character as they do when grown as trees.

LEUCADENDRON argenteum. Silver tree. Evergreen tree or large shrub. Pinch back young plant as new growth develops to achieve bushier growing habit. For more open habit, do not pinch but give only guidance required for shaping.

LEUCOPHYLLUM frutescens (*L. texanum*). Texas ranger. Evergreen shrub. Thin and shape in winter. If it becomes straggly, cut back to within few inches of ground and it will come back to form attractive, compact shrub.

LEUCOTHOE. Evergreen shrubs.

L. davisiae. Sierra laurel. Prune by removing old flower heads. If blossoms are removed before they can set seed, shrubs will bloom again in fall. If growth becomes too rank, cut to ground to give them fresh start.

L. fontanesiana (*L. catesbaei*). Drooping leucothoe. Left to their natural growth habit, they are likely to develop wild look by producing long sprays. Cutting these sprays for winter arrangements will strengthen and renew shrubs, force new growth, and keep them tidy. Easy to control by pinching and pruning. If they become too rank, cut to ground for fresh start.

LIGUSTRUM. Privet. Deciduous or evergreen shrubs or small trees. Can take heavy pruning and shearing. Most widely used in hedges. Clip into formal shapes or train as trees.

L. japonicum. (Often sold as *L. texanum.*) Japanese privet, waxleaf privet. Evergreen shrub. Keep low by pruning or allow to grow informally to its natural height. Clip young privet hedge 3 or 4 times during growing season to make thick and bushy at base. Good choice for tall hedge or screen, both informal or clipped. Remember to clip hedge so it is narrower at top than at base.

L. lucidum. Glossy privet. Evergreen tree. Takes kindly to pruning. Train to almost any shape and keep at any height. Hold plant low and full for informal effects or train as small shade tree.

L. ovalifolium. California privet. Semi-deciduous shrub; evergreen only in mildest areas. Clip early and frequently to encourage low dense branching. Thin carefully for distinctive pot plant that can be dwarfed in container for years.

L. o. 'Aureum' (*L. o.* 'Variegatum'). Golden privet. To get larger leaves and best color, prune back overgrown shrub severely before growth starts in spring.

WAXLEAF PRIVET in pot. 'Suwannee River' hedge at base. Both need shearing.

L. 'Suwannee River.' Evergreen shrub. Keep clipped as small hedge or prune into formal container plant.

LILAC. See Syringa.

LILAC, GATE. See Centranthus.

LILAC, WILD. See Ceanothus.

LILIUM. Lily. Bulb. Cut off faded flower heads before they form seed; otherwise, the plant's energy goes into seed formation and not into bulb growth.

LILLY-PILLY TREE. See Acmena.

LILY. See Lilium.

LILY, FORTNIGHT. See Moraea.

LILY, GINGER. See Hedychium.

LILY, PLANTAIN. See Hosta.

LILY-OF-THE-VALLEY SHRUB. See Pieris.

LILY-OF-THE-VALLEY TREE. See Crinodendron, Clethra.

LILY TURF. See Liriope and Ophiopogon.

LIME. See Citrus.

LINDEN. See Tilia.

LINGONBERRY. See Vaccinium.

LINOSPADIX monostachya. See Palm.

LION'S TAIL. See Leonotis.

LIQUIDAMBAR. Sweet gum. Deciduous trees. Trees branch from ground up and look most natural that way, but you can train them to form higher heads for easiest foot traffic. You'll need to do some training when trees are young in order to develop strong central trunks. Don't remove any side growth during the first 3 or 4 years. Pinch these side branches back during dormant season to divert growth to tops. After fourth year, remove lower branches to form heads of trees at desired height. (Don't try to force young liquidambar into bushier plants by pinching out tips. They just don't grow that way and will continue skyward by sending up more leaders.) If necessary, thin crown of trees during dormant season to encourage well-spaced framework of branches. Mature trees have beautiful natural forms and need no pruning except to remove stubs of broken branches.

LIRIOPE and OPHIOPOGON. Lily turf. Evergreen grasslike perennials. They become ragged and brown with neglect. Cut back shaggy old foliage after new leaves appear.

LITCHI chinensis. Litchi nut. Evergreen tree. Like citrus, litchi fruits are borne terminally on current season's growth and do not require much wood renewal. One good method of pruning is to gather fruit in traditional manner—

cutting off 10-12 in. long branches with fruit attached.

LITHOCARPUS densiflora. Tanbark oak. Evergreen tree. Needs early training for shape. Grows with multiple trunks but can be trained to single trunk by removing poorest trunks and keeping the best one. Corrective, preventive pruning is all that's required after it's established.

LIVISTONA. See Palm.

LOCUST. See Robinia.

LONICERA. Honeysuckle. Evergreen or deciduous shrubs or vines. All types respond well to heavy pruning, but bush forms are sufficiently self-contained to stay neat without severe pruning. How heavily you prune depends on whether or not you want the bushes to have definite shapes. Thin out some older branches during winter months to encourage fresh new growth. Cut out all branches you don't want, head others back slightly.

L. ciliosa. Deciduous vine. Becomes weedy if not controlled. Thin and head back, cutting out all wood that has borne blossoms.

L. 'Clavey's Dwarf.' Deciduous shrub. Slow growing, compact. Cut back to stems in winter if it becomes woody. New growth will emerge in spring.

L. fragrantissima. Winter honeysuckle. Deciduous shrub. Partially evergreen in milder areas. Willowy, requires considerable pruning, cutting back to keep within bounds. Good hedge plant but needs constant clipping, detracting from show of bloom.

L. heckrottii. Gold flame honeysuckle, coral honeysuckle. Deciduous, semi-deciduous vine or small shrub. Train on low fence, on wire along eaves, or as espalier.

L. hildebrandiana. Giant Burmese honeysuckle. Evergreen vine. Thin out older stems occasionally, removing some growth that has bloomed. Prune out overlong shoots. Frequently head back terminals to keep vine from becoming stemmy at base.

L. involucrata. Twinberry. Deciduous shrub. Densely foliaged, needs heavy pruning in winter to keep it looking attractive.

L. japonica. Japanese honeysuckle. Evergreen vine, partly or wholly deciduous in coldest regions. Very vigorous. Needs regular pruning to keep it from spreading like a weed and becoming tangled, shapeless mass. To prevent undergrowth from building up and becoming a fire hazard, cut the vine back almost to the basic framework once a year any time after the peak of bloom or in winter. If you don't control this plant, it will climb trees and its roots may invade sewer and drain lines.

L. maacki. Bush honeysuckle. Will grow up to 15 ft. high and as wide unless severely pruned each year.

L. nitida. Box honeysuckle. Evergreen shrub. Untidy if left alone but easily pruned as hedge or single plant.

L. tatarica. Tatarian honeysuckle. Deciduous shrub. You can let it reach its full 10 ft. or cut it back to any height.

LOQUAT. See Eriobotrya.

LOROPETALUM chinense. Evergreen shrub. Neat, compact habit, grows naturally into an attractive plant. Train while young as pot plant, a plant to drape over a wall, or grow it against a wall or fence. Little further pruning will be necessary.

LOTUS berthelotii. Trailing perennial. Vigorous plant. Prune heavily in spring and cut or pinch back stems occasionally to induce bushiness. Cut straggly branches off at base.

LUPINE. See Lupinus.

LUPINUS. Lupine. Annuals, perennials, shrubs. Cut to ground after bloom,

SHE'S CUTTING Yulan magnolia flowers for indoors, making cuts at branch base.

may flower again same year. Remove spent flowers from plants all during blooming period.

LYONOTHAMNUS floribundus. Catalina ironwood. Evergreen tree. Prune in winter to shape and control growth. It stump sprouts readily when cut or burned, so severe pruning will not hurt it. (In the country, hungry deer will do some pruning for you.) Trim off dead, brown flower clusters; they tend to hang on tree for a long time and may be unsightly. Can be pruned as hedge to any height you want.

LYSILOMA thornberi. Feather bush. Shrub or small tree. Evergreen in frostless areas, deciduous elsewhere. Train as dense shrub or as single-trunk tree. If frost damaged, cut out bad wood after danger of frost is past; plant should come back.

MAACKIA amurensis. Deciduous tree. Stake and prune to shape when young to develop clear trunk. Unpruned tree is shrubby looking.

MACADAMIA ternifolia. Macadamia nut, Queensland nut. Evergreen tree. Stake and shape young tree to central leader. Prune to space side branches about 6 in. apart vertically on trunk.

MACADAMIA NUT. See Macadamia.

MACLURA pomifera. Osage orange. Deciduous tree. Responds well to pruning, can be kept to any size from 6 ft. up. Pruned high, makes good desert shade tree. Fast growing, it can spread into thicket.

MADRONE. See Arbutus.

MAGIC FLOWER. See Cantua.

MAGNOLIA. Deciduous or evergreen trees and shrubs. Magnolias do not usually require much pruning. The type of pruning you do to train young plants depends upon what your objective is: if you want trees, prune to main frames; if you want shrubs, promote and protect new shoots from bases (however, shrubby forms, such as *M. kobus stellata*—star magnolia—do not make good trees). Magnolias should be pruned only lightly to maintain their desired shapes. Remove interfering branches and sucker growth, thin inside for light and air. Cut winter-damaged wood back to healthy tissue. You can prune at almost any time. Some gardeners like to prune during bloom period for cut flowers. Always cut magnolias all the way back to another branch. Do not leave stubs, for they are particularly susceptible to disease. Deciduous magnolias sucker freely in their early years. However, especially on young vigorous trees, shoots that originate above the graft may well be worth keeping (cut off those

from below). Since each shoot that appears is successively more vigorous, better wait until there are 2 or 3. Then choose the best shoot and cut out completely the weaker ones. The single remaining vigorous shoots will form the eventual trees. For bigger, better quality blooms, thin out excess flower buds.

MAHALA MAT. See Ceanothus.

MAHERNIA verticillata. Honey bell. Evergreen perennial or subshrub. May be short-lived. For longer life, cut off dead flowers. Cut back after bloom.

MAHOBERBERIS miethkeana. Evergreen shrub. Dense, upright growth. Gets leggy, but can be pruned back after spring bloom.

MAHONIA. Evergreen shrubs.

M. aquifolium. Oregon grape. Requires minimum of pruning when young. As plant matures, it tends to send out unbranched shoots 6 or more ft. long with foliage only near and at tip if left unpruned. To keep plant compact, cut these long shoots right to the ground in spring before new growth begins. Cut oldest, woody stems to ground at same time to keep fresh new growth coming. As rank new shoots emerge, pinch their tips part-way back so they will branch.

M. lomariifolia. Young plant tends to have a single vertical, unbranched stem; with age the plant produces more nearly vertical branches from near base. Cut stems at varying heights to induce branching. After that the plant needs little or no pruning, except for removal of old berry clusters in mid-year.

M. nevinii. Nevin mahonia. Normally loose, many-branched shrub, can be trained as hedge with regular pruning. Plant responds well to over-all pruning.

M. repens. Creeping mahonia. Spreading habit. Little pruning necessary except to keep it from spreading.

MAIDENHAIR TREE. See Ginkgo.

MALUS. Crabapple. Deciduous trees, rarely shrubs. Require regular annual pruning. Neglected, they tend to produce complicated tangle of branches. Too heavy pruning, on the other hand, stimulates growth of numerous unwanted shoots and dearth of flower buds for following spring. Pruning can be done at any time during dormant season, up to just before growth starts in early spring. Although you can prune after flowering, it's best to wait until branches are bare and you can easily see what you're doing, resulting in a much better, more balanced pruning job. During this same period, branches are lighter and somewhat easier to handle. If you like to use flowering branches in indoor arrangements, leave a few that you'd normally remove during dormant pruning, cutting them later when flower buds are beginning to show color. In addition to dormant pruning, some light thinning should be done throughout growing season. Instead of allowing unwanted growth to continue, literally "nip it in the bud" to allow time within same growing season for trees to direct their energy where growth is needed. The first step—as in pruning most trees—is to eliminate weak growth, conflicting and

AT TOP, tangled, twiggy growth on flowering crabapple. Below, plant after pruning.

tangled branches, and any wood that detracts from handsome shapes. Leave some stubby lateral branches, giving extra leaf surface to help thicken main branching and prevent sunburn.

Prune the crabapple you grow for jelly as you prune an apple, see Apple.

FLOWERING CRABAPPLE in pot doesn't grow much. Few cuts produced this form.

MANDEVILLA laxa (*M. suaveolens*). Chilean jasmine. Deciduous vine. Becomes topheavy, tangled mass of intertwining stems, and often base is quite bare of foliage. Thin heavily after leaves fall to keep tangle to minimum. This will produce a neater looking plant during winter, encourage abundant fresh spring foliage.

MANZANITA. See Arctostaphylos.

MANZANOTE. See Olmediella.

MAPLE. See Acer.

MAPLE, FLOWERING. See Abutilon.

MARANTA leuconeura. Prayer plant, rabbit tracks. Perennial house plant. In winter when the leaves become small and dry at tips, cut back to base. Will later begin sending up vigorous new growth.

MARGUERITE. See Chrysanthemum.

MARGUERITE, BLUE. See Felicia.

MATILIJA POPPY. See Romneya.

MAYTEN TREE. See Maytenus.

MAYTENUS boaria. Mayten tree. Evergreen tree. Has much side growth and tendency to sucker. Train it to single trunk by removing unwanted side growth. For multiple trunk effect, preserve and encourage some side branches and suckers. Responds well to heavy pruning in fall or spring. Thin center to keep tree open. Every 2 or 3 years, you may have to remove some low hanging branches for foot and lawn-care traffic under tree.

MEADOW SWEET. See Astilbe.

MELALEUCA. Evergreen trees and shrubs. Most are vigorous and fast-growing, need pinching back regularly. Control by cutting back unwanted branches to well-placed side branches. Avoid shearing; it makes them dense and lumpish. Smaller melaleucas are good screening materials; some large ones are useful as flowering or shade trees.

M. armillaris. Drooping melaleuca. Shrub or small tree. Clip as hedge or leave unclipped for informal screen. Can grow to 30 ft., but with training you can make it sprawling shrub or small tree.

M. decussata. Lilac melaleuca. Large shrub, small tree. Thin to show off trunk, branch character.

M. hypericifolia. Dotted melaleuca. Shrub. Clip into hedge, if you wish. Will bloom more profusely if left as informal, unclipped screen.

M. linariifolia. Flaxleaf paperbark. Tree. Young willowy plant needs staking, training. Prune out lower branches to shape.

M. nesophila. Pink melaleuca. Tree or large shrub. Versatile. Use it as big informal screen, train as vase-shaped tree, or shear as hedge. Can also be trained as multi-stemmed specimen using same method as described for *Feijoa sellowiana* (see page 42). End result is rangy, open tree-shrub with interesting shape.

MELIA. China-berry, Texas umbrella tree. Deciduous tree. Does not require much pruning beyond cutting out suckers or weak and damaged wood when dormant.

MELIANTHUS major. Honey bush. Evergreen shrub. If you want a sprawling mass rather than a tall-stemmed plant, prune to bring on new surges of foliage. As soon as canes start vertical growth, make cuts 12 in. from base of each cane. Do this at practically any time in mild winter climates. (It is not necessary to remove the terminal flower spikes after bloom.) If you want a tall plant, select 2 or 3 canes, staking and tying them to keep them erect; don't pinch them back. Keep dry, messy looking leaves picked or pruned off lower stems. Don't be afraid to take pruning shears to this plant, for it can get out of hand unless you tame it regularly by cutting back heavily. Prune it at any time, but most gardeners wait until after plant flowers. If plant looks shabby in fall, cut back severely to within 1 or 2 ft. of ground. This brings surge of new leaves that will look handsome during winter months.

MESCAL BEAN. See Sophora.

METASEQUOIA. See Chrysolarix.

METROSIDEROS. Evergreen trees or large shrubs. If you prune them annually, can be kept to 6-10 ft. shrubs or windbreaks. (Can also be trained as hedge, but other choices are better.) To bring into tree forms will require careful staking and pruning. These trees have same potential for sculptured multi-stem use as *Feijoa sellowiana* and can be trained by same method (see page 42). Remove lower side branches to about 6 ft. to encourage top growth. Leave about 3 stems for multiple trunk effect.

MEXICAN PALO VERDE. See Parkinsonia.

MEXICAN ORANGE. See Choisya.

MICHAELMAS DAISY. See Aster.

MICHELIA figo (*M. fuscata*). Banana shrub. Evergreen shrub. Slow growing, you can shape it almost at will. Shear as large evergreen hedge or espalier it. Left unpruned, it may reach 15 ft. high and 8-10 ft. across.

MICROCOELUM. See Palm.

MIRROR PLANT. See Coprosma.

MOCK ORANGE. See Philadelphus.

MONKEY FLOWER, SHRUBBY. See Diplacus.

MONKEY HAND TREE. See Chiranthodendron.

MONKEY PUZZLE TREE. See Araucaria.

MONSTERA deliciosa. (Often sold as *Philodendron pertusum*.) Split-leaf philodendron, it tends to get rangy and lose bottom leaves. If this happens and you want lower plant, air layer it, cut off top when new roots form, and plant it. New growth will also sprout from stump so you'll have 2 plants. Simplest method is just to cut it off lower down where you want new shoots. Or you can plant an overgrown plant in larger container and add younger, lower plant to fill in. On all plants, remove old fruit and spent leaves.

MORAEA iridioides. Fortnight lily. African iris. Corms or rhizomes. Have perennial stalks, producing flowers for many years unless they are completely cut off. When you cut stalks for arrangements, be sure to leave at least one node on remaining section of each stalk to carry flowers next season.

MORNING GLORY. See Ipomoea.

MORNING GLORY, BUSH. See Convolvulus.

MORNING GLORY, GROUND. See Convolvulus.

MORUS alba. White mulberry, silkworm mulberry. Deciduous tree. Train tree when young to form high head. Stake carefully because it develops large crown rather fast, and it may snap from slender young trunk in high winds. Branches may grow so long for first few years that they droop from their own weight. Shorten such branches by cutting back to well-placed upward growing bud. Thin out excess growth each winter, lightly cutting back tips of branches. This will encourage sturdy branches that resist wind damage. In parts of the Southwest, for some reason it once became a fad to prune mulberry trees back to stubs. This practice is unwise. It develops dangerously weak growth because of rotten or hollow centers in larger branches. Such pruning also prevents tree from achieving its own natural beauty. A better approach is to thin out excess growth and cut back tips lightly to produce better-balanced shade tree.

MOUNTAIN LAUREL. See Kalmia.

MOUNTAIN-MAHOGANY. See Cercocarpus.

MUEHLENBECKIA. Wire vine.

M. axillaris. Creeping wire vine. Low carpeting ground cover. Shear back if it grows out of bounds.

M. complexa. Mattress vine. Naturally a tangled, filmy mass of wiry stems and tiny leaves. Let it scramble and ramble at will or shear it back to thicken it or mold it into topiary shapes.

MULBERRY, SILKWORM. See Morus.

MULBERRY, WHITE. See Morus.

MURRAYA paniculata (*M. exotica*). Giant orange jessamine. Evergreen shrub. Hedge, large bushy or small tree. Grows slowly into compact upright shrub. Adapts well to any type of shearing or pruning. Can be sheared, trained easily into tree form. Left on its own, it is a handsome shrub.

MUSA. See Ensete.

MYOPORUM laetum. Evergreen shrub or tree. Attractive multiple-trunk tree if you stake and train it. Thin to prevent top-heaviness and wind damage. Cut back in spring to get lush, midsummer foliage. Heavily thin back old woody plant to rejuvenate it. If used as windbreak, prune side growth to keep heavy foliage at base coming.

MYRICA. Evergreen and deciduous shrubs. Respond well to heavy pruning, recovering rapidly.

M. californica. Pacific wax myrtle. Evergreen shrub or tree. Can also be used as screen, informal or clipped hedge. Grows most naturally as many-stemmed handsome and tidy shrub, 10-15 ft. high. (Waxy secretion may gum up pruning shears.)

M. pensylvanica (*M. caroliniensis*). Bayberry. Deciduous or partly evergreen

YOUNG UNPRUNED MULBERRY tree. Shorten branches to up-facing buds.

PRUNED MULBERRY (different tree from one shown at left) has developed strong framework branches from being thinned; head back repeatedly during growing season.

shrub. Though it responds well to heavy pruning, little is required beyond thinning and corrective pruning. Prune when most dormant.

MYRSINE africana. African boxwood. Evergreen shrub. Floppy when young, stiffens up into dense, rounded bush that can easily be kept at 3-4 ft. with moderate pinching and clipping. Responds well to pruning. Good for low hedges, clipped formal shapes.

MYRTLE, OREGON. See Umbellularia.

MYRTLE, TRUE. See Myrtus.

MYRTUS communis. True myrtle. Evergreen shrub. Very tolerant of pruning but can be left unpruned. Clip as formal hedge or thin to reveal attractive branches.

NANDINA domestica. Heavenly bamboo, sacred bamboo. Evergreen or semi-deciduous shrub. Some gardeners follow this rule of thumb: avoid pruning nandina until its foliage has turned from green to red, and then only if the plant is too tall for its location. To encourage strong, airy growth habit, cut old stems to 6-12 in. above the ground. This forces strong new growth from stubs, making plant bushier. Mature plant gets 6-8 ft. tall; keep it lower by cutting tallest stems right back to the ground. If nandina gets too tall and straggly all over, prune it down in two stages. First, cut half the stems to 6-12 in. above the ground. After new foliage appears below, cut remaining stems for a much lower shrub.

N. **'Nana'** ('Nana Compacta,' 'Lemon Hill'). Small, compact. Will stay below 3 ft.

NATAL PLUM. See Carissa.

NECTARINE. See Peach and Nectarine.

NECTARINE, FLOWERING. See Prunus.

NEPETA. Perennials.

N. **cataria.** Catnip. Shear back after bloom.

N. **mussinii.** Catmint. Shear off unsightly faded flower spikes.

NEPHROLEPIS. See Fern, Tender.

NERIUM oleander. Oleander. Evergreen shrub. Takes kindly to all types of pruning and can be grown as full, many-branched shrub. Also can be trained as handsome standard or multi-stem tree, growing as high as 20 ft. and sometimes spreading 15 ft. Looks neat as a hedge, but clipping with hedge shears also removes what would be flowering wood. If required, prune in early spring to control size and form. Cut out old wood that has flowered. Cut some branches nearly to ground. To restrict height, pinch remaining tips or prune back lightly. To prevent bushiness at base,

OLEANDERS trained as standards. There's room beneath for other plants.

OLEANDER SCREEN. With lower branches removed, plants could grow under it.

pull (don't cut) unwanted suckers. Caution children that all parts of plant are poisonous. Keep prunings, dead leaves, flowers away from hay or other animal feed; don't use wood for barbecue fires or skewers. Smoke can cause severe irritation and skewers have poisonous sap.

NET BUSH. See Calothamnus.

NEW ZEALAND CHRISTMAS TREE. See Metrosideros.

NEW ZEALAND FLAX. See Phormium.

NEW ZEALAND LAUREL. See Corynocarpus.

NIEREMBERGIA. Cup flower. Perennials.

N. **frutescens.** Tall cup flower. Can be trimmed to low, rounded, shrublike shape.

N. **hippomanica caerulea.** Dwarf cup flower. Plants usually form low mounds. If branches begin to get long and stringy after first long spell of bloom, cut them back with hedge shears to within 6 in. of the ground. New shoots will come out soon, and flowering will continue through fall.

NIGHT JESSAMINE. See Cestrum.

NINEBARK. See Physocarpus.

NORFOLK ISLAND PINE. See Araucaria.

NOTHOPANAX arboreum. Evergreen tree. Will grow moderately fast to 15-25 ft. tree, but can be trained as a multiple-stem small tree only 6-8 ft. high. Plant is stimulated by pruning.

NUTMEG, CALIFORNIA. See Torreya.

NYSSA sylvatica. Sour gum, tupelo, pepperidge. Deciduous tree. Part of charm is its crooked branches, twigs. Young tree has twiggy growth, with branches going in all directions. Remove crossing branches and any that might spoil shape. Very little pruning required once basic form is established.

OAK. See Quercus.

OCEAN SPRAY. See Holodiscus.

OCHNA serrulata (O. multiflora). Mickey Mouse plant, bird's-eye bush. Evergreen shrub. Trim young plant to keep it shapely and compact, nipping back long, jutting branches. As plant gets older, prune less and permit plant to spread. If too dense, thin branchlets to show off flowers and fruit to advantage.

OCTOPUS TREE. See Brassaia.

OLEA europaea. Olive. Evergreen tree. Tolerates heavy pruning or thinning and can be trained as a tree, shrub, or as large, dense hedge. For a tree, begin training early. To develop single trunk, prune out or shorten side branches below point where you want branching to begin, stake tree firmly, and cut off basal suckers when they appear. To train with several trunks, stake lower branches or basal suckers to continue growth at desired angles. Thin each year to show off handsome branch and trunk forms and to let more light and air through. Though thinning can be done anytime, if you wait until after flowering it will decrease production of fruit (usually a nuisance). Fruit can stain paving and harm lawn if not removed. Besides pruning, crop can be reduced by spraying with a plant hormone called naphthaleneacetic acid. Less efficient but easier is to knock off flowers with a good blast of water from the hose before they set fruit. If you want the crop, delay heavy pruning until after harvest.

OLEANDER. See Nerium.

OLEANDER, YELLOW. See Thevetia.

OLEARIA haastii. Daisy bush. Evergreen shrub. Shear or tip when necessary to keep plants shapely. Cut faded blooms or they will persist right through winter.

OLIVE. See Olea.

OLIVE, BLACK. See Bucida.

OLIVE, RUSSIAN. See Elaeagnus.

OLIVE, SWEET. See Osmanthus.

OLIVER'S SNAPWEED. See Impatiens.

OLMEDIELLA betschleriana. Guatemalan holly, Costa Rican holly, manzanote. Evergreen shrub or small tree. Very adaptable to pruning and shaping. If you want several stems and bushier growth, pinch out leader; if you want a single-trunked tree, encourage the strongest stem and keep side growth pinched back. As a shrub, it remains thickly foliaged to the ground and can be clipped or left unclipped to provide a tall hedge or privacy screen.

ORANGE. See Citrus.

ORANGE JESSAMINE. See Murraya.

ORCHID TREE. See Bauhinia.

ORCHID VINE. See Stigmaphyllon.

OREGON GRAPE. See Mahonia.

OSAGE ORANGE. See Maclura.

OSMANTHUS. Evergreen shrubs or trees. Though relatively slow growing, these plants do need to be pruned and shaped. Pinch stem ends regularly during spring and summer to force side growth. Remove branches that are topheavy or off balance.

O. armatus. Chinese osmanthus. Shrub. Once established, plant needs little pruning except to control height or remove straggly branches. Do this after flowers fade.

O. delavayi (*Siphonosmanthus delavayi*). Delavay osmanthus. Shrub. Easily controlled by little pruning if it has adequate growing room. Still blooms even when clipped as hedge, but natural habit is low and broad, with arching branches. Good espalier.

O. fortunei. Shrub. Good plant for large container. With occasional light pruning, you can keep it about 3 ft. high and about as wide.

O. fragrans. Sweet olive. Shrub. Can be trained as small tree, hedge, or espalier. Will grow to 10 ft. high (eventually

much more) and almost as wide, but you can keep it lower by pinching out branch tips in spring and summer.

O. heterophyllus (*O. aquifolium, O. ilicifolius*). Holly-leaf osmanthus. Shrub. Cutting handsome foliage regularly for arrangements will keep shrub from growing too lanky.

O. h. 'Variegatus.' Grows slowly, filling out as it gets older. Pinch branch tips once a year to help it fill in sooner.

OSMARONIA cerasiformis. Oso berry, Indian plum. As usually seen, it is a thicket that needs little pruning. Can be trained as single-stem tree by cutting out suckers.

OSMUNDA. See Fern, Hardy.

OSO BERRY. See Osmaronia.

OSTEOMELES schwerinae. Grows at least 10 ft. tall but can easily be kept down to 4 or 5 ft. with a little thinning and attention during year. Prune after plant flowers.

OSTEOSPERMUM. Evergreen subshrubs or perennials. Closely related to *Dimorphotheca* (Cape marigold) and often sold as such. Pinch tips of young plants to induce bushiness. Cutting back old, sprawling branches to young side branches will keep plants neat, often induce repeat bloom. Plants have tendency toward ranginess; can be minimized with regular pinching and occasional pruning.

OXERA pulchella. Evergreen vine or viny shrub. Leaves grow densely on arching, twining stems, reaching 10-20 ft. if supported. Not supported, makes a mounding shrubby mass about 6 ft. high. Train as vine along eaves, over entryway, on arbors or trellises. Trim for unusual pattern quality against wall. Vine takes much guidance; tie stems in direction you want them to grow. Prune lightly as you train vine, trimming out dead and broken branches as soon as vines finish flowering.

OXYDENDRUM arboreum. Sourwood, sorrel tree. Deciduous tree. Needs only minimum of guidance and training while young, corrective and preventive pruning later. If needed, prune while dormant. Remove freeze-damaged wood only after danger of frost is past.

PACHISTIMA. Evergreen shrubs. Low hedges, edgings, ground covers.

P. canbyi. Ratstripper. Lends itself to use as a ground cover and as a low clipped hedge or edging plant.

P. myrsinites. Oregon boxwood. Takes shearing well so is suitable for clipped hedge.

PACHYSANDRA terminalis. Japanese spurge. Evergreen subshrub. Underground runners may become somewhat invasive, but plant is easy to keep in

bounds with sharp shovel. Needs occasional light clipping or pinching in early spring to keep it compact. Do not cut all the way to the ground.

PACIFIC WAX MYRTLE. See Myrica.

PAEONIA. Peony. Herbaceous perennials and deciduous shrubs.

Herbaceous peonies. Perennials. Pick flowers as they fade but leave as much foliage as possible to nourish the plants. When foliage turns completely brown in the fall, cut it just below the soil surface. (Be careful not to damage next year's new buds or eyes 2 in. or so below ground level.)

Tree peonies. Deciduous shrubs. As flowers begin to fade, cut them off just above the topmost leaf. Before spring growth starts, cut back all stems to the uppermost healthy live eye or bud. Some growers advocate cutting 3 or 4-year old plants to ground. Do this in fall, when it is too late for new top growth to start. This practice strengthens underground eyes, stimulates root growth, and induces growth of more stems the following spring. Cut off winter damaged stems as new spring growth begins. Subject to botrytis; remove afflicted flowers, buds, and stems, cutting back into healthy stems.

PAINTED DAISY. See Chrysanthemum.

PAINTED-TONGUE. See Salpiglossis.

PALO VERDE, MEXICAN. See Parkinsonia.

PALM. Pruning of palms is mostly restricted to manicuring to keep them neat. Because this process is continual rather than seasonal, you may have to remove dead leaves on some types about every 3 or 4 months. Also remove fronds so damaged by disease, pests, storm damage, or freezing as to be unsightly. Feather-leafed palms require a split pruning operation. The yellow fronds should be cut off as close to the trunk as possible leaving the leaf bases. Some palms shed these old leaf bases on their own; others including arecastrums and chamaedoreas, may hold the old bases. The second stage is to remove the leaf bases, where necessary, by making shallow slices next to the trunk. Trunks of some palms wear a heavy overcoat of fiber. If you prefer the beauty of bare stems, the fibrous coat may be stripped off without injury to plant. Be careful if you trim shag skirts of fan palms, for you'll leave ugly scars if you cut up into live growth. Some palm admirers say that the dead leaves of Washingtonias should remain on the tree, the thatch being part of the palm's character. The most convincing argument for removal of the dead fronds is that they are a fire hazard. An attractive way to handle them is to cut lower fronds in a uniform way close

MUNICIPAL GARDENERS in Nice, France prune a Phoenix palm. Man at right is removing lowest tier of old fronds.

IN CUTTING old fronds, leave about 1 foot of leaf base. Just-cut fronds left white cut surfaces. Here, the men begin to remove leaf bases left from the year before, slicing clean at trunk. This method is useful for most feather palms.

THE KIND of tool they use in France.

THE JOB is almost complete. Last year's fronds have been sliced off right at trunk (see fresh scars between ropes and remaining bases). Here the men are putting decorative points on the bases from this year's pruning. Do this pruning in May.

COMPLETED JOB. Next year these bases will come off and next year's fronds will be cut off and their bases shaped.

to the trunk, leaving the trimmed leaf bases to present a rather pleasant lattice surface.

PALM, DATE. See Phoenix.

PALM, WINDMILL. See Trachycarpus.

PALMETTO. See Sabal.

PAMPAS GRASS. See Cortaderia.

PANDOREA jasminoides (*Bignonia jasminoides, Tecoma jasminoides*). Bower vine. Prune to direct or thin growth. Cut back frost-damaged wood when new growth begins in spring.

P. pandorana (*Bignonia australis, Tecoma australis*). Wonga-wonga vine. Prune ends of branches heavily after spring bloom.

PANSY. See Viola.

PAPAYA. See Carica papaya.

PAPER MULBERRY. See Broussonetia.

PAPYRUS. See Cyperus.

PARIS DAISY. See Chrysanthemum.

PARKINSONIA aculeata. Jerusalem thorn, Mexican palo verde. Deciduous tree. Young plants must be staked and trained to get a tree shape started (select strongest leader for central stem or trunk). Train it for high or low branching, as desired. As tree ages, dead branches may sometimes need to be removed from inside portions.

PARROT-BEAK. See Clianthus.

PARROTIA persica. Persian parrotia. Deciduous tree or large shrub. Densely foliaged branches spread wide and tend to grow in horizontal planes. Because of this, give special attention to pruning the young plant if you want to grow it as a tree. By shortening side branches during summer months, you can encourage it to grow taller and more tree-like in form. When tree reaches desired height, remove lower shortened side branches cleanly.

PARTHENOCISSUS. (Sometimes sold as *Ampelopsis*.) Deciduous vines. Boston ivy, Virginia creeper. Can be trained as either dense or open vines. Trim out at any time any long branches that obstruct view or walk-way. However, if vines have been pulled away from support, cut back to a firmly holding portion. Require annual pruning once they reach desired size; trim away from doors and windows. Cut off wandering branches that invade areas where they don't belong.

PASSIFLORA. Passion vine. Evergreen, semi-evergreen, or deciduous vines. If not controlled, these vines will grow rampant and may become thickly tangled masses of foliage with few flowers. They climb or crawl by wiry tendrils

that grab anything they can wrap around, including the vines themselves. Thin by brutally cutting wayward growth back to main structure at least once during growing season, and cut vines back before they get to nearby plants. In colder areas die-back acts as a natural annual pruning. But even in these areas, prune stems that are crowding and heading in wrong directions during rapid growth period to keep vines neat. If plants get out of hand, cut back all the way to ground after danger of frost is past in spring.

PASSION VINE. See Passiflora.

PAULOWNIA tomentosa (*P. imperialis*). Empress tree. Deciduous tree. If tree is cut back hard annually or every other year, it will grow as billowy mass of foliage with giant-sized leaves up to 2 ft. This kind of pruning, though, is done at expense of flowers and shade. Thin weaker wood to open up tree and provide interesting form. In colder areas, remove frost-damaged wood in spring.

PEACH AND NECTARINE (*Prunus persica* and *P. nectarina*). Trees. Peach and nectarine are the most vigorous growing fruit trees. This voluminous new growth of long, willowy shoots bears fruit the following summer. New growth bears only once (see bearing habits of fruit trees in the *Pruning Glossary*). Prune hard to encourage new growth; otherwise, fruit will be produced farther and farther out on the branches each year.

Cut off ⅔ of the previous year's growth by removing 2 of every 3

HORIZONTAL BRANCH

CUTS as marked for mature trees would remove ⅔ of last year's growth. On young tree, cuts at A or B would do same thing.

branches formed last year (cut right at base); or head back each branch to ⅓ its length. Actually you will probably prune ⅔ of last year's growth by heading back some branches and cutting out others. If picturesque shape is desired, wait until 2 or 3 years after planting (see *Training of Young Fruit Trees*, the *Pruning Glossary*), then give scaffold

VERTICAL BRANCH

OLD MATURE TREE

YOUNG GROWING TREE

CUTS on mature tree would also remove 2/3 growth. On young tree, cut A would widen it, cut B would extend it upward.

branches some special shape by twisting and tying them or by selectively removing secondary branches and leaving others that take off in angles to give some interesting shape to lower, visible part of tree.

PEACH, FLOWERING. See Prunus.

PEAR. Pear trees, like apples, produce fruit mostly from the ends of long-lived spurs. Pears are also similar to apples in their pruning requirements and pruning of mature trees consists primarily of cutting out the dead, twiggy and misplaced branches and encouraging new branches. Heavy pruning of pears will stimulate vegetative growth and may increase the danger of fireblight. Blighted branches should be removed below the dead wood, washing the pruning tools with disinfectant between each cut. After trees have been trained early to a good framework of main branches (see *Training Young Fruit Trees* in the *Pruning Glossary*), prune them lightly to keep good form.

PEAR, EVERGREEN. See Pyrus.

PEA VINE, AUSTRALIAN. See Dolichos.

PEARL BUSH. See Exochorda.

PECAN. See Carya.

PELARGONIUM. Geranium. Shrubby perennials. All the really common plants called geraniums are pelargoniums. All kinds require grooming and shaping, but timing and severity of pruning depend on the kind of plant and where it is grown. All but ivy geraniums grow as bushes but can be grown as single standards or trees by staking a single stem and rubbing out side buds until plant reaches desired height.

P. domesticum. Pelargonium, Lady Washington pelargonium, Martha Washington geranium, regal geranium. Pinch the growing tips of young plants to keep

OLDER PELARGONIUM needs pruning; branches should be cut back one half.

PRUNING almost finished. Most side branches should have 1 or 2 leaves.

them full and bushy and to increase flower production. Snap off uppermost tip just above node or joint. This will send growth out at sides of plant. When side branches develop, pinch them so that they will develop their own side branches. Each tip left to grow will develop a flower truss. (If you are growing plants indoors or in a sheltered place outdoors, stop pinching after late December or early January to get maximum spring bloom.) Remove faded flowers regularly to encourage new bloom. When peak bloom period is over in early fall, cut back plants about ½. Then, as new growth develops, resume shaping plants by pinching out tip growth. If plants are leggy, with woody stems, and are holding green leaves only at tips, renew them in one of the following ways: 1) Cut back plants gradually, starting right after heavy spring bloom. Prune each stem back to the lowest pair of leaves. When some new growth breaks below these leaves, cut back to the next pair of leaves. Continue cutting back as new leaves develop until plant is compact and well-shaped. 2) Cut plants down to within a few inches of the ground in spring after danger of frost is past to make them branch from the base. (You will lose bloom for one season this way, also may lose old woody plants if you cut them right to ground.) Some people like to replace old plants with new ones they grow from cuttings taken from old plant.

P. hortorum. Common geranium, garden geranium (including fancy-leaf geraniums). Pinch young, newly set plants to force side growth and bushiness (see *P. domesticum* above). Exception: don't pinch Carefree or other strains grown from seed; they are self-branching. Remove faded flowers regularly and occasionally cut back straggly branches to the lowest pair of leaves to force out lower growth. Cut back old, overgrown plants to reshape them. You can cut back in fall and root new plants from the wood you cut off, or cut back in spring after heavy frosts are past and plants are starting to grow. Cut back a little at a time so you can see what you are doing; don't prune all the way back to old wood. Retain some leaves on stems you prune. If possible, cut back just above a leaf bud. If no buds are visible, cut to lowest leaf and wait until buds break lower down, then cut back stub just above new bud break.

P. peltatum. Ivy geranium. Trailing, climbing, or hanging plant. Pinch growing tips to produce more stems. Not all varieties branch freely; some make long, trailing growth. Select compact ones for hanging baskets, longer, looser kinds as ground cover. Groom by cutting off faded flowers. Cut back stems that grow out of bounds.

Scented leaf geraniums. Many species of Pelargonium are grown for their scented foliage. They vary widely in appearance and habit but all take the same pruning: tip-pinch to keep plants compact and bushy, and shape to desired size and form by cutting out unwanted growth and shortening stems to lowest healthy leaf. Many are effective as standards.

PENNISETUM setaceum (*P. ruppelii*). Fountain grass. Perennial grass. You can cut the plant back to the ground at almost any time during its active growing season and see a fresh crop of leaves within a few weeks. If you let flowers set seed, you'll have seedlings popping up all over the garden. In colder areas, cut back dead and frost-damaged leaves in winter. New growth will emerge in spring.

PENSTEMON. Beard tongue. Perennials, evergreen shrubs and shrublets. Keep seed heads removed. Plants will then produce new growth, another set of buds and flowers throughout summer. Cut perennials back to base after final bloom period is over.

PEONY. See Paeonia.

PEPPER TREE. See Schinus.

PEPPERBUSH, SWEET. See Clethra.

PEPPERIDGE. See Nyssa.

PEPPERMINT TREE. See Agonis.

PEPPERWOOD. See Umbellularia.

PERIWINKLE, DWARF. See Vinca.

PERNETTYA mucronata. Evergreen shrub. Plantings spread by underground runners and can be invasive. Contain by root pruning or by putting plants in containers. Can be pruned heavily in late spring to keep bushy and well-rounded. Cut back straggling branches when necessary to keep neat and compact. Tends to grow many stems; cut back unwanted stems half-way to encourage branching.

PERSEA. Evergreen trees.
P. americana. See Avocado.
P. indica. Needs very little pruning. Dense and rather stiff growth may require thinning of branches to get proper shape.

PERSIAN PARROTIA. See Parrotia.

PERSIMMON (*Diospyros*). Deciduous trees. Very little pruning is required except that necessary to remove dead wood and to shape. It's possible, although difficult, to train as shade trees by removing lower branches. Because branches tend to droop, it's easier to train trees into semi-weeping forms by weighing down branch ends with rocks or half bricks. If you start consistent training program when trees are young, you can fashion them into very interesting informal espaliers. Watch branching patterns when young trees are developing and select laterals with strong-angled crotches so that brittle wood won't split under a heavy load of fruit. They split easily at a crotch, and important crotches should be safeguarded by lightening branches and cross-cabling. Persimmons tend to get dense in interior, causing fruit to be borne toward end of branches, so you must thin branches enough to allow sunlight to reach center. Thin before growth begins in spring to stimulate new wood which bears the fruit. Thin branches back to laterals, removing water sprouts (except when needed to fill in spaces). Do not prune heavily or stub back branches, for this will encourage vegetative growth at expense of fruits. Heavy pruning is recommended for old, neglected trees in order to force branching and new fruiting wood.

PHAEDRANTHUS buccinatorius (*Bignonia cherere*). Blood-red trumpet vine. Evergreen vine. Rampant growth once established; must be pruned annually to be kept under control. Do major pruning in late fall after bloom in mild winter areas; in early spring after danger of frost is past elsewhere. First remove all weak, damaged wood and then thin out crowded stems inside plant to provide good air circulation and light. Train vine on a wall, a high trellis, an arbor, or a chain link fence.

PHELLODENDRON amurense. Amur cork tree. Deciduous tree. Moderate growing. Requires minimum training when young and little pruning later. If young tree grows multiple leaders, remove all but one to make single-trunk tree, its lower branches at desired height.

PHILADELPHUS. Mock orange. Deciduous shrubs. All mock oranges need regular pruning as soon as possible after flowers fade. To keep shrubs airy and open, cut all spent flowering branches back to first bloom-free shoot or to a bud on stem being pruned. Unless you intend to grow a trimmed hedge, don't shear shrubs. On some more vigorous kinds, you can remove fair percentage of old flowering canes at ground level each summer when they begin to crowd center of bushes.

PHILODENDRON. Evergreen vines and shrubs. One big problem with vining philodendrons and their near relative *Monstera deliciosa* (the so-called split-leaf philodendron), is that they become rangy, lose bottom leaves, and outgrow their place indoors or in garden. Here are possible courses of action: 1) train plant to grow downward; 2) air layer (see *Pruning Glossary*) it to develop new plant; 3) cut back to make fresh start. The simplest way to keep a plant from getting too tall is to weight top growth down gradually until it makes a U-turn. Do by degrees so you don't break the stem. To fix leggy philodendron, you can air layer leafy top section, sever it, and replant when it develops roots. (You can encourage new growth from lower portion, as well.) If plant has become very straggly and sparsely foliaged, cut back to within 1 or 2 joints (leaf buds) from ground. New growth will develop from there. Prune in spring or summer.

PHLOMIS fruticosa. Jerusalem sage. Shrubby perennial. Cut back ⅓ each year in fall to keep it in shape.

PHOENIX. Date palms. For all species except the two below, see *Palm*.

P. dactylifera. Date palm. Suckers from base; remove these to keep tree single-trunked.

P. reclinata. Senegal date palm. Old leaves should be removed as they dry. After you have picturesque clump of 4 or 5 trunks, keep excessive suckers removed. You can direct growth to single trunk if you remove stem offshoots, but its clumping nature is part of its charm.

PHORMIUM tenax. New Zealand flax. Evergreen perennials. At least once each year, cut off dead or sunburned leaves close to ground and seal large cuts with asphalt emulsion. After a few years, clumps get quite thick. Thin out by cutting off some outside leaves at ground level. When it gets too large, divide in spring, using sharp spade or shovel to make cuts.

PHOTINIA. Evergreen or deciduous shrubs or small trees. Fast growing, photinias should be pinched and pruned to encourage spreading, dense growth and the colorful new foliage that comes every time new growth breaks. Light pruning at least 4 or 5 times a year will keep plants neat and full. For continuous supply of bright scarlet new growth, cut branch tips back once a month in late spring, early summer. Thin and head back to shape when required; never allow new growth to get away and make long, bare switches.

PHYGELIUS capensis. Cape fuchsia. Perennial shrubs. In mild winter areas where plants remain evergreen, trim off dead flower stalks to keep plants neat. Pinch out branch tips while plants are young to encourage sturdy upright stems. Root pruning may be necessary to control invasive roots.

PHYSOCARPUS capitatus. Ninebark. Deciduous shrub. Prune to make plant bushy. Remove old and heavy wood after bloom to encourage new growth from base. If you want attractive pods to develop after bloom, prune in dormant season. Can be renewed gradually by cutting a few of the oldest stems to ground each year.

PHYSOSTEGIA virginiana. False dragon-head. Perennial. Cut to ground after bloom. Divide every second year to control sprawling habit, keep in bounds.

PICEA. Spruce. Evergreen trees and shrubs. Prune to shape only. If two main trunks develop, cut one out. If a branch grows too long, cut back to well-placed side branch. Promote new side growth and make more dense by cutting new growth back about halfway. Cut out dead branches.

PIERIS. Evergreen shrubs. Respond well to heavy pruning and cutting back but this is seldom required. To keep plants looking neat, remove dead flower clusters and developing seed pods after blooming.

PIMELEA. Evergreen shrubs and shrublets. Light trimming after flowering is all that is normally required. Do not cut out too much foliage.

PINCUSHION FLOWER. See Scabiosa.

PINE. See Pinus.

PINE, FERN. See Podocarpus.

PINE, YEW. See Podocarpus.

PINEAPPLE GUAVA. See Feijoa.

PINK. See Dianthus.

PINK POWDER PUFF. See Calliandra.

PINUS. Pine. Evergreen trees, rarely shrubs. All pines can be shaped, and usually improved by some pruning. To slow a pine's growth or to fatten up a rangy one, cut back the candles (new growth) when new needles begin to emerge. Cut them back halfway or even more. Leave a few clusters of needles if you want growth to continue along the branch. To shape a pine in the oriental manner is trickier, but not really difficult; it's just a matter of cutting out any branches that interfere with the effect, shortening other branches, and creating an upswept look by removing all twigs that grow downward. Cutting the vertical main trunk back to a well-placed side branch will induce side growth, and wiring or weighting branches will produce cascade effects.

P. mugo mughus. Mugho pine. Shrublike, dwarf mugho pine isn't always as full and compact as you would like. Grows slowly, tends to be broader than tall at maturity. You can maintain or increase compactness by pinching back about half the candles as they begin to unfold in spring. To encourage taller growth and give the plant a more treelike character, remove most branches that lie close to the ground, and if necessary, cut out a few others to accentuate the interesting branch structure. If you prune carefully, the resulting miniature tree often resembles a true bonsai.

P. pinea. Italian stone pine. If you want an Italian stone pine to grow more dense, remove straggling, down-hanging lower branches. At the top of the tree, remove candles annually to force more growth inside the tree top. If you want to make an Italian stone pine look more open, remove several interior branches, cutting each one off where it joins the trunk or a main branch.

P. radiata. Monterey pine. The photographs across the top of the opposite page show how to create dense, Japanese-print looking individual branches in place of the rather amorphous, formless mass that the young or adolescent tree makes on its own.

SEVERAL UNPRUNED 10-year-old Monterey pines. At this size and age, these trees are undistinguished. Next day, the first pruning–photograph at right.

RIGHT AFTER PRUNING, trees look like picked chickens. (They soon fill out.) Many branches and branchlets were removed. Remaining ones headed back.

TWO SUMMERS LATER. Trees now have a shape and are ready for another pruning –to remove new vertical branches like those showing against upper skyline.

CANDLES (clusters of infant needles) on Mugho pine. Candles on other kinds of pines are generally smaller. As a pruner, you remove these candles to keep a pine plant at about the same size; leave them intact to let the pine extend its growth.

VENERABLE Italian stone pine. If tree were smaller, it could be improved by removing down-hanging lower branches.

Pistacia — Pittosporum

PISTACIA. Pistache. Deciduous or semi-evergreen trees.

P. chinensis. Chinese pistache. Deciduous tree. Mature, well-trained tree requires little more than corrective pruning. Young tree must be staked, then pruned and trained for several years to develop head high enough to walk under. Sometimes, branches tend to grow downward; cut them off at trunk. Train to a single trunk, and avoid crowding limbs in any one area on trunk during its youth. Avoid equal narrow crotches that may split later. This way, tree will require less bracing and limbs will not be so likely to split in its mature stages. If tree is budded or grafted, remove buds and suckers forming below graft. Where pendulous branches need stiffening, tie a piece of lath or similar material parallel and close to branch. It will serve as a splint.

P. vera. Pistachio, pistachio nut. Deciduous tree. Stake and train to form a head at desired height. Prune out branches that grow downward. When structure is formed, prune as little as possible, cutting out only weak or damaged wood and suckers below graft of bud (if tree is grafted or budded).

PITTOSPORUM. Evergreen shrubs and trees.

Pittosporum, tree forms (*P. eugenioides, P. tenuifolium, P. undulatum*). Will take all forms of pruning, thinning, or shearing. By clipping and heading back, you can grow them as a hedge and keep them at any level over 5 or 6

PITTOSPORUM EUGENIOIDES hedge being sheared back into formal shape (smooth top and sides). Pole at pruner's left is marked at 6 feet to help him keep top even.

SOFTER LOOKING hedge this way: cut out overly long branches at their bases.

PITTOSPORUM TOBIRA clipped into tiers in narrow space alongside driveway.

LESS-KNOWN, very handsome pittosporum–P. phillyraeoides, the tall plants here. Only pruning this one needs is to help it keep its weeping, ancient-tree look.

ft. almost indefinitely. To force bushiness, shear off 2-6 in. of plant tops several times each year between March and November. Begin shearing sides when necessary. Continue to do this 2 or 3 times a year until plants reach desired size. Then shear the surface whenever necessary—typically, once in spring, again in mid-summer, and again in October or early November. If you prefer a softer, more natural looking surface, prune overlong branches back to laterals or buds inside the body of the hedge. Leave those branches which terminate in approximately the plane where you want the soft and uneven surface.

If plants get woody at the base, prune heavily in spring to encourage new growth. Train pittosporum either as multiple or single-trunked tree.

Pittosporum, shrub forms (P. tobira, P. t. 'Variegata'). Will also tolerate much pruning, but excessive cutting can ruin the natural shape. Has same potential for handsome, multi-stemmed tree as *Feijoa sellowiana* (see page 42). Easily trained to any desired form, they can be grown as trees, used in clipped or informal hedges, kept in containers, or grown as single plants. If a wayward shoot grows above the desired height, pinch it back or cut it off at the base at any time. Pinching will encourage bushier plants.

P. crassifolium. Grows neatly enough so that you don't have to prune it often. Though it can grow to 25 ft. high in 8-10 years, it can be kept to 8 or 10 ft. and as narrow as 6-8 ft. with a yearly pruning. If hedge effect is not desired, selective removal of branches will produce handsome, vertical tree.

P. phillyraeoides. Willow pittosporum. Has weeping, trailing habit. Needs little pruning. Stake against winter storm winds; open up form by thinning out branches to permit winds to blow through.

P. rhombifolium. Queensland pittosporum. Needs little pruning. Grow either as large shrub with foliage to ground, or as single or multiple-trunked tree.

PLANE TREE. See Platanus.

PLANTAIN LILY. See Hosta.

PLATANUS. Plane tree, sycamore. Deciduous trees.

P. acerifolia. (Often sold as *P. orientalis.*) London plane tree. Can be pollarded yearly, after leaf fall, to create dense, low canopy; can also be allowed to grow naturally. Full grown trees require no pruning except to repair damage. Benefit from thinning of smaller branches to open form and expose interesting bark.

P. occidentalis. American sycamore, buttonwood. Has beautiful, natural form

in winter without leaves and needs little or no pruning. Thin out smaller branches to open up form.

P. racemosa. California sycamore. Stands heavy pruning in winter. Easily trained to any trunk and branch form you wish if you start when tree is young. Makes a picturesque multi-trunked clump if given careful early pruning. Remove dead sticks and erratic, reverse growth resulting from blight.

PLATYCLADUS. See Thuja.

PLATYCODON grandiflorum. Balloon flower. Perennial. Keep pinching off old flowers to prolong bloom but don't cut back stems until leaves have withered.

PLUM AND PRUNE. The two kinds of plums are Japanese (*Prunus salicina*), and European (*P. domestica*). Differences in pruning methods are discussed below:

Japanese plums. Belonging to this group are these varieties: 'Beauty,' 'Becky Smith,' 'Burbank,' 'Burmosa,' 'Duarte,' 'Eldorado,' 'Elephant Heart,' 'Formosa,' 'Howard Miracle,' 'Inca,' 'Kelsey,' 'Laroda,' 'Late Santa Rosa,' 'Mariposa,' 'Nubiana,' 'Peach Plum,' 'Queen Ann,' 'Santa Rosa,' 'Satsuma,' 'Shiro,' and 'Wickson.'

Trees make tremendous shoot growth, requiring severe pruning at all ages. Train young trees to vase shape. Cut back to lateral branches. If tree tends to grow upright, cut to outside branches; if it is spreading, cut to inside or vertical branches. Heavy bearing results in quantities of small fruit and possible damage to tree. Thin green fruit drastically as soon as it is big enough to be seen. Leave the remaining fruits 4-6 in. apart.

European plums (including Prune). The following are some of the most popular varieties: 'Damson,' 'French Prune,' 'Green Gage,' 'Imperial,' 'Italian Prune,' 'President,' 'Stanley,' 'Sugar,' 'Tragedy,' and 'Yellow Egg.'

Prune European plums to avoid formation of V-crotches. Mature trees require little pruning—mainly thinning out of annual shoot growth.

PLUM, FLOWERING. See Prunus.

PLUM, JAPANESE FLOWERING. See Prunus.

PLUM, NATAL. See Carissa.

PLUMBAGO auriculata (*P. capensis*). Cape plumbago. Semi-evergreen shrub or vine. Can be trained either as a shrub or a climbing vine. Heavy frosts will kill growth back, but recovery is good. Cut out damaged growth (or cut to ground if badly damaged) after frost danger is past. To train as a shrub, cut back to encourage side branching. Shrub can be

EACH WINTER all of these London plane trees are pollarded (see pages 92 and 93).

renewed by cutting oldest stems to ground each year after blooming. To train as a vine, encourage long growth by pinching back side branches and tying up main branches.

PLUMBAGO, DWARF. See Cerato-stigma.

PLUME CEDAR. See Cryptomeria.

PLUME CRYPTOMERIA. See Cryptomeria.

PLUME FLOWER, BRAZILIAN. See Jacobinia.

PODOCARPUS. Evergreen trees, shrubs.
P. andinus. Shrub or shrubby tree. Can be clipped like yew (*Taxus*) into hedge or screen.
P. falcatus. Tree. Prune it the same as *P. gracilior.*
P. gracilior. (Often sold as *P. elongatus.*) Fern pine. Tree, often grown as an espaliered vine. Responds readily to pruning. Can be encouraged to take various forms. If you start training early, it can be ground cover, vine, shrub, or tree. More than most trees, it needs staking when young until strong trunk develops. Slow to develop, but eventually gets big. Some espaliers have reached 40 ft., towering above walls they were trained against. For ground cover, peg down pliable stems and cut off vertical growth. Trees should be thinned out at regular intervals to show up the handsome gray branch structure. If not especially trained, fern pine becomes 25-30 ft. tree with graceful growth habit. If a plant becomes tall and spindly, cut it back to ground and it will stump sprout. Tree is excellent for multi-stem development or low-branching form. This requires selection

of desired leaders in first 2-3 years and the removal of competitive growth. An old, freely-grown tree can be shaped in same way if studied carefully before cutting. Generally do not require much pruning, though they respond well (will stump sprout if cut to ground) and can be trained as small trees or shrubs, green walls, espaliers, vines, ground covers, or container and house plants. Fairly slow growing, so pinching new tip growth is usually sufficient to keep them to desired size. If heavier pruning is indicated, do it in spring or fall. To grow compact shrubs or hedges, cut leggy branches to ground. When growing as espaliers, keep stems securely tied and remove unwanted growth as it develops.

P. macrophyllus. Yew pine. Shrub or tree. Let it go its way as a narrow, dense, upright tree, or train as hedge, screen, or topiary plant. Can take shearing or severe thinning as a sort of giant bonsai.

P. m. maki. Shrubby yew pine. Shrub. Slower to grow, smaller, shrubbier.

P. nagi. Tree. To preserve weeping look, prune only to remove dead and damaged wood or extra leaders.

P. totara. Totara. Tree. Prune it the same as *P. andinus.*

POINSETTIA. See Euphorbia.

POKER PLANT. See Kniphofia.

POLYGALA. Evergreen shrubs, shrublets. Respond well to heavy pruning, though a light trimming after bloom is all that is normally required. Head rangy plants back to bring down to size.

POLYGONUM. Knotweed. Evergreen and deciduous perennials and vines.

P. aubertii. Silver lace vine. Freezes to ground in winter in most regions and can be cut to ground at that time each year if desired (this will delay bloom until late summer). Where it doesn't freeze to ground, wait until spring to prune; thin out side shoots and cut all main and secondary stems back to third or fourth bud of last year's growth. Fast growing; prune and pinch tips as necessary in summer to keep in bounds.

P. capitatum. Evergreen perennial. This tough ground cover will invade other beds unless confined by edging boards or curbs. It also spreads by seeding. If it mounds up too much, you should whack it back. If burned by frost, don't prune. It will come back nicely.

P. cuspidatum. Japanese knotweed. Perennial. Extremely invasive. Cut to ground in late fall or winter. Underground roots must be controlled to keep plant in bounds.

POLYSTICHUM munitum. See Fern, Hardy.

POMEGRANATE. See Punica.

POMPON TREE. See Dais.

POPLAR. See Populus.

POPPY, MATILIJA. See Romneya.

POPPY, YELLOW HORNED. See Glaucium.

POPULUS. Poplar, cottonwood, aspen. Deciduous trees. Roots extremely invasive; some have reputation for invading and breaking sewer lines. Most produce suckers freely, especially if roots are cut. Nevertheless, it has to be root pruned (see page 92) to stop greedy roots. Rapid growing, with easily-broken limbs. Give usual training while young, maintenance pruning later. Responds well to heavy pruning when required. Some gardeners prefer to let it grow naturally.

PORCELAIN GINGER. See Alpinia.

PORTUGAL LAUREL. See Prunus, Evergreen.

PORTULACARIA afra. Elephant's food, purslane tree, spekboom. Succulent. Pruning not necessary, though it can be pruned and shaped into an informal screen, unclipped hedge, or high-growing ground cover. Responds well to opening up and is willing subject for almost any form. In containers, terminal growth will take on weeping character if placed in shade for 2 or 3 months and then returned to sun. Some pruning may be necessary to prevent plant from becoming topheavy or to bring symmetry to lopsided plant.

POTATO VINE. See Solanum.

POTENTILLA. Cinquefoil. Evergreen and deciduous perennials and shrubs. Shrubby types respond well to heavy pruning, although they require almost none beyond removal of any damaged wood in early spring.

PRAYER PLANT. See Maranta.

PRIDE OF MADEIRA. See Echium.

PRIMROSE TREE. See Lagunaria.

PRINCESS FLOWER. See Tibouchina.

PRIVET. See Ligustrum.

PRUNE. See Plum, European.

PRUNUS. Deciduous and evergreen trees and shrubs. The edible-fruit trees that belong to *Prunus* are better known as the "stone fruits" and are listed elsewhere in this encyclopedia under their common names (see Almond, Apricot, Cherry, Peach and Nectarine, Plum and Prune).

Take away the fruit trees and you have left two classes of ornamentals: evergreens, and deciduous flowering fruit trees and shrubs.

QUAKING ASPEN (typical of Populus) looks handsome with lower branches off.

EVERGREEN FORMS

P. caroliniana. Carolina laurel cherry. Evergreen shrub or tree. Slow growing, needs little pruning if grown as upright shrub. Pinch back wayward shoots that develop above main body of the plant. It can be well branched from ground up and useful as formal, clipped hedge or tall screen. Can be sheared into formal shapes. Trained as small tree, will become broad-topped and reach 35-40 ft. Requires average pruning to shape; heading back causes it to spread.

P. ilicifolia. Hollyleaf cherry. Evergreen shrub or small tree. Use as small tree, tall screen, or formal clipped hedge of any height (for hedge training procedures, see *Pittosporum*). Stands pruning well.

P. laurocerasus. English laurel. Evergreen large shrub or small tree. Stands heavy shearing, but at expense of considerable mutilation of leaves and loss of flowers and fruit. Unless grown as formal, sheared hedge, needs some pruning to open dense canopy of foliage. For low hedges or screens, plant dwarf varieties. Best pruned not by shearing but one cut at a time, just above a leaf on overlong twigs. Untrimmed plant will grow 18-30 ft. tall, occasionally more. If too large, reduce size by selective pruning over a season or two. To transform overgrown shrub into tree, see *Viburnum*.

P. l. 'Zabeliana.' Zabel laurel. Evergreen shrub. With branches pegged down it makes effective bank cover. Can be espaliered or grown flat against an entrance wall; clip twice yearly. Moderately fast growing—to 4 ft. high

THESE FLOWERING CHERRIES have been pruned to emphasize the open and sparse growth habit that is typical of all the forms. The tree at left could yield as many as 10 or 12 cut branches-in-bloom for indoor display without hurting its form. They could have been cut for that purpose before buds opened.

WEEPING CHERRY grafted high on standard trunk. To keep form, pinch out any wild upright twigs and rub out all sprouts growing from trunk below graft.

SHEARED HEDGE of Prunus ilicifolia. Plants spaced 18 inches apart were headed back often when young to force low branches. Now, shearing just maintains size.

NATURAL HEDGE of Prunus lyonii. Plants were spaced 5 feet apart. Here, 12 years later, they are 15 feet high. Prune only to remove broken or ungainly limbs.

and usually wider—but can be held lower by removing vertical branches. Then branches fan out, reaching no more than 2 ft. high, much wider.

P. lusitanica. Portugal laurel. Evergreen shrub or tree. If left to grow naturally, becomes densely branched large shrub 10-20 ft. high or many-trunked spreading tree to 30 ft. However, can be kept to 6 ft. or under without difficulty. Sometimes used as formal hedge, but clipping mutilates its 5-in. leaves, destroys grace, and eliminates flowers and fruit. Cut branches for indoor arrangements at any time since it stands heavy pruning and topping. Makes an unusually neat and controllable tub plant and can be trained into formal tree or espalier while kept in container.

P. l. azorica. Grows into gigantic columnar bush 20 ft. high and half as wide.

P. lyonii (*P. integrifolia, P. ilicifolia integrifolia*). Catalina cherry. Evergreen shrub or tree. Can be held to any height desired by regular pruning and can be trimmed to any shape.

FLOWERING FRUITS

Flowering Cherry. Fast growing deciduous tree 20-25 ft. high and as wide. Should be headed up if canopy wanted; tends to branch close to ground. Do as little pruning as possible. Remove sucker growth—any buds or branches that appear below the graft. Cut branches while tree is in bloom for use in arrangements. Remove awkward or crossing branches. Pinch back an occasional overly-ambitious shoot to force new growth. If diseased branch dies back, prune out affected area. To be on safe side, disinfect pruning tools between cuts. Pruning in early years to force multiple branching can correct its rather open and sparse growth habit.

Flowering Nectarine. Pruning procedures are the same as for Flowering Peach (see below).

Flowering Peach. Training and growth habits are same as for fruiting peach (see Peach and Nectarine). Heavy pruning is required for good show of flowers. Cut branches back to 6-in. stubs at or immediately after flowering time. With lighter pruning you avoid sheared-back look but reduce next year's flower display. Entire top growth flowers on 1-year wood. Thin out old wood, dense or crossing branches, and dead growth. Remove suckers from understock.

Flowering Plum. Prune young tree to establish a head at height you can walk under. Remove suckers that appear below graft. As tree develops, prune out crossing and inward-growing branches. Remove vigorous vertical branches that shoot up from inner parts of tree (water

sprouts) unless one is needed to replace a broken or damaged branch. Densely branched, so must be pruned to prevent twigginess. Do heavy pruning when trees are dormant. Prunings can be taken inside for forcing into bloom. Light trimming after flowering controls shape. To put in container, prune roots heavily and thin top branches to an open frame.

P. glandulosa. Dwarf flowering almond. (See also *P. triloba*.) Deciduous multi-stem shrub. Flowers carried on year-old wood, so prune back hard either just after blooming or when in bloom to get long whips for next year's wands of bloom.

P. mume. Japanese flowering apricot, Japanese flowering plum. Deciduous tree. Prune heavily after flowering. Cutting back long, one-year, whip-like growth forces laterals which produce heaviest crop of flowers. Let grow for a year, then prune back all shoots to 6-in. stubs. The following year cut back half of young growth to 6-in. stubs; cut back the other half the following year, and continue this routine in succeeding years. When roots are restricted, the plant puts on less vegetative growth.

P. triloba. Flowering almond. Small tree or treelike large shrub. Usually grows slowly to about 15 ft. high, with equal spread. Cut branches as soon as flowers fade in spring. At the same time, remove any old wood and dead growth. If grafted and trained as small standard tree, remove suckers below graft and rub off buds along trunk.

PSEUDOTSUGA menziesii (*P. taxifolia*). Douglas fir. Conifer. As a garden tree, its height is difficult to control; you can't keep it down without butchering it. To slow the growth, pinch young growth as described on page 92. Trees need guidance when young. Be sure a good, strong single leader is formed. If young leader is damaged, select best upper horizontal branch, brace and train it upright to become new leader. Roots are greedy and invasive, need occasional pruning. You can plant young trees close together, top them, and trim into a 10-12 ft. hedge.

PSIDIUM cattleianum. Strawberry guava. Evergreen shrub or small tree. If it gets tall and unmanageable, it can be pruned by removing whole branches to shape into small tree or cut back to make bushy shrub. Thin small branches to make an informal pattern. Makes a good informal hedge or screen, fine bonsai subject. Can also be trained into interesting multi-stem form (see *Feijoa sellowiana*).

PTEROSTYRAX hispida. Epaulette tree. Deciduous tree. Will grow up to 40 ft.

but can be held to shrub height of 15-20 ft. and width of 10 ft. Needs normal guidance to shape while young (see training procedure for young trees, page 95). Cut out winter damaged wood in spring.

PTYCHOSPERMA macarthuri. See Palm.

PUNICA granatum. Pomegranate. Deciduous tree or shrub. If you buy a bare-root pomegranate, cut it back hard before planting to restore balance between large, bushy top and roots which have been severely cut back in digging. Whether it becomes a thicket, shrub, or tree depends upon how you train it. If not pruned each year by removing suckers at the base, it becomes a formless thicket. You can select the number of stems you want and hold it to those as a shrub, or you can force it to become tree-like by cutting away all but its strongest single stem when you plant it, each year cutting out any new growth from the base. To train as an espalier, select a few strong shoots and fasten fanwise to a support. Suppress suckers, and shorten side branches to hold plant in bounds. Dormant pruning consists of thinning out oldest, weakest wood. Old, neglected plants are good subjects for pruning into interesting shapes.

P. g. 'Chico.' Dwarf carnation-flowered pomegranate. Compact bush, can be kept to 18 in. tall if headed back occasionally.

P. g. 'Nana.' Dwarf pomegranate. Rounded, dense, and twiggy, will grow to 3 ft. tall but can easily be kept at 2 ft.

PURPLE CONEFLOWER. See Echinacea.

PURPLE HEART. See Setcreasea.

PURSLANE TREE. See Portulacaria.

PUSSY WILLOW. See Salix.

PYRACANTHA. Firethorn. Evergreen shrubs. Blossoms and fruits are produced on short spurlike branches growing from 2-year-old wood. Withstands severe pruning. Degree and timing depend somewhat on gardener's objectives. Normally grown as bushes or espaliered (formally or informally) against walls and fences. Can also be trained as standards, clipped into hedges or topiary, though many gardeners feel clipping spoils plant's rugged informality (it will probably also curtail the colorful berry crop). Low growing varieties are good ground covers; on these, shorten any runaway vertical shoots. Size and form can be controlled from the start by pinching new young growth in spring and shortening overly long branches that tend to develop during the years. During bloom period, pinch out flowering branches just above first flower clus-

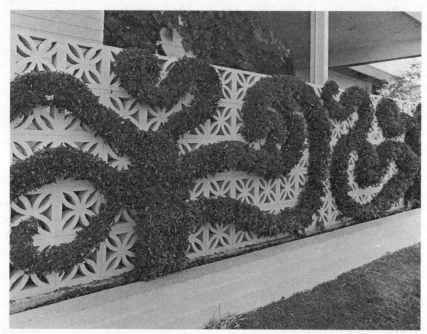

PYRACANTHA in stylized shape. Original trunk and selected side shoots are tied in place to make the pattern. Side shoots cut back regularly to hold pattern.

ter. This will produce neat little packages of berries to form in following fall and winter and will keep plant in check. Cut branches that have borne berries back to a well-placed side shoot (don't leave stubs to die back and cause rot). For maximum fruit crop, remove all bearing wood as soon as berries have dropped. To keep plant vigorous and renewed, cut oldest wood to ground in most dormant period (between berry drop and the beginning of new growth). In areas where temperatures occasionally drop below 24°, prune after March 1. When cutting berried branches for decoration, let cutting serve as constructive pruning. Thin out crowded centers and try not to alter basic shape of shrub. Don't try to grow pyracantha in small area or you'll be continually butchering it to keep in bounds.

PYRETHRUM. See Chrysanthemum.

PYROSTEGIA venusta (*P. ignea, Bignonia venusta*). Flame vine. Evergreen vine. Fast grower; prune in spring before new growth begins to keep it under control.

PYRUS kawakamii. Evergreen pear. Evergreen shrub or tree. The way it accommodates pruning makes it a most versatile plant. You can make it take almost whatever form you wish: limber-limbed sprawling shrub; formal or informal espalier; neat, middle-sized spreading street or lawn tree as tall as 30 ft.; screen; or container plant. The first year or so it grows rather bushy and needs staking. Without support,

evergreen pear becomes a broad, sprawling shrub, or in time, a multi-trunked small tree. With willowy young branches fastened to fence or frame, it makes a good-looking espalier. Evergreen pears trained as trees take a couple of years to outgrow young gawky stage but in 10 years can be 20 ft. wide and reach as high. To make a tree of it, stake one or several trunks, remove side growth, and keep staked until trunk is self-supporting. Beef up framework branches by shortening (when young) to upward facing buds or branchlets. For a thick screen, space plants 10 ft. apart. For espaliers, just bend long limber branches where you want them to go, thin out growth that will not become part of structure, and shorten long stems. Continuous pruning can keep a plant small enough for a trellis or in a formal candelabra shape but may curtail or prevent flowering. You can train a plant to grow flat against a wall by supporting it with a wire framework and cutting off branches that head out. Vigorous plants trained like this can sometimes cover the side of a two-story house in 7 or 8 years. Spring pruning can encourage more flowers. After bloom, cut ⅔ of previous year's growth off each branch. Plants are susceptible to fireblight; remedial pruning is the same as for *Pyracantha.*

QUEENSLAND KAURI. See Agathis.

QUEENSLAND NUT. See Macadamia.

QUEENSLAND POPLAR. See Homalanthus.

QUEENSLAND UMBRELLA TREE. See Brassaia.

QUERCUS. Oak. Deciduous or evergreen trees. Young oaks tend to grow twiggy. Growth is divided among so many twigs that none elongate fast. To promote fast vertical growth, pinch off tips of unwanted small branches, retaining all leaf surface possible in order to sustain maximum growth. A young healthy oak that is heavily thinned will often grow at a much faster rate than one that is left alone. If the young oak has been shaped and trained properly, annual pruning will be primarily corrective and preventive: removing dead branches, spurs of broken branches, suckering growth, or diseased and weak wood, and thinning out to avoid wind and storm damage. Oaks can be pruned at just about any time. Where mildew is a problem on evergreen oaks, prune in winter to reduce mildew-susceptible new growth. Some tree experts feel you can do a better job on deciduous types when they are in full foliage. Large cuts on oaks and other trees should be treated with sealing compound (repeat yearly for cuts over 4 in. until they have healed over).

Q. palustris. Pin oak. Deciduous. May require more attention than other oaks. As a young tree it may need help to develop natural leader. Older tree often requires removal of down-sweeping lower branches to permit foot traffic under it. Lower branches tend to support each other. Removing lowest tier may not be enough if higher ones later drop lower.

QUILLAJA saponaria. Soapbark tree. Evergreen tree. Tends toward multiple trunks and excessive bushiness but responds quickly to pruning. Prune to shape as necessary. Can be pruned as tall hedge if desired.

QUINCE, FLOWERING. See Chaenomeles.

QUINCE, FRUITING. Deciduous shrub or small tree. Prune only to form a trunk and shape the frame. Keep the center open for air and light, and thin out and cut back only enough to stimulate new growth. Heading back will reduce the crop since fruit is borne on new wood at the tips. It's desirable to have many small shoots on the tree.

RABBIT TRACKS. See Maranta.

RAPHIOLEPIS. Evergreen shrubs. Require little pruning or training, but for bushier, more compact plants prune them from start. Pinch back tips of branches at least once each year, after flowering. For more open structure, let grow naturally, sometimes thinning out branches. Encourage spreading by shortening vertical branches. Pinch side branches to encourage upright growth. Occasional pinching of stem ends will control their shape. Some raphiolepis have been budded on quince rootstock; you may have to cut off quince shoots occasionally. They will appear from below the graft with light green, soft leaves. As plant grows and base becomes shaded by foliage, suckering is less frequent. Encourage rather flat growth by removing the central or crown branches. Or encourage erect growth, leaving vertical branches intact and removing some side branches.

RASPBERRY. Most popular and heaviest bearers are red raspberries that have erect canes and do not branch readily. They can be grown as free standing shrubs, staked, or tied to wires or trellises. At planting time, cut the 1-2 ft. cane back to about 8 in. This young cane serves mainly as a marker; new shoots arise from its base. Let shoots grow undisturbed through one growing season. Next spring, just before growth starts, cut out small and weak canes and cut back remaining canes to 5 ft. (They will probably have to be tied to a stake or trellis to keep them from whipping in the wind.) Beginning the second year, prune plants as follows: remove all canes that have fruited immediately after harvesting. This pruning makes room for new canes to develop freely. Leave about 7 canes on an average mature plant, more on an especially vigorous one, fewer on a weak one. Tie selected canes in a bunch in fall to protect over winter. Do major pruning in spring before buds begin to swell. (In areas with strong winter winds, head back in fall.) In the spring, head back canes to 4½-5 ft., shorten side branches to 2 in. Retie individual canes for support. As soon as red raspberries begin active growth, they start sending up suckers. Leave canes that come up where you first planted them, pull others up by roots to prevent too rampant growth. Fall-bearing varieties differ slightly in pruning needs. Fruit laterals form and bear fruit near top of the current year's cane. Cut off upper portion that has borne fruit instead of taking out entire cane. Lower parts will then fruit next spring. Cut out cane only after it has fruited along its entire length.

Black raspberry (Blackcap). These have a branching growth habit. New plants form when arching cane tips root in the soil. Red raspberries, in contrast, come up from roots. This is why growers tip pinch black raspberries during growing season to encourage branching. Tip pinching red raspberries, on the other hand, tends to encourage more sucker growth instead of more branch-ing. Post-harvest care of black raspberries is similar to that of red raspberries: cut out portions that have borne berries. Dormant pruning and training are quite different, though. With black raspberries, encourage branching by heading back or pinching new shoots when they reach 2-2½ ft. Completely remove any new canes that appear during or after harvest. Dormant season pruning consists of shortening side branches on headed canes to from 5-8 buds.

RATSTRIPPER. See Pachistima.

RAUWOLFIA samarensis. (Often sold as *Alstonia scholaris*.) India devil tree. Semi-deciduous tree. Cut off any limbs that tend to grow toward the center of the tree in a way that would be incongruous with the natural skeleton. Remove lower branches that have died from overhead shading. It is normal for rauwolfia to become high-headed. Under no circumstances permit shearing, for the charm of this plant is an open structure that displays pale gray areas between layers of elegant foliage.

RED CEDAR, WESTERN. See Thuja.

RED CHOKEBERRY. See Aronia.

RED VALERIAN. See Centranthus.

REDBERRY. See Rhamnus.

REDBUD. See Cercis.

RED-HOT POKER. See Kniphofia.

REDWOOD. See Sequoia.

RHAMNUS. Evergreen or deciduous shrubs or trees.

R. alaternus. Italian buckthorn. Evergreen shrub. Can be kept in bounds with minimum of training. Easily shaped or sheared as screen or tall clipped hedge. Can also be trained as single-stem small tree.

R. a. 'Variegata' (*R. a.* 'Argenteo-variegata'). Has leaves edged in creamy white. To retain striking appearance, cut out plain green branches that occasionally appear.

R. californica. Coffeeberry. Evergreen shrub. Doesn't require much pruning. To keep dwarf varieties low and compact, pinch or prune out upright growth.

R. crocea. Redberry. Evergreen shrub. Will stand a lot of shearing. Untrimmed, it may reach 3 ft.

R. c. ilicifolia. Holly-leaf redberry. Evergreen shrub to 15 ft. Prune to shape and to increase density of foliage.

R. frangula. Alder buckthorn. Deciduous shrub or small tree. Set 2½ ft. apart for tight, narrow hedge that needs minimum of trimming and can be kept as low as 4 ft.

RHAPIDOPHYLLUM. See Palm.

RHAPIS. See Palm.

RHODODENDRON (including azalea). Evergreen or deciduous shrubs, rarely trees. If plants have been pinched and trained for proper branching and shape from an early stage, later major pruning chores will be corrective and limited to the removal of damaged or dead wood.

To keep mature plants healthy and productive, continue a regular program

PINCHING to make an azalea bushy. First, pinch as at upper left, then upper right.

of pinching shoots and cutting the flowers. The major difference between azaleas and rhododendrons is the azaleas have growth buds all along their stems, just under bark surface. As a result, new growth will originate close to any cut you make. (Some growers therefore give azaleas a "butch haircut" by clipping with hedge shears.) Cuts on rhododendrons, on the other hand, should always be made just above leaf rosettes since new growth emerges from dormant eyes there. If you have to cut into the stem below any leaf rosettes, look for faint rings on bark that mark where there once were leaves at the ends of previous growth periods. Small bumps under the bark there are growth buds, and cuts should be made just above these rings. Winter or spring is the preferred pruning season in mild climates; spring, after frost no longer threatens, is preferable where winters are severe. Best pruning time for maximum bloom is just after flowering (or during bloom if cut flowers are to be used). Winter and pre-bloom pruning is likely to remove some of bloom unless pruning is

SOME EVERGREEN AZALEAS, especially the Kurume types, naturally maintain themselves in neat mounds like this. On others, lanky branch tips sometimes mar the outline. Clip back such errant growth to maintain an outline like this.

DEADHEADING on a rhododendron. Bend back old flower clusters and pull. Don't touch growth buds below flowers.

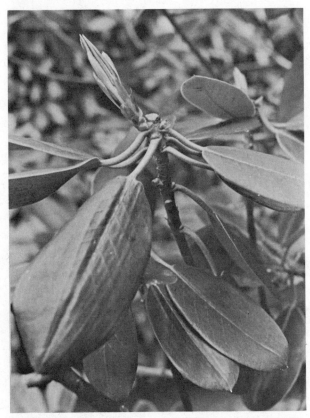

NEW GROWTH here came from growth bud beneath flower truss such as shown in photograph at upper right.

REMOVING heavy branch on a rhododendron. Branch has been pre-cut all around so falling limb can't tear bark from trunk.

very light and selective, allowing many flower buds to remain.

One good pruning technique when plants are in bloom is to cut out crossing, awkward branches that destroy the symmetry of the plants, using them as cut flowers. To conserve plants' energy, remove faded flower trusses on rhododendrons before seed pods form. Be careful not to damage the buds just starting growth at the base of the flower stem. (These will form next year's flowers and leaves.)

After azaleas' main blooming period, you can (if the plants need pruning) pinch out tips of new growth or shear the surface with hedge shears. This produces bushy, uniformly branched plants with a crop of flower buds uniformly distributed over the surface. Both azaleas and rhododendrons respond well to restorative pruning. Stems of deciduous azaleas often become woody and unproductive as they grow older. They will remain vigorous and give you lots of flowers if you systematically remove old, declining wood each year. At any indication of reduced vigor, cut weakening stem to ground; new growth will soon replace it.

You may also rejuvenate overgrown evergreen azaleas and rhododendrons in the same way. Cut back oldest, heaviest limbs to a foot or less (but always above growth rings on rhododendrons); from these, strong new shoots will grow to fill in plants. By doing this progressively over 3 seasons, removing about ⅓ of old growth each year, you can transform rangy, open, overgrown shrubs into compact and colorful ones. The entire plant can be cut back in one operation (sometimes it is necessary to treat a damaged plant this way). However, you will lose all flowers for a year or two and run a greater risk of losing the plant. Be sure to cut out old weak stems entirely. These will not improve under better care.

RHODOTYPOS. Jetbead. Deciduous shrub. Will withstand heavy pruning, preferably after flowers and berries are gone. Prune to shape as required, cutting out some oldest canes to ground every few years to renew.

RHOICISSUS capensis (*Cissus capensis*). Evergreen grape. Evergreen vine. Needs to be controlled to keep in bounds. Do this with constant pinching back of tips during growing season rather than pruning severely at one time; heavy pruning may cause dieback.

RHOPALOSTYLIS. See Palm.

RHUBARB. Perennial. It's best to harvest stalks by grasping near base and pulling sideways and outward. Cutting with a knife is supposed to leave stubs

that will decay (it doesn't always happen). Cut out flower stalks as soon as they appear, or plant's energy will go toward producing them at the expense of foliage.

RHUS. Sumac. Evergreen or deciduous shrubs or trees. Pruning and training varies with type and function.

R. aromatica. Fragrant sumac. Deciduous shrub. Should be pruned each year in early spring. Because fast spreading stems root and sprout readily, some root pruning may be necessary to keep in bounds.

R. glabra. Smooth sumac. Deciduous large shrub or small tree. Treated best as shrub. Can be invasive; root prune and pull or dig out suckers if plant spreads too far. Cut back hard in early spring to control form.

R. lancea. African sumac. Evergreen tree. Can be trained in several different ways: with foliage to the ground, with a single trunk, or in an interesting multiple-stemmed effect (its natural way to grow).

R. laurina. Laurel sumac. Evergreen shrub. Gets rangy unless trimmed frequently. If it freezes, it will recover quickly and grow back from stump. Can also be trained as espalier or trimmed as hedge.

R. ovata. Sugar bush. Evergreen shrub. Can be pruned as small tree but is adaptable only to light pruning. Slow to fill in if heavily pruned or after limb breakage.

R. typhina. Staghorn sumac. Deciduous shrub or small tree. Best trained as small tree. One attractive feature is bare-branched winter form, so prune lightly in early spring and remove only weak, crossing, or unattractive limbs.

RIBES. Currant, gooseberry. (See these entries for fruiting kinds.) Deciduous and evergreen shrubs.

R. aureum. Golden currant. Deciduous shrub. Shape by pruning after bloom. Can be rejuvenated in fall by cutting back to the ground the oldest, weakest stems. Do not head back branches in the fall or you'll remove next spring's flowers.

R. alpinum. Alpine currant. Deciduous shrub. Usually sheared as hedge. Best pruned in late spring after new growth is established.

R. sanguineum. Pink winter currant, red flowering currant. Deciduous shrub. Responds well to pruning after blooming period.

R. s. 'glutinosum.' Pink flowering currant. Can take any amount of pruning after flowering.

R. viburnifolium. Catalina perfume, evergreen currant. Spreading evergreen shrub. Will take a moderate amount of pruning. Can be used as a ground cover,

trailer, or low-spreading border shrub. Cut out upright growing stems to keep low. It can also be trained against a wall, but its slender stems must be supported.

RICE PAPER PLANT. See Tetrapanax.

RICINUS communis. Castor bean. Annual in colder areas, perennial in mild climates. Can be pruned severely to keep it bushy and under control. New growth shoots out readily along the cut-back stems. In areas of light frosts, where plant is fairly well-established, it will break out new growth from lower portions of stems in the spring. After new growth has progressed, cut frost-killed leaves and stems back to green wood. In frost-free areas, you may want to renew plant's vigor by cutting it back to 4 or 5 ft. each spring. The beans are highly toxic, so it is best to cut them off. If it gets too woody, dig it up and start a new one.

ROBINIA. Locust. Deciduous trees or shrubs. Fast growing, brittle wood. Need training and pruning for structure and shape in early years. Roots are aggressive, and plants will spread by suckers if not contained.

R. hispida. Rose acacia. Deciduous shrub. Has spreading, suckering habit. Prune to keep in bounds. Umbrella-shaped tree grafted on black locust will need careful staking to prevent breakage, blowover.

R. pseudoacacia. Black locust. Deciduous tree. Attractive bare-leafed form in winter can be considerably improved by selective branch removal after bloom. Wood is brittle; corrective pruning is sometimes required for broken, damaged limbs.

ROCKCRESS. See Arabis.

ROCKROSE. See Cistus.

ROMNEYA coulteri. Matilija poppy. Perennial. Flowers, cut in bud, will open in water and last a few days. Plant dies back each winter and should be cut nearly to the ground in early fall. New shoots will emerge, and next spring you'll have a much more vigorous plant with better blossoms than if you had left plant to its own devices. Vigorous, spreading roots may need curbing.

RONDELETIA. Evergreen shrubs. Cut back as soon as flowering season is over, especially when young. Remove old leaves that tend to hang on, as well as faded flower custers, to keep plants neat and encourage longer blooming.

ROSA. Rose. Deciduous, bushy or climbing shrubs (a few evergreen in warm climates). Rose plants require pruning to make them produce good flowers and to keep them from growing into hopeless thorny tangles. Some gardeners favor only a light annual pruning, others advocate cutting roses back heavily each year.

Pruning requirements for the different types of roses vary. Some climatic factors also influence pruning methods. Generally, however, most rose growers have come to favor a light to moderate pruning instead of the hard cutting back which was once the accepted practice.

Timing. The best time for pruning roses is toward the end of the dormant season when growth buds along the canes begin to swell. In general, you should do the pruning in winter or early spring but not so early that the tender new growth which follows will be damaged by late frosts.

Basic objectives are to develop an attractive framework and to encourage growth of new, flowering wood. Here are a few basic guidelines for pruning the various types of roses:

Bush roses: Hybrid Teas, Grandifloras, Floribundas. Remove all dead wood and all weak, twiggy branches. If an older cane produced nothing but weak growth, remove it right at its base —at the bud union.

Open up the center of the bush by removing all branches that cross through the center. This gives you a "vase shaped" plant. It's a slender or a fat vase, depending on how upright or spreading the variety grows. The vase should be free of twigs and leaves in the middle where insects could hide.

Remove up to ⅓ of the length of all growth that was new during the previous year. A convenient rule-of-thumb: don't cut into growth of the past season that is bigger around than a pencil.

If you live where winter protection is necessary and you use a method that requires reducing the bush size to fit the protector, you will probably have to remove more than ⅓ of the past year's growth. Cut out *all* damaged wood regardless of how low this leaves your bushes. Prune all stems and canes back to wood that is light green to cream-white in the center. Even though a cane may be green on the outside, if the center is brown it is damaged.

Make all cuts ¼-in. above a leaf bud and at a 45° angle, with the lowest point on the side of the stem opposite the bud.

Paint all cuts larger than pencil size with a sealing compound. This is especially important for cuts to the bud union.

Cutting flowers. Any removal of flowers can be considered pruning, with a few guidelines of its own. Remember that leaves help provide nutrients for the plants, so you must leave a good supply on the bush. When you want a few long-stemmed beauties for inside, cut each stem so that you leave *at least* two sets

of leaves on the branch from which you cut the flower. Otherwise, when you remove faded blooms from the bushes, cut down only as far as the first five-leaflet leaf that points away from the bush's center.

New rose bushes and weak or small plants that you're trying to build up need all possible leaves to manufacture nutrients. With these plants, just snap off the faded flowers and cut no blossoms with stems for the house.

Climbing Hybrid Teas, Grandifloras and Floribundas. Several distinct growth and flowering habits are grouped in the category of "climbing rose." What they all have in common is long, flexible canes which produce flowers along their length. For their first 2 or 3 years in your garden, just tie new canes into position, remove dead canes, weak growth, and spent flowers. Then, after growth patterns are established and some wood has matured, you can begin to prune plants.

In several years' time, the plant will consist solely of long canes produced after you planted it in your garden. From these canes will come side branches (laterals) which will bear the flowers. Beginning then, prune to encourage growth of more flowering laterals and to stimulate production of new canes to gradually replace the oldest and less productive ones. Varieties differ in this respect; some will always throw out new canes from the base each year while others get woodier and produce long new cane growth from higher on the plant. Don't cut back the long canes at all unless any of them are growing too long for the allotted space. Whenever any long canes or branches grow in a direction you don't want, train them into place. If you can't train them, remove them. But remember—the long growths produce the flowering laterals.

For the annual pruning, remove only old, unproductive wood. Then cut back to 2 or 3 buds all laterals that bore flowers during the last year. Best blooms grow on laterals from 2 or 3-year-old wood.

During the flowering season remove all spent blooms. Cut them back to a strong bud 2 or 3 leaves away from the flowering shoot's point of origin.

Pillar Rose. Two sorts of climbing roses are grown as flowering pillars up to about 10 ft. tall. One is the Hybrid Tea or Floribunda climber which grows short climbing canes (about 8-10 ft. long); the other is a natural pillar type which grows 6-10 ft. upright canes that will flower along their length. Pruning objectives and methods are the same as for climbing Hybrid Teas; the principal difference is that you will want to train all long new growth vertically.

Large-Flowered Climbers. Some of these bloom only once a year (examples: 'Dr. W. van Fleet' and 'Paul's Scarlet Climber'). After they finish flowering, cut out the least productive old wood and any weak or entangling branches. New growth will come from the base, and other strong new growth will come from older canes that you leave. From this strong new growth come most of the lateral branches that will carry next year's flowers.

Large-flowered climbers that repeat their bloom throughout the growing year include such favorites as 'Don Juan,' 'Golden Showers,' 'Kassel,' and 'New Dawn.' They produce flowers from new canes and laterals as well as from wood more than a year old. Prune them like climbing Hybrid Teas (see this page).

Ramblers. Each year after spring bloom Rambler roses produce many long, vigorous, and limber canes from the base of the plant. Next spring's flowers come from this new growth. Typically, flowers are small but in large clusters or trusses and come only once annually. However, this spring flower display can be overwhelming.

Wait to prune Ramblers until flowering has finished and new growth is underway. Then, cut out all canes that just flowered and show no sign of producing any long, vigorous new growth. As the new canes mature, train them into correct position.

These are perhaps the highest-maintenance plants among roses because they renew themselves almost completely each year and require annual training to look their best.

Training Climbing Roses. The most profuse bloom comes from Climbers whose canes are trained horizontally or are trained upward and arched over. A long climbing cane left alone will continue to build new tissue to increase only its upward growth. This is a situation known as *apical dominance*: the topmost growth continues at the expense of any lateral growth. However, when a long, upright cane is arched over or bent down to a horizontal position, many eyes along the cane will begin to grow—each one growing upward. These laterals off main canes and long branches make flowers.

If you have a high fence, wall, or side of a house to cover, let the vertical canes grow to about 10 ft. long. Then spread them out at an angle from the plant's base, spacing them evenly, and arch each one and tie it in place with the end pointing downward. Flowering shoots will come from the arched sections of the canes.

Climbers trained horizontally along a low fence or wall will tend to produce

CLIMBING ROSE 'Mrs. Sam McGredy' ready for winter pruning in a mild California climate (leaves and flowers still on).

FLOWERING SHOOTS cut back to spurs about 6 inches long. Note how canes are arched with ends pointing down.

DORMANT PRUNING on Hybrid Tea. Here a cut to remove crossing branch. Remove other crossing branches and weak twigs.

LAST CUT on same Hybrid Tea. Strong canes remain; side shoots shortened. About ⅓ of last year's growth removed.

TREE ROSE before pruning. Growth to be removed: twiggy and crossing branches, close branches, damaged branches.

PRUNING COMPLETED. Branches fairly evenly spaced; crown symmetrical. All cuts made to outward facing buds.

flowering shoots from most buds in the horizontal portions of the canes.

Pruning Shrub and Old Roses. These durable and venerable species and varieties represent so many types and growth habits that it is difficult to make many generalizations. Most, however, are vigorous growers which may need some thinning and shaping each year but very little actual cutting back. As most of these roses are used for showy shrubs or in hedges, the main pruning should be to trim and shape them to fit their place. Cut back any shoots which mar the general pattern and remove any old, unproductive canes. Removal of weak or damaged wood completes the job.

Pruning Standard Roses. Objective in pruning tree roses is to keep crowns symmetrical and branches evenly spaced. First remove all leaves, rose fruits (hips) and dead, weak, and damaged branches. Next, cut out small twiggy growth and crossing branches. Then, cut back branches in crown back to a promising, outward facing bud. (Make slanting cuts, just above the bud.) If you remove an entire branch, cut it flush to the trunk or stem. Be careful not to remove branches that are essential for a balanced crown. Finally, remove any suckers that have formed below bud union. Retie plant to its stake if necessary.

ROSE. See Rosa.

ROSE ACACIA. See Robinia.

ROSE APPLE. See Syzygium.

ROSE OF SHARON. See Hibiscus.

ROSEMARY. See Rosmarinus.

ROSMARINUS officinalis. Rosemary. Evergreen shrub, herb. Under good growing conditions, growth can get rather leggy without adequate pruning. Control growth by frequent tip pinching when plant is small. Prune older plant lightly, making all cuts to side branches. Some varieties can be clipped as hedges. Head back after bloom to encourage new growth. Leave bushy to ground or cut off lower branches to expose one or more gnarly trunks. Gnarly old branches need no pruning.

R. o. 'Prostratus.' Dwarf rosemary. Low growing, needs little pruning. Thin out old wood after bloom to keep new growth coming. Can be pinched or sheared to keep as flat cover.

ROYAL TRUMPET TREE. See Distictis.

RUBBER PLANT. See Ficus.

RUDBECKIA hirta. Gloriosa daisy, black-eyed susan. Biennial or short-lived perennial. Cut plant back down to ground after it finishes blooming in fall and before it goes to seed; or remove spent flowers before seeding.

R. laciniata 'Hortensia.' Golden glow. Perennial. Spreads aggressively by underground stems. Root prune to keep in bounds.

RUSSIAN OLIVE. See Elaeagnus.

SABAL. Palmetto. Fan palms. On some types, dead leaves are shed; on others, they fold and hang down. Only pruning required is removal of dead leaves for appearance.

SACRED FLOWER OF THE INCAS. See Cantua.

SAGE. See Salvia.

ST. JOHN'S BREAD. See Ceratonia.

ST. JOHNSWORT. See Hypericum.

SAINTPAULIA ionantha. African violet. Evergreen perennial. As plant sheds its lower leaves it may develop an awkward trunklike stem. You can shorten the stem and restore plant to more pleasing appearance by taking off the lower row of leaves and cutting off rosette with an inch of stem. Plant that piece to make it root again. If bare part of stem is not long enough for this procedure, take plant out of pot and cut off bottom of the root mass. Scrape bare stem slightly above remaining roots (dust with rooting hormone) and repot to about ¼ in. below bottom row of leaves. As new roots develop quickly, you'll have greatly improved plant.

Separate multiple-crown plants into single crowns and repot. Carefully trim off side growths (suckers) and root them for new plants.

SALAD BURNET. See Sanguisorba.

SALAL. See Gaultheria.

SALIX. Willow. Deciduous trees or shrubs. Because all forms have invasive roots, they need to be root pruned occasionally to keep them in bounds. On any willow, at any time, cut out branches that are dead, diseased, or infested with borers.

S. alba 'Tristis' (*S. babylonica aurea, S. 'Niobe'*). Golden weeping willow. Tree. Left to its own way, it will head too low to furnish usable shade. Stake up a main stem and keep it staked right up to 15-18 ft. Shorten lower side branches and remove them as they lose their vigor; keep growth directed into a tall main stem and high-branching scaffold limbs. This treatment will give you a tree you can walk under.

S. babylonica. Weeping willow. Tree. Train to full-fledged weeper as described under *S. alba* 'Tristis.'

S. caprea. French pussy willow, pink pussy willow. Shrub or small tree. Can be kept at shrub size by cutting to ground every few years. Forces easily indoors and can be cut for winter arrangements.

WEEPING WILLOW this open and pretty needs no pruning. Mostly on mature trees, you cut ugly or crowded branches.

S. discolor. Pussy willow. Shrub or small tree. Large and spreading shrub, grows 6-8 ft. a season if cut to ground after flowering. If not pruned back each year, will grow to 20 ft. Heavy pruning is recommended to keep in bounds and to encourage a large crop of catkins on long new shoots for use in winter arrangements.

S. gracilistyla. Rose-gold pussy willow. Shrub. Cut stems for indoor decoration in the winter to help curb size. Or cut it back every few years to keep it lower and less wide-spreading. It's best to cut back the whole plant to short stubs every 3 or 4 years. You'll be rewarded by especially vigorous shoots with large catkins.

S. matsudana 'Tortuosa.' Twisted Hankow willow, corkscrew willow. Prune to give a head of branches you can walk under. Thin and shape by cutting picturesque bare branches in winter for indoor arrangements.

S. purpurea. Purple osier, Alaska blue willow. Shrub. Usually grown as a clipped hedge and kept 1-3 ft. high and equally wide.

SALTBUSH. See Atriplex.

SALVIA. Sage. Annuals, perennials, shrubs.

A. azurea grandiflora (*S. pitcheri*). Perennial. Should be pinched back when young to promote bushy growth. Can also be cut back in late spring or early summer to make plants bushier. Plants grow to 4 ft. high.

S. clevelandii. Shrub. In summer, after the plant finishes blooming, prune back about half of the most recent growth to shape plant and to encourage new flowering wood when growth starts again. You may also correct plant's shape in spring after danger of frost is past, but you will sacrifice some bloom.

S. gracilistyla. (Often sold as *S. rutilans.*) Pineapple sage. Perennial herb. Cut back after bloom in fall. Use leaves (fresh or dried) as seasoning.

S. leucantha. Mexican bush sage. Shrub. Cut old stems to ground; new ones bloom continuously.

S. officinalis. Garden sage. Perennial herb. Cut back after bloom. Use leaves (fresh or dried) as seasoning.

SAMBUCUS. Elderberry. Deciduous shrubs or trees. Rampant, fast-growing, wild looking but can be tamed to a degree. To keep dense and shrubby, prune hard every dormant season. New growth sprouts readily from stumps.

S. caerulea (*S. glauca*). Blue elderberry. Shrub or tree. If thinned to single or multiple trunk, becomes a graceful rounded tree with slightly weeping branches. If cut back to within a few feet of the ground, tree will stump sprout readily. To keep it from becoming dense and cluttered, thin out excess twiggy growth in fall. To grow it as shrub, prune drastically every year.

S. canadensis. American elder, sweet elder. Deciduous shrub. Makes a number of shoots from the base each year. Tip pinch these during following winter to force heavy branching for bloom and fruit. Cut out unproductive 2-3 year-old shoots at soil level in fall or winter.

S. racemosa. Red elderberry. Bushy shrub. Grows as a 2-6 ft. spreading shrub. If cut back to within few feet of ground, will stump sprout readily. To keep it from becoming dense and cluttered, thin out excess twiggy growth in fall. To grow as shrub, prune drastically every year.

SANDHILL SAGE. See Artemisia.

SANGUISORBA minor (*Poterium sanguisorba*). Small burnet, salad burnet. Perennial herb. Keep blossoms cut or it will self-seed too freely. Don't cut plant back more than half, though.

SANTOLINA. Herbs, evergreen subshrubs. Good as ground covers, bank covers, or low, clipped hedges. Look best if kept low by pruning. Clip off spent flowers. Cut back in early spring. May die to ground in coldest areas but roots will live and resume growth.

S. chamaecyparissus. Lavender cotton. Brittle, woody stems. Can reach 2 ft., but makes a better hedge if kept trimmed to 1 ft. As a clipped hedge, it probably won't develop flowers, but it may be just as attractive without them. If you want blooms, prune plant in early spring and again in late summer after it flowers.

S. virens. Compact little evergreen 2 ft. high and wide. Most often seen as a clipped dwarf hedge. Needs at least a yearly trimming to keep it from becoming woody.

SAPIUM sebiferum. Chinese tallow tree. Deciduous tree. Prune only to correct shape. Tends toward shrubbiness, multiple trunks, suckering, but easily trained to single trunk. Usually winter freezes deaden a few twig ends; cut them off in spring or let new growth cover them.

SAPPHIRE BERRY. See Symplocos.

SARCOCOCCA. Evergreen shrubs. Slow and orderly growing, generally need no more than shaping to stay neat and compact; but it may be desirable to remove old stems to encourage younger growth. If corrective methods are needed, don't be afraid to cut to ground. Will sprout from roots.

S. ruscifolia. Will form a natural espalier against a wall, sheared boxwood-like hedge, or a trained single shrub.

SASSAFRAS albidum. Sassafras. Deciduous tree. Normal training while young, prune only as required for shape when mature. Suckers tend to pop up if roots are cut in cultivating; should be removed when they appear.

SATUREJA montana. Winter savory. Perennial or subshrub. Keep clipped. Clip at start of flowering season for drying. In fall shoots can be cut down to near ground level to produce new growth next season.

SAWLEAF ZELKOVA. See Zelkova.

SAXIFRAGA. Saxifrage. Perennials. Shear off faded blooms to keep plants looking neat.

SAXIFRAGE. See Saxifraga.

SCABIOSA. Pincushion flower. Annuals, perennials. Bloom begins in midsummer and continues until winter if flowers are cut.

SCARLET KADSURA. See Kadsura.

SCARLET WISTERIA TREE. See Daubentonia.

SCHINUS. Pepper tree. Evergreen and semi-deciduous trees.

S. molle. California pepper tree. Evergreen tree. Young tree needs training: prune for high branching if you wish to walk under it. Once a California pepper grows branches as thick as your arm, don't saw them at all except in case of real emergency. (Tree is very susceptible to troubles.) If you have to saw, keep large cuts sealed with pruning compound. Greedy and invasive roots have been known to get into sewer lines and crack pavement. Plant where it has room to spread. Young pepper trees can be planted 2 ft. apart and pruned into graceful, billowy hedge. Even a 20-30-year-old hedge can be kept pruned to 4 ft. height. It will be graceful and well-behaved, with branches and leaves easily controlled by pruning.

S. polygamus (*S. dependens*). Peruvian pepper tree. Evergreen or semi-deciduous tree. Occasional thinning of excess twiggy growth and thinning inner branches of tree will make branch pattern and structure more interesting. Be careful pruning and handling branches —small hidden spines can hurt.

S. terebinthifolius. Brazilian pepper. Evergreen tree. Better behaved than *S. molle.* Bushier, stiffer looking in its youth. Tends to get topheavy if not kept thinned out but with little training makes a broad, umbrella-shaped crown. Stake young trees well and prune to make a fairly high crown. To reduce possibility of storm breakage, shorten overlong limbs and do some late summer thinning so wind can pass through. Young tree may be killed back to main trunk in a heavy freeze.

SCIADOPITYS verticillata. Umbrella pine. Evergreen tree. Versatile, lends itself to bonsai, container use, and special training and pruning. Can be left unpruned or can be thinned to create Oriental effect.

SCIMITAR SHRUB. See Brachysema.

SEA PINK. See Armeria.

SEDUM. Stonecrop. Succulent perennials or subshrubs.

S. amecamecanum. Mexican sedum. Looks brown for about 6 weeks after flowers fade, but it should not be cut back. The dried flowers drop down through foliage and make good moisture-holding mulch.

S. spectabile. Dies back in winter. Divide clumps after bloom in fall or early spring. Plant and remove old stems. New growth will soon appear.

S. spurium 'Dragon's blood.' Keep neat by cutting off dead flower stalks at base.

SEMELE androgyna. Climbing butcher's broom. Evergreen vine. Prune occasionally to keep it from getting too dense and to retain inherent graceful and emphatic foliage pattern. Remove dead wood.

SENECIO. Perennials, shrubs, vines.

S. cineraria. Dusty miller. Shrubby perennial. Old growth tends to become leggy and brittle, so best procedure is to cut back plant in spring and encourage new shoots from close to ground level. New foliage will be fresher gray-green and usually more deeply cut than the old.

S. greyii. Evergreen shrub. Keep it compact and stimulate new wood by removing oldest or damaged growth. Use pruned-off branches for indoor arrangements.

S. leucostachys. (Often sold as *S. cineraria* 'Candidissimus.') Pinch tips of young plant to keep it compact.

S. petasitis. Velvet groundsel, California geranium. Perennial or shrubby perennial. Prune hard after bloom to limit height and sprawl. Can be kept 2-4 ft. tall in big pots or tubs.

SENNA. See Cassia.

SEQUOIA sempervirens. Coast redwood. Evergreen tree. Mature trees normally require little more than corrective pruning. If you want to walk under the tree, remove lower branches high enough to give head room. To make a beautiful hedge, plant trees 3-4 ft. apart, top them at least once a year.

SEQUOIADENDRON giganteum (*Sequoia gigantea*). Big tree, giant sequoia. Evergreen tree. Tree tends to grow so precisely that little pruning is necessary, aside from occasional obvious training while young.

SERVICE BERRY. See Amelanchier.

SETCREASEA purpurea. Purple heart. Perennial. If tops killed back by frost, growth will resume in warm weather. Remove dead portions to base.

SHADBLOW. See Amelanchier.

SHADBUSH. See Amelanchier.

SHASTA DAISY. See Chrysanthemum.

SHELL FLOWER. See Alpinia.

SHEPHERDIA. Buffalo berry. Prune lightly after it blooms if required for shaping.

SHRIMP PLANT. See Beloperone.

SHRUB ALTHAEA. See Hibiscus.

SIBERIAN PEASHRUB. See Caragana.

SIERRA LAUREL. See Leucothoe.

SILK OAK. See Grevillea.

SILK TREE. See Albizia.

SILKTASSEL. See Garrya.

SILKWORM MULBERRY. See Morus.

SILVER BELL. See Halesia.

SILVER LACE VINE. See Polygonum.

SILVER TREE. See Leucandendron.

SILVERBERRY. See Elaeagnus.

SIMMONDSIA chinensis. Jojoba, goatnut. Evergreen shrub. Slow compact growth, requires little or no training. Many branched stems from base form compact, rounded mound 4-6 (even 10) ft. high. Like boxwood, can be kept at height you want by shearing back. Plant is not damaged by frequent shearing and trimming. If you are patient, it will also make a handsome 4-6 ft. high clipped hedge or compact unclipped screen.

SKIMMIA japonica. Evergreen shrubs. Don't have lanky tendency of many shrubs and need to be pruned only to shape, remove dead wood. Make rounded, spreading shrubs to 5-6 ft. high.

S. reevesiana (*S. fortunei*). Dwarf form, won't go over 30 in. and can easily be kept under 16 in. without looking overtrimmed.

SKY FLOWER. See Thunbergia.

SMALL BURNET. See Sanguisorba.

SMOKE TREE. See Cotinus.

SNAPDRAGON. See Antirrhinum.

SNEEZEWEED. See Helenium.

SNOWBALL, COMMON. See Viburnum.

SNOWBALL, JAPANESE. See Viburnum.

SNOWBERRY, COMMON. See Symphoricarpos.

SNOWDROP TREE. See Halesia.

SNOWDROP TREE, JAPANESE. See Styrax.

SNOWFLAKE TREE. See Trevesia.

SNOW-IN-SUMMER. See Cerastium.

SOAPBARK TREE. See Quillaja.

SOLANDRA hartwegii. (Usually sold as *S. guttata*.) Cup-of-gold vine. Evergreen vine. Prune to induce laterals and more flowers. Can be cut back to make rough hedge, or pegged down as coarse bank cover.

SOLANUM. Evergreen and deciduous shrubs and vines.

S. jasminoides. Potato vine. Evergreen or deciduous vine. If allowed to grow free, many stems will interlace and twine to 30-ft. tangle. Cut back severely in fall or early winter to prevent tangling, promote vigorous new growth, and keep new flowering wood coming. Control rampant runners that grow along ground.

S. rantonnetii. Evergreen or deciduous shrub or vine. Can also be staked and trained as tree form, or left to sprawl as ground cover. Bushy and straggly, it needs a severe cutting back every year to produce new growth. Prune severely to keep it a neat shrub; tie to a support if you want a vine. Can be cut back to the ground in early spring to encourage better blooms, new stem growth.

SOLLYA fusiformis (*S. heterophylla*). Australian bluebell creeper. Evergreen shrub, vine, or ground cover. Unless trained, its stems will spill out over ground, twining about each other or any object within reach. To make the most of its growing habit, use it as a ground cover. To grow as a shrub, keep pinching back vine-like shoots that grow out of bounds. As a vine, encourage strongest shoots and cut out all others that develop at the base of the plant. Thin and prune after danger of frost is past in spring.

SOPHORA. Deciduous or evergreen trees or shrubs.

S. japonica. Japanese pagoda tree, Chinese scholar tree. Deciduous tree. Usual training while young for form. Little or no pruning later. You may want to remove seed pods to prevent staining of a patio and tidy up tree after flowering in fall.

S. secundiflora. Mescal bean, Texas mountain laurel. Evergreen shrub or tree. Tends to grow shrub-like but with training it will eventually grow 25 ft. high with narrow head, slender trunk, and upright branches. Untrained, makes good large screen or bank cover. Scarlet seeds in gray pods are attractive but poisonous; remove before they mature.

SORBUS aucuparia. European mountain ash. Deciduous tree. Prune young trees (if necessary) to help them achieve mature form—erect with drooping outer branches.

SORREL TREE. See Oxydendrum.

SOUR GUM. See Nyssa.

SOURWOOD. See Oxydendrum.

SPARMANNIA africana. African linden. Evergreen shrub, tree. This vigorous grower will stand severe pruning at almost any time. Having rangy habit, it needs to be thinned out and headed back regularly to promote bushiness. Prune heavily every few years to give desired height and to control legginess. Tends to throw many trunks from base if frosted back or pruned back for size control.

SPEKBOOM. See Portulacaria.

SPICE BUSH. See Calycanthus.

SPIDER PLANT. See Chlorophytum.

SPIRAEA. Deciduous shrubs. For the many different spiraeas, the rule is to prune according to form and time of bloom. Most spiraeas will take severe pruning or cutting back to near ground level. Those with loose, graceful look need annual renewal of new growth. Thin some branches, head others back to young laterals. Remove some of the oldest wood that has produced flowers, cutting back to ground. Most shrubby types require less severe pruning. Prune spring-flowering kinds when they finish blooming. Prune summer-flowering species in late winter or very early spring. If in doubt, wait for plant to bloom, then prune at proper season; missing one pruning won't hurt. Some forms will produce second set of blooms if pruned immediately after flowering.

S. douglasii. Western spiraea. Suckering shrub that needs drastic control. Hard to eradicate once it gets out of hand.

S. prunifolia 'Plena.' Bridal wreath spiraea, shoe button spiraea. Flowers in the spring on last year's wood; prune right after flowers fade. Responds well to heavy pruning. Renew part of plant each year by removing oldest stems. Cut back wood that has just flowered to strong buds or new lateral growth. You may train and clip it as hedge if flowers are not of first importance.

SPIRAEA, FALSE. See Astilbe.

SPRUCE. See Picea.

SPURGE. See Euphorbia.

SPURGE, JAPANESE. See Pachysandra.

SQUAW CARPET. See Ceanothus.

STACHYS olympica (*S. lanata*). Lamb's ears. Perennial. Cut back in spring.

STACHYURUS praecox. Deciduous shrub. Slow growing, shrub needs little pruning.

STAR BUSH. See Turraea.

STAR JASMINE. See Trachelospermum.

STAUNTONIA hexaphylla. Evergreen vine. Can become a tangled mess if not pruned occasionally after spring flowering. Train on trellis or grow on pillars.

STENOCARPUS sinuatus. Firewheel tree. Evergreen tree. Needs only pruning to shape in early years.

STENOLOBIUM stans (*Tecoma stans*). Yellow bells, yellow trumpet flower, yellow-elder. Evergreen shrub or small tree. Cut faded flowers to prolong bloom, prune to remove dead and bushy growth, control size and form.

STEPHANANDRA. Deciduous shrub. After frost danger is past, take out freeze-damaged wood. Cut some oldest wood to ground, head other branches back to strongest laterals.

STEWARTIA. Deciduous shrubs or trees. Slow growing; need some training while young, practically no pruning thereafter.

STIGMAPHYLLON ciliatum. Orchid vine. Evergreen vine. Moderate to fast grower. Prune as required to keep in bounds. Cut out any dead or weak wood.

STOKES ASTER. See Stokesia.

STOKESIA laevis. Stokes aster. Perennial. Will continue to bloom if old flowers are cut off as they fade. Or cut it back after main bloom for second crop in fall.

STONECRESS. See Aethionema.

STONECROP. See Sedum.

STRANVAESIA davidiana undulata (*S. undulata*). Evergreen shrub. Irregularly shaped plant about 5 ft. tall and 6-8 ft. wide. You can keep it to 3 ft. by cutting back taller and wider growing stems to lower and close-to-center laterals. Prune at Christmas if you want to use berried branches for holiday foliage.

STRAWBERRY. Most are reproduced by offset plants at ends of runners. Pinching off all runners results in large plants and small yields of large berries; allowing offset plants to take root and grow gives heavy yields of smaller berries. (Pinch off further runners when plants have made enough offsets.)

STRAWBERRY GUAVA. See Psidium.

STRAWBERRY TREE. See Arbutus.

STRELITZIA. Bird of paradise. Evergreen perennials.

S. nicolai. Giant bird of paradise. Keep dead leaves cut off and thin out surplus growth. If it gets too tall, remove main stem and allow lower growing suckers to take its place. As large trunk-like stems mature, you can remove old leaves and leaf stalks, cutting close to trunk as you would on palms.

S. reginae. Bird of paradise. Needs a yearly clean-up of old, torn, sun-burned leaves. Cut off old spent flowers and stalks to within 1 in. of clasping leaf sheath.

STREPTOSOLEN jamesonii. Evergreen viny shrub. Responds well to heavy pruning, but normally you only need to cut back dead wood after last frost in spring, thinning and pruning to shape. (Don't wait too long because it blooms on new wood formed in spring.) Cut back leggy, spindly plants to promote thicker growth below.

STYRAX. Deciduous trees.

S. japonica. Japanese snowdrop tree, Japanese snowbell. Prune after flowering to control shape; tends to be shrubby, but by early pinching and pruning, lower side branches can be suppressed so that it will form single-trunked tree with wide spreading, horizontal canopy (sometimes twice as wide as tree is high).

S. obassia. Fragrant snowbell. Prune after flowering. Branching pattern is more upright than that of *S. japonica*, does not require as much pruning to keep it a well-formed tree. Because branches tend to be brittle, it may require thinning to protect it against strong winds.

SUMAC. See Rhus.

SUMMER FORGET-ME-NOT. See Anchusa.

SUMMER HOLLY. See Comarostaphylis.

SUMMERSWEET. See Clethra.

SUNROSE. See Helianthemum.

SWAN RIVER PEA SHRUB. See Brachysema.

SWEET GUM. See Liquidambar.

SWEET OLIVE. See Osmanthus.

SWEET PEA. See Lathyrus.

SWEET PEPPERBUSH. See Clethra.

SWEET SHRUB. See Calycanthus.

SWEETLEAF. See Symplocos.

SWEETSHADE. See Hymenosporum.

SWORD FERN. See Fern, Hardy.

SYCAMORE. See Platanus.

SYMPHORICARPOS. Common snowberry, coral berry, Indian currant. Deciduous shrubs. All send out vigorous underground shoots from which suckers grow. Control suckers and shoots by pulling (or digging) them up. Prune out fruited branches in early spring when berries lose their attractiveness. Cut older growth to ground, leaving younger shoots. You can also cut the entire plant back to ground in early spring to prevent legginess. Do such cutting back annually or every 2 or 3 years.

SYMPLOCOS paniculata. Sweetleaf, sapphire berry. Deciduous shrub, small tree. Thin as required to prevent brushy look.

SYRINGA. Lilac. Deciduous shrubs. Control growth during early years by pinching and shaping. Flower buds for next year form in pairs where leaves join stems. After bloom, remove spent flower clusters just above points where buds are forming. Heavier pruning will result in loss of much of next year's bloom. Lilacs require only minimum amount of pruning. When you cut flowers in spring and remove faded flower clusters, you have given the young plants all the pruning they need. Keep suckers cut off at ground level around grafted plants. If plants are on their own roots and you want to increase your lilac planting, let suckers remain until they strike roots. Then plant them. Early spring is best time to prune to promote bush growth, but some bloom will then be sacrificed. To rejuvenate old plants, remove a third of the old wood each spring. When you do this, the shrub is never without some flowers during bloom period, and after 3 years all wood has been replaced. Old plants grown on their own roots can also be cut back hard (to about 18 in.) in late winter. This gives them a growing season to recover and ripen new wood before next dormant season so they can produce blooms subsequently. Grafted plants should be rejuvenated over several seasons, for they may not have enough strength for this treatment and might send out shoots from the rootstock.

SYZYGIUM. Evergreen shrubs or trees.

S. jambos (*Eugenia jambos*). Rose apple. Slow growth means little or no pruning is necessary.

S. paniculatum (*Eugenia myrtifolia*, *E. paniculata*). Brush cherry, Australian brush cherry. Can take severe pruning and is frequently used as a clipped hedge, column, topiary plant or espalier. But it also makes a beautiful moderately large tree if allowed to go untrimmed. During its early years, stake main stem to a sturdy support and allow all side branches to stay on. If the terminal stem divides, allowing 2 or more upright stems to form, cut out all but the strongest. When the plant reaches 8-10 ft. high, it will require no further training. Do heavy pruning after danger of frost is past.

TABEBUIA chrysotricha. (Sometimes sold as *T. pulcherrima*.) Golden trumpet tree. Briefly deciduous, sometimes evergreen tree. Growth habit is awkward. Stake while young and keep plant to single leading shoot until 6-8 ft. tall. Prune annually after spring blooming period to shape. Cut back any branches that get out of line and give tree lopsided look.

TALLOW TREE, CHINESE. See Sapium.

TAMARISK. See Tamarix.

TAMARIX. Tamarisk. Deciduous and evergreen-appearing shrubs and trees. Time of pruning varies, depending upon whether they are spring-flowering or summer-flowering, as noted below. All have greedy roots and need to be root-pruned occasionally for control. Spring flowering varieties—*T. africana*, *T. juniperina*, *T. parviflora*, and *T. tetrandra*—

REJUVENATE a lilac plant if it gets much bigger than this. Reduce its size by removing growth in spring (see text at left). This decreases mildew.

should be pruned after blooming in spring to control shape and size and to maintain graceful effect. This pruning will limit height and produce new flowering wood. Cut oldest stems to ground to promote growth of new wood. Summer flowering varieties are *T. chinensis*, *T. gallica*, *T. hispida*, *T. pentandra*, and *T. odessana*. These spreading feathery shrubs grow to 6 or 12 ft. if pruned to ground in early spring. Flowers are borne on wood of current season, so this type of pruning will not only keep plants down but will also produce mass of flower plumes from July to fall.

TANACETUM vulgare. Common tansy. Perennial herb. Thin clumps yearly to keep in bounds.

TANBARK OAK. See Lithocarpus.

TARO. See Colocasia.

TAXODIUM distichum. Bald cypress. Deciduous tree. Requires only such corrective pruning as removal of dead wood and unwanted branches.

TAXUS. Yew. Evergreen shrubs or trees. Slow growing, long-lived, tolerant of much shearing and pruning, though they don't normally require much. Trim anytime, doing most drastic cutting in late winter before new growth starts. (That is best time to shape them if they look straggly or lopsided.) Keep plants looking neat by making cuts so that they're

well concealed by surrounding foliage. These are the plants commonly used for topiary work—fashioned into birds, baskets, or free form sculptures.

If you let them grow to the desired height, you can trim them into the neatest of formal hedges.

Young yew hedges should be sheared in midsummer, removing about half the new growth. As the hedge begins to reach full size, prune 2 or 3 times a year—once in late winter before growth starts, then in late May or early June when new growth has reached full length, and then again (if needed) in late summer.

Columnar Irish yews tend to spread outward with age; slow the tendency by pruning back any branches that fall outward to a sturdy vertical side branch. Tie together branches of very large plants with wire. Join branches on opposite sides of the plants, so that wires run through the center of the plants.

TEA TREE. See Leptospermum.

TECOMARIA capensis (*Tecoma capensis*). Cape honeysuckle. Evergreen vine or shrub. Can be trained as vine, espalier, or large shrub. Fast growing, it can scramble to 15-25 ft. if supported. Its natural sprawling form makes it adaptable as large-scale bank planting. Can be held to 6-8 ft. upright shrub with hard pruning.

TERNSTROEMIA gymnanthera (*T. japonica*). Evergreen shrub. While young, pinch out tip growth to keep shrub compact and full-foliaged. Can be used as a big landscape shrub, informal hedge, or tub plant.

TETRAPANAX papyriferus. Rice paper plant. Evergreen shrub. Tends to have ungainly stems. In general, keep the number of stems thinned out for more interesting structural effects. Extra suckers should be removed to keep plant from taking over a bed. Cut off flowers after blooming, to keep foliage large for more effective display and to prevent tall branches from falling over. However, if you allow flowers to stay and set seed, there is less tendency for the plant to form suckers. Cut back at any height to force it to branch. New buds break readily, forming new leaf clusters. Pull off yellow leaves. Can sometimes prove hard to eliminate because of deep root system that sometimes sprouts long after tops have been cut off. Digging around roots stimulates suckering.

TETRASTIGMA voinierianum (*Cissus voinieriana, Vitis voikeriana*). Evergreen vine. Travels by strong, steely tendrils and sends out long, trailing, pendulous branches. Cut back these long branches to keep under control.

TEUCRIUM. Germander. Evergreen shrubs or subshrubs. Respond well to pruning and shearing.

T. chamaedrys. To keep neat, shear back once or twice a year, forcing growth at sides. This will make a dense mass of foliage right down to ground. If trained as a hedge, shear twice in midsummer when plants are well-established. Pruning at this time keeps plants from blooming and keeps them in shape.

If you aren't growing it as a hedge, you can enjoy its loose spikes of rose or purple-red bloom in summer and then shear it to shape after it flowers.

T. fruticans. Bush germander. Makes a neat, easy to trim hedge. Thin and cut back in late winter, early spring. Its slender branches seldom get woody and hard to cut. An electric hedge clipper does a fast, efficient job of shearing it. Plant normally grows as a rather loose shrub about 4-6 ft. high and wide.

TEXAS MOUNTAIN LAUREL. See Sophora.

TEXAS RANGER. See Leucophyllum.

TEXAS UMBRELLA TREE. See Melia.

THERMOPSIS caroliniana. Perennial. Cut to ground after bloom.

THEVETIA. Evergreen shrubs, small trees. Fast-growing.

T. peruviana (*T. nereifolia*). Yellow oleander. Shallow-rooted; selectively remove branches to lessen wind resistance. Can be grown as tree or cut short into 6-8 ft. hedge or screen. Pruning is seldom necessary unless you want plants kept in hedge form or kept more compact. If top is frozen, hold off pruning until plant begins to put out new growth. New growth appears rapidly from uninjured basal wood, will bloom same year. Head back and prune to shape after bloom.

THREADLEAF FALSE ARALIA. See Dizygotheca.

THRIFT. See Armeria.

THUJA, PLATYCLADUS (*T. occidentalis,* American arborvitae, and *Platycladus orientalis,* Oriental arborvitae). Evergreen shrubs or trees. Arborvitaes can stand heavy shearing. Shape in late

winter or early spring before new growth starts if they look straggly or lopsided. Try to make cuts so that they're well concealed by surrounding foliage. Prune again if necessary in summer to control size and shape. Brown, dead foliage inside dense thuja is normal. Although it's not necessary to remove it, a good hosing will sometimes blow it out.

T. plicata. Western red cedar. Evergreen tree. Tall-growing giant, it can be held to compact 6 ft. hedge. Has greedy roots that must occasionally be pruned to control.

THUNBERGIA grandiflora. Sky flower. Perennial vine. Vigorous, needs pruning to keep under control. Will come back to bloom in a year if frozen back.

THYME. See Thymus.

THYMUS. Thyme. Ground covers, erect shrubby perennial herb. Restrain plants as needed by clipping back growing tips.

T. serpyllum. Mother-of-thyme, creeping thyme. Ground cover. To restrain, clip around margins of clump.

T. vulgaris. Common thyme. Shrubby perennial herb. Prune after flowering.

TI. See Cordyline.

TIBOUCHINA semidecandra (*Pleroma splendens*). Princess flower. Evergreen shrub or small tree. Minimize legginess by light pruning after each bloom cycle, heavier pruning in early spring. Pinch tips of young plant to encourage bushiness and continue pinching back new growth during summer for more compact plant. Will sprout from stump if it dies back in winter. Wait until danger of frost is past and new growth has a good start before pruning out freeze-damaged wood.

TEUCRIUM CHAMAEDRYS, infrequently sheared, produces branches that give a soft, irregular, casual look.

SAME PLANT, kept as a sheared hedge alongside steps, acts as a white curtain at night. Shear twice each summer.

TILIA. Linden. Deciduous trees. Young trees need staking and shaping. Older trees need only corrective pruning.

TIPU TREE. See Tipuana.

TIPUANA tipu. Tipu tree. Deciduous or semi-evergreen tree. Fast and awkward grower. Needs staking and pruning for attractive form when young. Can be pruned to emphasize natural umbrella shape or headed back to make narrower, denser crown.

TORCH-LILY. See Kniphofia.

TORREYA californica. California nutmeg. Evergreen tree. Train early and then it will require only occasional pruning. Withstands heavy pruning and will usually send up new growth from stumps. Full grown tree may reach 50 ft., can be kept smaller by pruning.

TOYON. See Heteromeles.

TRACHELOSPERMUM (*Rhynchospermum*). Star jasmine. Evergreen vines or sprawling shrubs. Used as ground covers, spillers, or climbers.

T. jasminoides. Can take a great deal of pruning but seldom needs it. Without support and with some tip pinching, it becomes a spreading shrub or ground cover, 1½-2 ft. tall and 4-5 ft. wide. To

WESTERN HEMLOCK (Tsuga heterophylla) as a tall, wide hedge. Clipping once a year will keep it dense like this.

STAR JASMINE'S roles. As shrub or ground cover, needs pinching or pruning.

grow as a vine, do not tip pinch, and give stems some support. Older plant should be cut back about ⅓ each year to prevent inner growth from becoming too woody and bare. You can also cut it back to main branch framework; in a year, new growth and flowers will replace it. To grow as ground cover, cut back upright shoots to keep it low.

TRACHYCARPUS fortunei. (Sometimes sold as *Chamaerops excelsa*.) Windmill palm. Prune only to cut off occasional dead frond. Sometimes develops a skirt of dried foliage that should be removed to keep palm neat in appearance.

TRADESCANTIA. Trailing or clumping perennials.

T. fluminensis. Wandering Jew. Trailing evergreen for pots, baskets, window boxes. Pinch tips or cut back to shorten stems. Cut pieces root easily in water. Can spread fast as ground cover in mild climates; hoe or pull out by shallow roots if it invades other plantings.

TRANSVAAL DAISY. See Gerbera.

TREE-OF-HEAVEN. See Ailanthus.

TREVESIA. Snowflake tree. Evergreen shrubs or small trees. Little pruning is required.

TRICHOSTEMA lanatum. Woolly blue curls. Evergreen shrub. Blooms in late spring; prune in bloom for arrangements. Pinch tips of new growth frequently when young to develop a fuller bush.

TRINIDAD FLAME BUSH. See Calliandra.

TRISTANIA. Evergreen trees.

T. conferta. Brisbane box. Leaves tend to crowd toward ends of branches, so trees should be pruned or pinched occasionally to make them bush out more, give better leaf distribution. With each pruning you should also shape to retain an attractive branch pattern.

T. laurina. Tree is easy to train and takes shearing. Young plant is densely shrubby and can be kept that way with a little pinching. To make a tree, stake plant and shorten side branches. Remove shortened side branches when treelike growth pattern is established; then only some light shaping will be necessary.

TRITHRINAX. See Palm.

TROCHODENDRON aralioides. Slow growing multiple-stem shrub or small tree. Needs only corrective pruning.

TRUMPET CREEPER. See Campsis.

TRUMPET TREE, GOLDEN. See Tabebuia.

TRUMPET VINE. See Campsis.

TRUMPET VINE, BLOOD-RED. See Phaedranthus.

TRUMPET VINE, ROYAL. See Distictis.

TRUMPET VINE, VANILLA. See Distictis.

TRUMPET VINE, VIOLET. See Clytostoma.

TRUMPET VINE, YELLOW. See Anemopaegma, Doxantha.

TSUGA. Hemlock. Coniferous evergreen trees and shrubs. Mostly large trees but can be kept small by pruning new growth to shape desired. If you want a tree, keep a single leader and prune out competitors. Will tolerate hard pruning and shearing.

T. canadensis. Canadian hemlock. Normally a graceful tree for screen or background, but can be clipped into an outstandingly beautiful clipped hedge 3-15 ft. tall. Give hedge main pruning in late winter or early spring before new growth begins. Shear again in mid-summer if you want a dense (as opposed to a feathery) effect.

T. heterophylla. Western hemlock. Normally a fast-growing, tall, pyramidal tree. Good for background use, or can be pruned as hedge or screen.

T. mertensiana. Mountain hemlock. Slow growing in home gardens. Adaptable to shaping into horizontal, twisted form. Use in rock gardens, containers, as bonsai subjects.

TUCKEROO. See Cupaniopsis.

TUPELO. See Nyssa.

TUPIDANTHUS calyptratus. Evergreen shrub or small tree. Can be pruned into almost any form. Can easily be trained as a semi-vine or shrub. For multiple stem effect, prune plant severely back to its base to produce several stems. If you prefer shorter and more bushy plant, cut top and encourage lower branching. Can also be trained into an interesting bonsai.

TURRAEA. Star bush. Evergreen shrub. Slow growing, adaptable. Responds well to pruning and can be grown as a shrub, sheared as a hedge or trained as a ground cover by removing vertical growth and encouraging horizontal spreading.

UGNI molinae (*Myrtus ugni*). Chilean guava. Evergreen shrub. Young plant may sprawl awkwardly, but usually fills out with age to make attractive shrub. To use as hedge or informal low screen, shorten overlong branches back into foliage mass.

ULMUS. Elm. Deciduous or partially evergreen trees.

U. americana. American elm. Deciduous tree. This tall-growing tree and the similar English, Dutch, and Scotch elms respond well to pruning, but mature trees require little pruning if carefully trained to desired shape while young. Do major pruning in dormant season; groom, remove weak and damaged wood at any time. Because roots are fast spreading, you may have to root prune occasionally for control (they have been known to lift pavement). Remove suckers with spade or mattock. Remove and destroy diseased wood as soon as you can spot it.

U. parvifolia. (Often sold as *U. p.* 'Sempervirens.') Chinese elm, Chinese evergreen elm. Evergreen or deciduous according to winter temperature and tree's heredity. Train when young to branch at desired height and to encourage graceful weeping habit. Branches tend to be brittle and form dense crown.

Thin some of these crowded branches in winter to cut down wind resistance. Leading shoot should be staked and headed higher than in other shade trees to compensate for weeping tendency. Rub or cut out small branches along trunk for first few years. Shorten overlong branches or strongly weeping branches to strengthen tree scaffolding. Older tree may need thinning to lessen chance of storm damage. Rapid growth can take it to 40 ft. or more, but you can cut and prune almost at will to hold it back or to shape or thin it out. Often planted on slopes where it is cut back and forced to branch low for controlling weeds.

U. pumila. Siberian elm. Can be pruned and trained similarly to *U. parvifolia*. However, wood is more brittle, and tendency to develop weak crotches should be checked. Prune mature tree yearly to lighten weight on branches, prevent breakage. Root system can also be troublesome in gardens and requires root pruning to control. Tends to have much dead and diseased wood that should be removed. Tree responds well to pruning. Can also be sheared as hedge and kept to 3-4 ft. height.

UMBELLULARIA californica. Pepperwood, California laurel, California bay, Oregon myrtle or myrtlewood. Evergreen tree. Though it responds well to heavy pruning and will readily stump sprout, mature tree usually needs no pruning at all. Under certain circumstances, it may need shaping, thinning and removal of weak, diseased wood. Tends to cast very dense shade unless thinned. Good for screening or tall hedges. Often forms several trunks. Good patio or street tree when thinned to one or a few trunks.

UMBRELLA PINE. See Sciadopitys.

UMBRELLA PLANT. See Cyperus.

VACCINIUM. Evergreen and deciduous shrubs.

V. ovatum. Evergreen huckleberry. Evergreen shrub. Can be trimmed into hedge or grown in container. Takes heavy pruning; cut branches are attractive in arrangements. Selectively head back branches to maintain desired shape every year after new growth has lost its bronzy tints.

V. parvifolium. Red huckleberry. Deciduous shrub. Slow growing. Little pruning needed; how you prune depends upon whether blossoms (for arrangements) or showy, delicious berries are most important. Prune in bloom to get branches for indoors (this will, of course, reduce berry crop). Remove some oldest wood, weak and crossing branches in dormant period.

V. vitis-idaea. Lingonberry, mountain cranberry. Evergreen shrub. Slow grow-

ing, needs very little pruning, but may have to be clipped back occasionally to contain it. Spreads by underground runners. Cut these if necessary with spade or hoe them to keep plants from spreading into other areas.

VANILLA TRUMPET VINE. See Distictis.

VELVET GROUNDSEL. See Senecio.

VERBASCUM. Mullein. Perennials. Remove spent flowers as soon as you can, then cut spikes to ground after blooms are faded. Plants may flower again the same season.

VERBENA. Perennials, some grown as annuals.

V. hybrida (*V. hortensis*). Garden verbena. If used as perennial, prune severely in winter or early spring.

V. peruviana (*V. chamaedryfolia*). Perennial, often grown as annual. Ground cover. To keep it looking its best, cut back once a year after frost with shears or rotary mower. Occasional pinching during growing season will help to maintain compact growth.

VERBENA, LEMON. See Aloysia.

VIBURNUM. Deciduous or evergreen shrubs, rarely small trees. All viburnums can be pruned heavily without injury, though some in this large and diverse group need more than others. Deciduous varieties are usually rapid and vigorous growers, benefit from having old wood pruned out every second or third year. May also be necessary to cut out any thin, weak wood in spring in order to maintain their form. Evergreen forms usually require little pruning, but shaping or pruning some plants that are awkward or rangy looking in youth will bring them to graceful maturity.

V. burkwoodii. Deciduous shrub in coldest areas, nearly evergreen elsewhere. Light, whippy wood makes it a good and easily trained espalier or wall plant. Early growth is straggly and rather weak, and plant can become a tangle if not pruned and trained when young. Flowering branches make fine display. Prune quite heavily during or after flowering for more compact shrub. Selectively head back branches to laterals or promising buds.

V. carlesii. Korean spice viburnum. Deciduous shrub. Little pruning necessary. Remove weak branches and occasionally remove older wood to ground to renew. Not unattractive as bare plant in winter, can be shaped and pruned to make most interesting bare branch pattern of light brown wood.

V. dentatum. Arrow-wood. Deciduous shrub. Fast, vigorous grower, requires thinning out frequently. Prune during, after flowering; remove some of oldest stems to ground.

V. odoratissimum. Sweet viburnum. Evergreen shrub. Useful as thick screen or can be trimmed to form neat, lustrous hedge.

V. opulus. Highbush cranberry, European cranberry bush. Deciduous shrub. Prune out oldest wood to renew. Normally many stemmed, can easily be trained to small, single-trunked tree.

V. o. 'Nanum.' (Dwarf form of above.) Needs no trimming as low hedge.

V. o. 'Roseum' (*V. o.* 'Sterile'). Common snowball. Normally a large, upright, many-stemmed shrub, it can be easily trained to a small, single-trunked tree. If trained to tree form, pinch leader when it reaches proper height to encourage branching.

V. plicatum (*V. tomentosum* 'Sterile'). Japanese snowball. This and *V. p.* 'Sterile,' doublefile viburnum, are deciduous shrubs. Instead of transplanting or discarding a shrub that has grown too large, transform it into tree instead. To do this, remove all but strongest upright stem and all side growth to the height desired, bracing with strong stake. Or keep it lower by trimming back to one of the side (unflowered) branches after flowering. (Don't prune shrub lower than 4 ft. or it will lose its natural shape and become bushy.)

V. rhytidophyllum. Leatherleaf viburnum. Evergreen shrub. Instead of pruning at or right after flowering as with other viburnums, wait until new growth is stronger in late spring, early summer.

V. suspensum. Sandankwa viburnum. Evergreen shrub. This rapid growing, vigorous shrub benefits from pruning. Cut out old wood every second or third year during winter months. Cut out any thin or weak wood in spring to maintain desired form.

V. tinus. Laurustinus. Evergreen shrub or small narrow tree. Usually grown as screens, clipped or unclipped hedges, densely foliaged shrubs, or shrubbery borders. Will take heavy pruning. Cut flowering branches freely for indoor decoration and delicate fragrance. If grown as a hedge, clip frequently to maintain desired shape. Having dense foliage right to ground makes it good plant for clipped topiary shapes. In wet climates, clipping and shearing may aggravate the mildew susceptibility of the plant, so it's best to let it grow more naturally.

VINCA. Periwinkle, myrtle. Evergreen perennials.

V. major. Fast growing, long trailing stems root as they spread. To restrain, cut when necessary. When used as ground cover, shear close to ground occasionally to bring on fresh new growth.

V. minor. Dwarf periwinkle. Becomes more compact when sheared back an-

nually in spring. It keeps the plants dense, compact, and free blooming.

VIOLA. Violet, pansy. Perennials, some treated as annuals. Keep picking flowers and faded blossoms of pansies and violas to keep them blooming.

V. cornuta. Viola, tufted pansy. Cut back after spring bloom, feed and water heavily, and they will produce a second crop of flowers lasting well into summer. Pinch violas if leggy. Keep blooms picked off until plants are established. If plants are bushy and making plenty of sideshoots, let them have their head. Once in full bloom, pick flowers as often as you can.

V. odorata. Sweet violet. Easy to keep under control by cutting off runners you don't want. Shear rank growth in late fall for better spring flower display.

V. tricolor. Johnny-jump-up. **V. t. hortensis.** Pansy. Cut blooms freely for house, taking long stems with foliage. Will then spread and bloom much better. Regularly remove faded flowers before they set seed.

VIOLET. See Viola.

VIOLET TRUMPET VINE. See Clytostoma.

VIRGINIA CREEPER. See Parthenocissus.

VITEX. Chaste tree. Deciduous and evergreen shrubs or trees.

V. agnus-castus. Chaste tree. Deciduous shrub or small tree. Summer and fall blooming. Heavy pruning in midwinter assures good show of flowers following summer (wait until spring in colder areas to minimize chances of frost damage). Dies back in severe winters but new growth will spring from roots. Prune out dead wood.

V. lucens. New Zealand chaste tree. Evergreen tree. Requires little pruning. Groom when necessary, cutting out weak, damaged wood.

WALNUT (*Juglans*). Deciduous trees. Mature walnut trees require very little pruning. You may need to prune to maintain shape, also removing water sprouts, suckers, dead, weak and diseased wood. Thin out crowded and crossing branches as necessary. Young walnut trees require careful training. Following procedure is generally accepted for a central leader tree. *At planting*, head the whip back severely to 3-5 buds and 2-4 ft. in height (even lower where summer sunburn is a problem). As young tree develops, select a single shoot for leader and subdue all others by pinching back. As young tree grows, keep some shoots along trunk and branches to protect against sunburn. These can be pinched back and eventually removed when tree top has grown enough to shade and protect trunk.

In first dormant season the selected leader should be headed back (preferably to a bud facing toward prevailing summer winds) to stimulate growth of laterals below. *In second dormant season* and later, select the primary scaffold branch from 5-6 ft. off the ground to fix clearance as high as you want. Scaffold branches above should then be selected to form spiral pattern around trunk with vertical separation of 18-24 in. (If closer, they will crowd and shade branches below.) As tree grows, continue to head back leader (always to a bud facing toward prevailing summer winds) until tree structure and height are where you want them. At that point, you may allow the leader to bend down and assume the position of topmost scaffold branch.

Laterals that develop on walnuts the same season as the parent branch tend to form narrow angles and weak crotches. These new buds are soft and have a definite "neck"; they should be pinched off and permanent laterals chosen from those which form the following year. A good rule to follow in training a young walnut: remove all laterals developing the same year as the parent branch.

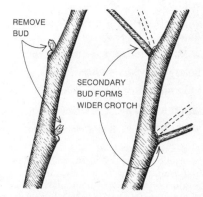

ELIMINATE "necked buds" on young walnut. Secondary buds make better branches.

WASHINGTONIA. See Palm.

WEEPING CHINESE BANYAN. See Ficus.

WEEPING WILLOW. See Salix.

WEIGELA. Deciduous shrubs. Vigorous growers, require considerable pruning. After flowering, prune branches that have bloomed back to unflowered side branches. Leave only 1 or 2 of these laterals to each stem. Cut most wood older than 2 years back to ground to keep plant renewed and vigorous. Save only strongest and healthiest new shoots that develop, removing others at base. Prune any time to remove weak, injured or dead wood. In colder climates, remove injured wood in spring. It may also be necessary to lightly prune tips in midsummer to keep these rangy growers under control. Older specimens can be renewed by cutting to ground, then selecting sturdiest canes that appear.

WESTRINGIA rosmariniformis. Evergreen shrub. Prune lightly to shape after main blooming period in spring. Blooms most of year in mild areas.

WHITE FORSYTHIA. See Abeliophyllum.

WHITE SAPOTE. See Casimiroa.

WIGANDIA caracasana. Treelike, woody perennial. As plant gets older, it becomes smaller leaved and ungainly. You can keep fresh new growth coming if you cut old canes off at base each spring. Even when plant is frozen down, new growth usually springs up from crown in early spring. Wigandia is rank grower, but it can be kept small by cutting to ground occasionally.

WILD BUCKWHEAT. See Eriogonum.

WILD LILAC. See Ceanothus.

WILGA. See Geijera.

WILLOW. See Salix.

WILLOW, AUSTRALIAN. See Geijera.

WILLOW MYRTLE, AUSTRALIAN. See Agonis.

WINDMILL PALM. See Trachycarpus.

WINTER HAZEL. See Corylopsis.

WINTER SAVORY. See Satureja.

WINTER'S BARK. See Drimys.

WINTERSWEET. See Chimonanthus.

WISTERIA. Deciduous vines. Can also be trained as trees and shrubs. Pruning and training are important for bloom production and control of plant's size, shape. Let newly set plants grow to establish framework, and remove stems that interfere with desired shape. Pinch back side stems and long streamers, rub

TREE-FORM WISTERIA. Buy one like this or make it yourself. Text and drawings below and on page 87 tell how to make one by training and pruning.

off buds that develop on trunk. Wisterias can be trained as big shrubs or multi-stem, small, semi-weeping trees. Aim for well-spaced branches to form the framework. Shorten side branches and nip long streamers. Pinch or cut back all errant shoots to second or third leaf whenever you see them. If you leave them, they may grow as much as 50 ft. in a season and form a tangled mass. Even after your wisteria has developed a permanent structure, it will need additional attention. Prune regularly every winter by cutting back or thinning out as necessary the side shoots produced off the main or structural stems and by shortening to 2 or 3 buds the flower-bearing laterals off these side shoots. You won't have any trouble recognizing short, fat-budded spurs that will carry next spring's flowers. A meticulous pruner who wants a clean-looking vine also knocks or cuts off dry slender stems that carried last season's flowers (these hang on tenaciously for months). To be

well-groomed, a wisteria also needs summer pruning. Cut off long green winding stems (gardeners often call them streamers or trailers) before they start getting tangled up in main body of vine. Best, and in the long run, easiest way to control these unruly growths is to keep a pair of pruning shears handy and snip these stems off whenever you see them.

The above procedure may be varied somewhat in warmest areas, such as Southern California. Here, many gardeners prune most heavily at the end of spring bloom. This allows another crop of shoots to form for bloom later in summer. In fall, following second bloom, head back these new shoots to control the plant and encourage more large clusters of flowers.

Tree wisterias can be bought ready made or you can train your own. Remove all but one main stem and stake this one securely. Tie stem to stake at frequent intervals. When plant has

PLANT IN 5 GAL. CAN AS FOUND IN NURSERY — STAKED, TIED, CUT BACK TO ONE STEM — TRAINING STARTS WHEN SHOOTS APPEAR — FIRST YEAR: PINCH TIP — SECOND YEAR: REMOVE SUCKERS, SHORTEN BRANCHES — FOURTH, FIFTH YEARS: PINCH STREAMERS, SHAPE HEAD

THE SIX STEPS in converting young wisteria plant into a tree. Photo above shows the kind of tree you get.

reached height at which you wish head to form, pinch or prune out tip to force branching. Shorten branches to beef them up. Pinch back long streamers, rub off all buds that form below head. Container grown wisterias thrive indefinitely but need faithful watering and hard pruning. If plants in open ground grow too vigorously and fail to bloom, prune roots by cutting around plant with spade.

WITCH HAZEL, CHINESE. See Hamamelis.

WONGA-WONGA VINE. See Pandorea.

WOODWARDIA. Chain fern.
  W. fimbriata. See Fern, Hardy.
  W. orientalis. See Fern, Tender.
  W. radicans. See Fern, Tender.

WOOLFLOWER, CHINESE. See Celosia.

WOOLLY BLUE CURLS. See Trichostema.

WORMWOOD, COMMON. See Artemisia.

WORMWOOD, FRINGED. See Artemisia.

XANTHOCERAS sorbifolium. Hyacinth shrub. Deciduous. Cut flowered branches back to good lateral immediately after bloom. Thin by taking out some of oldest branches, heading back others to a good lateral to keep an attractive form. Weak and crossing branches can be removed in winter, but heavy pruning at this time will reduce bloom.

XANTHORHIZA. Yellowroot. Deciduous shrub, ground cover. Prune as needed to check spreading, cut back with scythe (or mow) to thicken.

XYLOSMA congestum (*X. senticosum*). Evergreen or partially deciduous shrub or small tree. Pruning requirements depend upon your objective. Easily trained as an espalier, or stake the shrub, pruning side growth to make into a 15-30 ft. spreading tree. Can be shaped into attractive, multi-stemmed, large arching shrub or single-trunk tree; ground or bank cover (prune out erect growth), clipped or unclipped hedge (twine long branches together to fill in gaps faster). If left alone, plant develops angular main stem that takes its time zig-zagging upward. Eventually it forms a loose, spreading, graceful shrub, 8-10 ft. high and about as wide, with long, graceful side branches, arching and drooping to ground. As indicated by its various uses, xylosma responds with new growth rapidly after heavy pruning. You can prune it (in February or after frost danger in colder area) back to skeleton of main framework branches, and in about 4 months, bare branches become almost completely concealed by fresh,

vigorous new growth. With pruning shears and a discerning eye, you can transform ordinary looking plant into interesting one. Start by thinning out weak, crowded stems and twiggy growth; step back every now and then to survey what you've done and decide where to make the next cut. Little by little, you'll see basic branch structure you didn't know was there.

UNPRUNED
PRUNED

TOP, too-big xylosma. In circle, skeleton with new shoots. Below, the result.

YARROW. See Achillea.

YELLOW BELLS. See Stenolobium.

YELLOW HORNED POPPY. See Glaucium.

YELLOW OLEANDER. See Thevetia.

YELLOW TRUMPET FLOWER. See Stenolobium.

YELLOW TRUMPET VINE. See Anemopaegma, Doxantha.

YELLOW WOOD. See Cladrastis.

YELLOW-ELDER. See Stenolobium.

YELLOWROOT. See Xanthorhiza.

YESTERDAY - TODAY - AND - TOMORROW. See Brunfelsia.

YEW. See Taxus.

YEW, KOREAN. See Cephalotaxus.

YEW PINE. See Podocarpus.

XYLOSMA trained in vertical bands up wall, tied in place, clipped to pattern.

YUCCA filamentosa. Adam's needle. Evergreen perennial. After flowering, remove flower stalk. New plant will grow from side suckers. You may wish to thin plant, making it less bushy, by removing some of these suckers.

  Y. aloifolia, Y. gloriosa, and other yuccas with tree-like growth should have dead flower stalks removed. Prune out or tie back trunks or branches that might jab passersby with sharp leaves. *Y. recurvifolia* can be pruned to a single trunk.

ZANTEDESCHIA. Calla. Rhizome. Nearly evergreen in mild areas, deciduous where winters are cold. Cut off old droopy leaves and dead flower stalks to keep plant neat during growing season. Cut plant to ground after bloom (this is optional where mild winters favor all year growth). If you don't want plant to self-seed (it's prolific), remove old flowers before seed heads form.

ZANTHORHIZA. See Xanthorhiza.

ZAUSCHNERIA. California fuchsia, hummingbird flower. Perennials or subshrubs. Need control, for they tend to be rangy, spread their invasive roots into other garden beds, and reseed themselves. Cut or shear back to about 5 in. from ground in fall to keep in bounds. Cut off dead or frozen growth in spring.

ZELKOVA serrata. Sawleaf zelkova. Deciduous tree. Young tree needs careful training to develop strong framework. Head back excessively long, pendulous branches to force side growth, thin competing branches to permit full development of the strongest.

ZIZYPHUS jujuba. Chinese jujube. Deciduous tree. Prune while dormant to shape, encourage weeping habit, reduce size. Remove suckers from base of tree.

The Pruner's Glossary

AIR LAYERING. A method of propagating used for plants that are difficult to root from cuttings and for tall, lanky, single-stemmed plants that cannot be bent to the ground for tip layering or that offer no side shoots for cutting material. Make a cut in the stem just below a node. Cut ½ to ⅔ of way through stem. Brace the stem with a splint so it will not snap off at weakened point. Place a small amount of sphagnum moss in the cut. Place a couple of handfuls of it around the stem. Wet the moss thoroughly, wrap it in polyethylene plastic, and tie it securely into place at top and bottom. When roots form and show through the moss, sever the rooted portion from parent plant and plant it.

ALTERNATE BEARING. A characteristic of some plants to bear flowers and fruit more heavily one year than the next. The differences may be slight or quite marked. Some apple trees, for example, will bear heavily one season, little or none the next, and then heavily again.

AXIL, LEAF AXIL. The angle between leaf stem and main stem in which are located the lateral and axillary buds. It is these buds that can be stimulated into growth by pinching (see *Pinching*).

BEARING HABITS OF FRUIT TREES. Fruit trees have distinct flowering and bearing habits. These habits determine how you prune. Here are how some of the common deciduous fruit trees bear their crops:

Peaches and nectarines bear their fruit laterally along wood formed the previous season. Wood closer to the tree's center from where fruit is forming bore fruit in previous seasons and is now barren. Wood that will bear fruit for the next year forms on new growth of the current season. This bearing habit is peculiar only to peaches and nectarines. On no other fruit is each year's bearing portion stretched over so much new wood. Heavy annual pruning is necessary both to force out long new growth and to keep the ever lengthening bearing area as close as possible to the center of the tree.

Apricots. As on the peach tree, fruit and vegetative buds on apricots are borne along new wood, and the following summer some will develop into fruit while others will grow into short twigs. The difference between peach and apricot growth habits becomes noticeable in winter when, after the leaves fall off, fruit spurs can be seen. A fruit spur is a short stocky shoot, seldom more than three inches long, with fruit and leaf buds packed fairly close along it. Spurs develop from vegetative buds. (On the peach, these buds grow into shoots.) Fruit buds on these spurs, as well as those along new growth, will produce fruit the following summer. As on the peach tree, apricot wood that has borne fruit will not bear again. On the apricot, however, fruit continues to be borne on spurs that grow out of the wood which has previously produced. The spurs put on only a little growth each year, and each year's growth bears fruit. Apricot spurs are comparatively short-lived, rarely producing fruit for longer than four years, so regular pruning is essential to replace them continually. Prune selectively, allowing newer branches to grow, replacing the older branches as they become unproductive.

Cherry. The bearing habit of sweet cherries is radically different. Cherries grow from the same spurs for as long as 10 to 12 years. These spurs grow very slowly, putting on a short annual terminal growth and even shorter lateral growths. Because of the longevity of the cherry fruit spurs, there is practically no need for renewal of fruiting branches. As a matter of fact, cherries require less pruning than any other deciduous fruit trees.

Apples and pears grow mostly from the ends of spurs. The spurs start from vegetative buds on new shoots and, while they are growing, next year's fruit buds are forming on the ends. Spurs begin producing fruit in their second year. The following spring, spurs put out a little growth and set other terminal fruit buds. The spurs often go through this growing and fruit setting process over a period as long as 20 years. Because of the long bearing life of apple and pear spurs, pruning consists primarily of thinning old, weak, and crowded branches and heading others back to vigorous laterals.

BLEED, BLEEDING. Some plants tend to bleed sap when cut. The sugar maple is a classic example. Esthetically this is not pleasing, but generally it is not very harmful to the tree.

BONSAI. A Japanese term for one of the garden fine arts—growing dwarfed, carefully trained plants in containers designed to harmonize with the plants. The bonsai craftsman meticulously wires and prunes branches and trims roots to get the desired effect: the character of an ancient, weathered tree on a miniature scale.

BRUSHING OUT. The removal of dead wood and brush-like growth from trees and shrubs.

BRACTS, FLOWER BRACTS. Modified leaflike structures that grow in a flower cluster or around a flower.

BUDS, EYES. The place where all vegetative and flower growth begins. Most important to pruners are the *terminal buds*. These growing buds on the ends of all shoots draw plant energy to themselves and grow, adding length to the stems. Remove the bud (see *Pinching*), and one of the buds below it will draw plant energy to itself. Buds along the branch below the terminal bud are *lateral buds*. These lateral buds have an alternate or opposite arrangement. Plants on which buds grow opposite each other generally respond to a pruning cut by making a slingshot-shaped growth—both buds grow. Some lateral buds break out and develop during the same season as the terminal bud, and some (known as *dormant buds*) do not. If dormant buds do not begin growth after one season, they become known as *latent buds*. It is these dormant and latent buds which can be stimulated into growth by making pruning cuts above them. These buds are

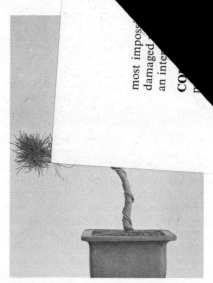

NURSERY PINE becomes a bonsai. Peel can, and remove lower branches.

ENCIRCLE TRUNK with 2 strands of #8 copper wire on trunk, 1 on branch.

BEND TRUNK, remove more branchlets, cut back needle clusters, pot the plant.

nature's reserve growth points, ready to develop under certain conditions (such as damage or a pruning cut farther out on the limb). Unlike all the above, which are formed in normal positions, *adventitious buds* may be found almost anywhere on the plant. With some stimulus, they too may break into growth.

MAKING BUDS do their thing. Pinch back where marked and the next several buds below make growth as shown.

CAMBIUM. A thin but vital layer of tissue between the bark and wood. Cambium layers of scion and stock must meet for successful graft.

CANE. As used in pruning language, cane means the long, vigorous stem of a raspberry, blackberry, or similar plant.

CANOPY. Refers to the top, shade producing structure— the branches and foliage—of a tree or shrub.

CONIFERS. These evergreens fall into two broad classes: those with branches that radiate out from the trunk in whorls, and those that grow branches in a haphazard, random fashion. Pine, spruce, and fir are examples of the whorl type; arborvitae, hemlock, juniper, and taxus (yew) are examples of the random branching conifers.

Conifers in general do not require as much pruning as deciduous trees, though they respond well if you abide by a few rules. Generally, you can shear the random branching types, but you should prune selectively (back to another branch or to a bud) on the whorl branching types.

On the whorl branching types, you can induce branching and thicken the tip growth by pinching back the candles of new growth about halfway.

Avoid damaging the central leader in conifers unless you want to limit height. If the central leader is damaged, you can stake one of the next lowest branches vertically and train it as a new leader.

How conifers should be pruned also depends on how they are to be used in the landscape. When they are used in a screen, hedge, low divider, ground cover, or a vertical form, you need only trim to keep them neat and in scale with their surroundings.

When some conifers get to within a foot or so of the size at which you want to hold them, cut back the new growth so that about 1 inch of it remains. This will produce enough small side branchlets to make full, dense foliage. Once this bushy growth has been established at the ends of the branches, you can hold the plant to the same size year after year by cutting off all new growth that develops beyond the line you want to hold.

For some conifers—*Cedrus deodara*, for instance— there are other specific ways to prune to maintain size. Look for these methods under the plant names in the Pruning Encyclopedia, pages 13-87.

Another way to slow growth is to prune some of the roots before the early spring growth begins. Do this by thrusting a sharp spade down through some of the roots or by digging a trench and severing some of them with an axe.

You can either shorten a branch a little or take it off altogether. If you cut beyond the last green growth, back to the bare wood, you usually limit the branch to that length. Most species won't develop a new shoot if they have been cut back this far.

When a conifer has been damaged by cold or breakage, you may have to remove entire limbs. Then it is al-

...ble to restore its natural shape. However, a ...plant can often be trimmed and trained to make ...esting sculptural form.

...RDON. A space-saving way to grow fruit trees. The ...ethod originated in Europe, where it is still in use. The name, meaning rope or cord, refers to the tree's appearance. The cordon differs from the espalier in that the tree is trained to a single main stem, with laterals carefully controlled. A cordon may be trained vertically, horizontally, or obliquely.

For training a dwarf as a cordon, buy 1-year-old whips. Cut back to 18 inches at planting time to force side shoots to develop. Use the uppermost shoot as a leader and tie it to the cane. If side growth was poor the first season, cut back the leader halfway to force a new one. This new leader should be on the opposite side of the stem from the first one.

In June or July, pinch back all fully developed side shoots to 4 leaves. Repeat in September, shortening those that weren't fully developed earlier and any late growing shoots.

Curtail the previous year's growth in winter. Remove all wood beyond the fat fruit buds on a spur. Where there are no fruit buds, keep laterals shortened to 3 or 4 leaves until buds form, then cut back. Thin fruit bud clusters when they are too thick.

On most fruit trees, break over or cut all mature laterals by mid-July. Cut laterals from side shoots to one leaf, leaving the immature shoots to be pruned in September. Cut secondary growth from summer-pruned shoots to one leaf in early autumn or winter.

CROTCH. The angle formed between the trunk and the scaffold branch or between a pair of trunks. This is an area of tremendous stress, especially when branches are being whipped in the wind. The branches most likely to split and break are those that form a tight angle with the trunk of the tree—a V-shaped crotch—rather than a more open angle—a U-shaped crotch. The weak, V-shaped crotches often form when a branch grows from a latent bud after several years of dormancy. The wood in such a branch is not continuous with the central wood of the parent branch. The stronger, U-shaped crotch, on the other hand, usually forms when the branch grows at the same time as the parent branch so that the wood is a continuous, integral part of the parent.

CUTS. By definition, pruning is the removal of plant parts. You remove the parts by making cuts—with your thumbnail or fingers, with shears or saw. The effectiveness of your pruning will be determined by how and where you make these pruning cuts. Using the right tools (see page 8) and using them properly is important to pruning effectively. Hand shears and loppers, particularly, must be held correctly to avoid leaving stubs. Stubs, whether above a bud or another branch, will die back to the growing point and can open the plant to infection. The cut that is generally accepted by experienced pruners as the best is one that is slanted at about a 45 degree angle just above the bud. Always cut back to a growing point, such as a bud or another branch. The growth will then continue along established channels.

Cuts in this book's illustrations are marked with thin black rectangles.

DISBUD, DISBUDDING. Certain varieties of camellias, roses, and other shrubs produce more buds than they can mature properly. For this reason, many gardeners disbud by removing some of the buds so that the plant's energy can be concentrated in the remaining buds, resulting in bigger, showier blooms. There is no point in disbudding, however, in the case of plants famed for their multiplicity of smaller or medium-sized flowers.

DORMANCY, DORMANT. The period in a plant's annual cycle when growth and development slows and seems to be suspended.

DOUBLE LEADER. When two trunks or main stems compete for the dominant, leading position, the tree is said to have a double leader. A second leader usually arises from the trunk at a very narrow angle, resulting in a weak crotch that is likely to split as the tree matures. It also spoils the natural, single leader shape of the tree. Remove or discourage these growths as they appear and head back branches that threaten to compete with the chosen leader. You would, however, want to encourage a second leader to replace the original one in case of damage to it.

ESPALIER. The practice of training a tree or shrub to grow flat—against a wall or along a fence, wire, or trellis. You can espalier in formal, rigid patterns or more informally, letting the plant's natural growth habit guide you. Almost any tree or shrub that is not too rigidly upright or formal in growth can be espaliered by continually removing growing points that would take growth in the direction you don't want, and allowing the rest of the growing points to have their own way.

Espaliering is an exacting but rewarding art. Fruit trees make good subjects because espaliering exposes a maximum of branch surface to the sun, stimulating heavier flower and fruit production.

Points to remember about espaliering: in cool summer areas, give espalier as much sun as possible by planting against a south wall or fence. Reflected heat will stimulate flower production and help to ripen the fruit. Where

ESPALIERED APPLE, fastened to wires on sunny wall. This 10-year-old is trained in a U-shaped pattern.

summer temperatures consistently hit the high 90's, reflected heat is likely to damage the plant or sunburn the fruit, so espalier on a free-standing trellis with an eastern exposure.

FLOWER TRUSS. See *Truss.*

FORCE (VERB), FORCING. In pruning, force and forcing refer to the deliberate direction of growth into a selected bud (or buds), branch (or branches) by removal of other buds or branches.

FRAMEWORK. The part of a tree or shrub made of mature, thick, woody growth—the trunk and main branches.

FREEZE DAMAGE. Examine plants for live leaf buds. Buds that are withered and brown are dead. Location of first live bud indicates how far back from the tip the plant has been damaged.

FREEZE DAMAGE being removed from a princess flower (Tibouchina). Cuts are made into areas showing new growth.

If you can't identify the live buds, examine the tissue between the bark and the wood. Make a small scrape through the bark. Brown cambium indicates that the tissue is dead.

Many plants killed to the ground have growth buds just below the surface; these will frequently grow. Where it's reasonable, give plants a year to activate these buds before discarding them. If it is a budded or grafted plant, make sure that the growing bud is from above the graft and not the understock.

If a conifer shows bare twigs or brown needles in spring, you can blame it on a damaging freeze the previous winter. If ⅓ or fewer of the needles dropped but the buds are not destroyed, the tree is probably unharmed and will recover fast. After new growth starts, cut into the twigs that have dropped their needles. If they show green inside, they are alive and will grow. If the twigs are brown and dry, they are dead. If terminal buds were killed, new leaders will develop from dormant side buds. To reshape the tree, you'll need to prune it for a year or two.

If ⅔ of the needles dropped, the tree is extremely weakened and if more than ⅔ of them dropped, it will need much care to bring it back.

FRUIT THINNING. You must thin some fruits to give them enough space to mature fully. Thinning is needed with apples, apricots, peaches, and Japanese plums. Leave 6 or 8 inches between apples, about 4 inches between peaches or nectarines.

GREEN WALL. This infrequently used term designates just what it says—a wall of living green leaves. It can also be just a row of plants with a naturally vertical growth habit. Or it can be a fence or wall covered with a leafy vine.

HEAD (VERB), HEADING BACK. A pruning term for cutting a branch back to a bud or side branch to increase the number of shoots or to make the plant bushier. For a method that produces roughly the opposite effect, see *Thinning.*

If you find it necessary to remove a sizable limb, avoid splitting it by making three cuts as shown here. Make

the first cut from underneath, halfway through the limb. Then make your second cut from the top until the limb breaks off. The short stub remaining can then be removed without splitting or tearing the bark on the trunk. Let the cut surface dry for a few days before applying a coat of pruning compound. A second coat applied in a few weeks will help prevent checking and admission of moisture.

HEDGES. There are two types of hedges—formal and informal. An informal hedge can be simply a row of one kind of plant. It should be allowed to grow naturally, with only an occasional pruning, shaping, or pinching back to keep the plants bushy and in bounds. Formal hedges are quite another matter. They should be sheared regularly all their lives, and proper training for them begins at planting time. It is a mistake to allow a formal hedge to reach the size you want before shearing it.

If your formal hedge plants are densely branched (or have no branches), cut them back drastically to 3 to 4 inches above the ground. By next spring, more growth will have come forth. At that time, cut plants back to within 3 to 6 inches of the previous cuts. Then in midsummer, cut back ½ to ⅔ of the new growth that has developed. You can cut back the new growth again in the fall, but don't do it too late in heavy freeze areas because the new growth that is stimulated may be damaged by the early frosts. The purpose of all the early shearing is to make the plants spread as widely as they can and to develop as dense and low-branched a framework as possible.

If at planting time the young plants are already nicely branched, you do not have to cut them back so severely. Head back the tops and sides as necessary to induce branching. Continue this procedure over several seasons until you have the desired shape and size. Subsequent trimmings and shearings would remove as much of the new growth as possible to keep hedge from growing too big.

At all stages of growth, hedges should be maintained so that their sides are either vertical or, even better, sloping in some from bottom to top. If a hedge flares out toward the top, the lower leaves won't get enough light. This will cause them to drop off, leaving you with a hedge that is open, twiggy, and leggy at the bottom.

INTERNODE. See *Node.*

LATERAL. Lateral means side. A lateral branch is a side branch. A lateral bud is a side bud. Statements such as "cut back to a lateral" usually refer to a lateral branch.

LAYERING. There are two ways of doing it; see *Air layering* and *Tip layering.*

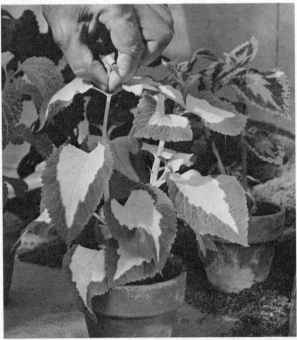

PINCHING OUT a stem tip. The pinching will force growth from the side buds, making the plant grow bushier.

LEADER. The dominant, central branch of a tree, easily recognizable in many conifers as the extension of the trunk. If an uninterrupted vertical trunk is essential, carefully watch and respect the leader. If necessary, train it into a dominant position in a young tree.

LEGGY. Vertical plants or stems that have their leaves or side branches too far apart, making the stems themselves too visible, are said to be leggy. Legginess is frequently caused by the plant or the plant part getting less sunlight than it needs.

NODE. A joint in a stem; the point where a leaf starts to grow. It is usually marked by a slight swelling that is easily detectible on young branches. Internode is the space between the nodes.

PINCHING, PINCH, PINCH BACK, PINCH OUT. Using thumb and forefinger to nip tips of branches in order to force side growth and make plants bushier.

PLEACH. To interweave and plait branches of trees together to form a hedge or arbor. You can pleach any tree that has branches and branchlets tough and supple enough to be bent and interwoven without breaking. To get an arbor of pleached trees as shown in the photograph, build a sturdy framework of wood, angle iron, or galvanized pipe on which to train the trees. You will need as many vertical supports as trees, as well as sufficient material to build a pergola-type trellis between the tops of the uprights.

Plant and tie a tree to each vertical support. (These should be 9 to 15 feet high.) Remove side branches that develop along trunk. When foliage is abundant and reaches well into the overhead framework, you are ready to start training.

Remove all upright growth. Don't leave any stubs. Lead all side branches toward those of the neighboring trees, bending them down to the framework and tying as necessary. You can also weave them under and over the wires or with other branches. Where branches cross, intertwine them; they'll form natural grafts.

Each year, bend, tie, or weave the new growth to keep the plane of canopy level.

POLLARD. Shearing off the top of a tree so that it puts out a dense head of slender shoots. Results of pollarding can be unsightly, but it can be attractive and beneficial, too. It all depends on the tree you choose to pollard and how you do it. More popular in Europe than here, pollarding is more a practical sort of pruning than a decorative one, and unless you have to keep a tree a certain size, there's little reason to pollard. Here's how to proceed:

When young trees produce trunks about 8 feet high, with branches high enough to walk under and about the thickness of a man's wrist, cut the branches down to 2 to 5 feet long and let them callus over.

Each spring the tree will produce more slender long branches. Each winter remove these and let the cuts callus over. Eventually knobs at the ends of the short branches will become very large.

PRUNING COMPOUND. See *Sealing compound.*

ROOT PRUNING. In one usage, this means cutting off some of a plant's roots to prepare it for transplanting. In

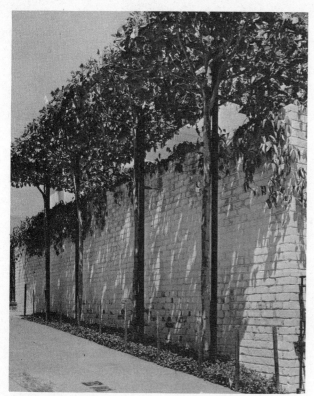

PLEACHING is shown here. Branches at the top are interwoven through themselves and through the iron framework.

POLLARDING brought this result. People often confuse it with pleaching. See midyear pollarded tree on page 67.

another, it means to sever invasive, greedy roots. Where roots have invaded adjacent planting areas and are competing for available water, first prune the roots and then make it impossible for them to grow back into the area. Small roots (up to the diameter of your thumb) can be cut quickly and easily by making a trench with a rented power trencher. Bigger roots will have to be cut by hand. After roots are severed, line trench with roofing paper, replace soil and replant any plants that were removed.

SEALING COMPOUND. Also called pruning compound, this is a thick, dense substance (usually black and tarry) that you scoop out of the container and spread across the face of a fresh saw cut or a freshly repaired wound. The material dries hard and protects the wood beneath from being dried out by the elements and from possible damage by insects or other organisms.

SELECTIVELY. Used as in "prune selectively," "thin selectively," "head back selectively." It means you should select the branch, the fruit, the flowers, or whatever you want to keep and then prune, thin, or head back the parts that you don't want to keep.

SHAPE (VERB), SHAPING. Pruning to emphasize a plant's natural shape or to assist in its development. As opposed to shearing, shaping is generally done by removing some whole branches or branchlets and leaving others untouched. Shearing, on the other hand, generally removes all the terminal buds on all the outer growth.

SHEAR (VERB), SHEARING. Using hedge shears or grass shears to clip leaves, stems, and branches on one plane at one time.

Shearing has a substantial place in gardening—mostly in keeping hedges neat, shearing grass, and reducing voluminous vines and ground covers (such as ivy) back to their minimum size again.

Shearing becomes unpleasant to many beholders when it converts a tree or shrub from its natural form or a near-natural form to a completely artificial and needless form—such as a globe. One form of such shearing is more acceptable under some circumstances—see *Topiary.*

SPUR. As used in pruning, the word applies chiefly to the stubby, fruit-bearing twigs up to 3 inches long that bear fruit each year on apple, pear, and cherry trees and in some cases on apricot, peach, and plum. The role of spurs and their relationship to other kinds of bearing wood are discussed under *Bearing habits of fruit trees.*

STANDARD. A plant, not naturally growing as a tree, that is trained into a small treelike form with a single, upright trunk and rounded crown. The tree rose is the most familiar example.

There are three ways you can acquire a standard:

One way is to come into ownership of a plant that has already been trained that way.

A second way is to start by growing a single stem up a stake. Let it grow up the stake until it reaches the height you want, then nip out the terminal bud. Remove lower branches and retain the upper branches that make a tree shape.

The third way is to prune a standard from a bushy shrub. Select one superior vertical stem, cutting out the

TWO YOUNG PLANTS being trained as standards (one at right is further along). Main idea is to extend terminal growth and allow no lateral growth below the top.

CAMELLIA STANDARD made from bushy plant. Lower branches were removed.

others. Next, cut off the lower side branches on the selected vertical stem, leaving the upper branches intact. Then head them back and thin them out as necessary to make a nice looking top.

STUB. A needlessly long section of branch or stem between a pruning cut and a bud, leaf, branch, or trunk. Such a stub will die back, as explained in *How Plants Grow*, see page 6. Leaving stubs to rot exposes the plant to disease and possible deterioration.

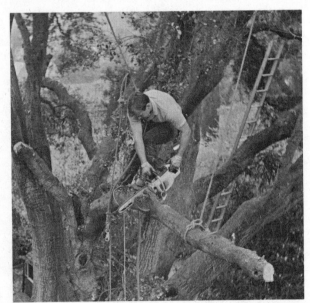

COMMERCIAL TREE PRUNER removing stub after branch was cut off. He cuts it in sections. Rope prevents tearing.

SUCKERS. Any unwanted shoot—it may come up from underground, appear on the lower part of the plant, or even pop out on the trunk or large branches (in which case it's called a watersprout). Suckers are vigorous and often outstrip older shoots.

Sucker growth arising beneath a bud or graft can slow top growth of the grafted variety by diverting growth substances to itself. If neglected, it can also kill the grafted or budded top by shading it out.

If a sucker arises *above* a bud or graft union (which may remove it from the category of suckers by some definitions) and if it is more vigorous than an older trunk and in other ways more desirable than the trunk, keep the sucker and cut out the older trunk. In some plants, suckers are a valuable means of increasing the plant.

If you catch suckers when they are very small and tender, you can snap them off or rub them off. Larger ones should be broken from the plant with a firm, brisk outward and downward snap.

If you have to cut off a sucker with pruning shears, try to leave no stub whatever. Any stub you leave behind will sprout again. On fairly good-sized trees you can cut off suckers with a chisel.

TERMINAL BUDS. The buds on the ends of stems or trunks and at the ends of branches. They extend growth. If you remove side buds, you channel energy into terminal buds. If you remove terminal buds, you cause growth in side buds to increase, making for denser, bushier plants.

The act of pinching (also called pinching out, pinching back, and tip pinching), defined under *Pinching*, centers upon the terminal buds. When you pinch the end of a branch, you remove that branch's terminal bud.

THINNING, THINNING OUT. Removing entire branches—large ones or small ones—clear back to the main trunk or side branch. The object is usually to make the plant more open. Sometimes the object is to let more air get through the plant to make it stand stronger in the wind or to let more light through it so that plants beneath it or on the north side of it can grow better.

In the case of fruit trees, thinning refers to the intentional removal of young, half-mature fruit to make the remaining fruit grow bigger; see *Fruit thinning*.

TIP LAYERING. A method of rooting plants that are hard to root from cuttings and don't come true from seed. Select a healthy branch near the ground or one flexible enough to bend to the ground. Cut a slit near the end of the branch and just underneath a node. Wedge it open with a pebble. Dig a hole beneath the notch, bend the notch into it, fasten in place with a wire loop, fill the hole with planting mix, stake branch tip, and cover earth in hole with a brick or stone. When layer is well rooted, sever from parent plant. With some easy-rooting plants, you can lay the whole branch in the ground, with branchlets projecting upward; the individual branchlets will root and can be cut off.

TIP-PINCH. See *Pinching*.

TOPIARY. The technique of shearing trees and shrubs to geometric shapes such as pyramids, spheres, and cones or to bird and animal shapes. Plants normally used as hedge material lend themselves well to topiary because they hold a sheared shape well. Choose from such plants as boxwood, chamaecyparis, cotoneaster, juniper, privet, olive, podocarpus, pittosporum, pyracantha, and yew.

Examine plants carefully, parting the foliage, to find a basic branch form you can work with. Cut off all nonessential limbs, leaving just the trunk and branches that you want to keep. Wherever you want to form a clump along the middle parts of a trunk or branch, leave some side branches, shearing them into approximately the outline of the clump that you desire. Of course, there must be a clump at the end of each branch that you keep, so shear the terminal branchlets there into clumps of the shape that you want.

Remove all little twigs and leaves along the branches between the clumps.

Typically, at first the clumps won't be full—they may look quite rangy and sparse. But if you keep the tree or shrub growing strong, new branches and leaves will fill out the clumps in a season or more.

Watch for new branches that may arise from hidden buds along the parts of the branches that are supposed to remain bare. Snip or rub them off whenever they form.

TRAINING YOUNG FRUIT TREES. Three named methods are described here. They were developed and named by commercial growers—for orchard efficiency. Home gardeners usually care as much about their fruit trees looking good as they do about fruit production. But there are no specific named methods for growing a handsome, productive home garden fruit tree. Here are the commercial methods:

(1) *Central leader system.* Essentially, with this method you leave the central leader intact and the scaffold branches grow out from it (a fruit tree version of a

Christmas tree). Such a tree is strong, but the center tends to be too shady.

(2) *Open center system.* In this one, you remove the top of the central leader, forcing big side branches to grow out and become the basic framework of the tree. This results in a tree that is not as strong as a central leader tree but one that is good for fruit production. The open center admits more light.

(3) *Modified leader system.* Here, the central leader is cut back but not as low as on the open center method. It makes a tree that should have both a central leader and strong scaffold branches.

TRAINING YOUNG TREES. Pruning is extremely important to the proper growth and development of a young tree from the moment you place it in the soil.

Young trees come in three kinds of packages, and you prune each kind in a different way. The amount and type of early training and pruning required will also depend upon the growth habit and your objective. You can purchase trees bare root, balled and burlapped, or in containers.

Bare root trees (most of the deciduous kinds) are dug, sold, and planted during the dormant season—December into or through March. Because bare root trees have undergone the most root removal, you should prune back the tops to compensate. Usually, nurserymen do this for you, and it involves selecting and heading back the best scaffold branches; heading back or thinning the others. If the bare root tree is a whip with no branches, it should be allowed to grow just above the height where branches are desired and then pinched back a couple of inches. This will stimulate the buds below into growth.

Balled and burlapped. Many conifers, broad-leafed evergreens, and a few deciduous plants with touchy roots come with roots in a ball of earth, wrapped in burlap. These will not normally require much pruning of the top, though these plants may also have lost some roots and would benefit from some top pruning to compensate. Pruning back lightly to a promising bud is all that is normally required.

Trees in containers should not have suffered any root damage, and you can plant them as you bring them home, with little or no top pruning when they are planted (unless, of course, you damage the root ball when you remove it from the container).

Whatever the planting method, once the tree is planted and the top has been pruned as necessary, give it proper watering and feeding and then relax and watch it grow. *Don't be in a hurry to establish the ultimate shape of the tree at this point* except to correct faults, such as a potential double leader. If you want the tree to grow rapidly, don't remove leaf shoots or unwanted laterals along the trunk. Young trees need all the leaves they can get to manufacture food for growth. Some tree experts claim that if the tree is to be trained to branch high above the ground, you should wait until the third year to remove lower trunk branches that are unwanted. By that time, the selected branches higher up will have enough leaf structure to supply the plant. On fast growing trees, you may want to start your training earlier. In this case, select carefully the type of growth to remove. Try to strike a safe balance between leaving more leaf surface and removing those branches which would build a framework closer to the ground than desired.

You may also have to pinch back new growth on laterals you plan to keep in order to induce secondary branching. Another good reason for leaving surplus leaves and branches on a young tree is that strong sunlight will sometimes injure exposed trunks of newly planted trees. Citrus and walnut, for example, are particularly susceptible to sunburn.

After the second or third year, begin to think of the tree's ultimate form. Your best guide in selecting the permanent framework will be the inherent form of the tree. Remove branches on the trunk below those you have selected as the lowest scaffold branches. Remember that branches always remain the same distance above the ground and will not get higher as the tree grows.

If you want a tree with a strong central leader, select and encourage the most upright stem, and cut out competing branches.

Remove scaffold branches that come off the trunk at a sharp angle and form a narrow crotch. Aim for good branch spacing, radially as well as vertically on the trunk. You can train the developing tree into the shape you want if you keep an eye on it and cut and pinch when you see it straying out of line.

Let's say you want an umbrella-shaped tree for the patio—a tree that you can walk under. And let's assume that you choose a shade tree with a slow to moderate rate of growth. (The fast growers, such as willow, poplar, Chinese elm, mulberry, and fig, are exceptions to the usual training rules—they are so vigorous that they will often reach the height at which you want horizontal branches before you know it.) With the moderate to slow growers, you get the umbrella stage most efficiently this way:

1. Choose a type that naturally has a good share of horizontal branches—flowering dogwood, Washington thorn, silk tree, apple tree, almond, and the like.

2. First spring: allow the tree to grow.

3. First midsummer: select the upright shoot that is to be the trunk and pinch back any competitors around it; also pinch out tips of vigorous side branches. Repeat pinching wherever new growth takes over.

4. First winter: if the tree has formed strong, overly developed side branches, cut them back to a small side shoot. Don't remove the summer-tipped lower branches.

5. Second summer: if main stem is 8 feet or more, pinch out the tip. Tree should be tipped 1 to 1½ feet above the height you want the branches. Continue to pinch back tips of lower branches.

6. Second winter: select framework of top branches and prune out other top branches. Shorten but do not remove side branches below the top.

7. Third summer: keep side branches tipped, except those of the top frame that you selected in winter. Allow the top frame branches to develop as strongly as they will.

8. Third winter: supplement the second winter procedure.

9. Fourth winter: top should have enough leaf surface to go it alone. Remove all side branches up to the point of desired branching.

Now relax and enjoy your tree, keeping an eye out for new, unwanted growth.

TRUSS. A cluster of flowers, usually rather compact, at the end of a stem, branch, or stalk.

VEGETATIVE. This adjective is used in pruning language to distinguish a bud that will become a leaf or stem from a bud that will become a flower (and the flower that will become a fruit). It is also used to distinguish lengths of stems that carry only leaves from those that have (or can have) flowers and fruits. In this instance, the stem is called vegetative growth.

WATERSPROUT. See *Sucker.*

WOOD, OLD AND NEW. New wood consists of stems (and the leaves and branches attached to them) that formed since the beginning of the current growing year. Most plants (even evergreens) cease growth during winter—making it easy to distinguish "year-old" from "new."

WOUND TREATMENT. See *Sealing compound.*

PHOTOGRAPHERS